MW01634366

Exploring Canada
Learning from the Past, Looking to the Future

Vivien Bowers
Diane Swanson

General Editors
Carol Langford
Chuck Heath

Teacher Consultants
Vicki Green
Jan Maynard Nicol

Explorations A Canadian Social Studies Program for Elementary Schools

Douglas & McIntyre (Educational) Ltd.
1615 Venables Street
Vancouver, British Columbia V5L 2H1

Printed and bound in Canada. 91 92 93 94 RP 6 5 4 3

Canadian Cataloguing in Publication Data

Bowers, Vivien, 1951–
Exploring Canada

(Explorations : a Canadian social studies program for elementary schools. Exploring Canada's past, present and future)
Includes index.
ISBN 0–88894–871–9

1. Forests and forestry — Canada — Juvenile literature. 2. Communication — Canada — Juvenile literature. 3. Canada — Politics and government — Juvenile literature. 4. Canada — Emigration and immigration — Juvenile literature. I. Swanson, Diane, 1944– II. Title. III. Series.

FC58.B69 1985 j971 C85–091061–7
F1008.2.B69 1985

We wish to thank the following people, who reviewed parts of the manuscript or illustrations, for their helpful comments and suggestions:

Unit I: *Exploring the Forest Resource*

Bruce Devitt, Chief Forester, Pacific Forest Products

Victor Heath, Founder and Former Department Head, Department of Forest Resources, B.C. Institute of Technology

Dr. Roy Strang, Executive Director, Forest Research Council, Province of British Columbia

Fred Thiessen, Recreation Officer, Nelson Forest Region, Province of British Columbia

Unit II: *Exploring Communications*

CBC National TV News Staff, Toronto

Dr. Dennis Dicks, Chairman and Associate Professor of Education, Concordia University

Dr. Rowland Lorimer, Department of Communication, Simon Fraser University

Unit III: *Exploring Government*

Dr. Pauline Jewett, M.P., New Westminster–Coquitlam

Dr. J. Terence Morley, Department of Political Science, University of Victoria

Unit IV: *Exploring Immigration*

Dr. Jack Kehoe, Department of Social and Educational Studies, Faculty of Education, University of British Columbia

Suniti Khosla, Assistant Regional Coordinator, Canada World Youth of British Columbia

Dr. Peter Stephenson, Department of Anthropology, University of Victoria

A Message from the Authors

What we enjoyed most about writing this book was gathering the information for it. Some of the most interesting information came from the people we talked to and the places we visited. For instance, we hiked through a forest where the trees were hundreds of years old. We talked to someone in charge of Search and Rescue operations. We could feel how excited he was. He had rescued a pilot from his crashed plane just that morning. In Victoria, we went to see Canada's oldest Chinatown. We heard how the people had worked with their city council to restore it. And, in court, we repeated the Oath of Citizenship with people from 19 different countries as they became Canadian citizens.

This book describes a lot of different places. Of course, we couldn't possibly visit all of them. But it seemed as if we could by reading and by talking to people. It even seemed as if we could travel through time—back to the past and ahead to the future.

As you read this book, we hope you'll travel to these times and places in your imagination, too. We also hope you'll do a lot of real exploring one day. Canada is a big place and there is a lot more to see than we could possibly fit into one book.

Contents

UNIT III

Exploring Government

UNIT IV

Exploring Immigration

Introduction

Welcome to *Exploring Canada: Learning from the Past, Looking to the Future.* This book is about the country you live in—Canada. Canada is an enormous country, the second largest in the world. It stretches from the Atlantic Ocean to the Pacific Ocean, and from the border with the United States to the frozen Arctic Islands. It has scenery that can take your breath away—mountains, rivers, lakes and prairies. It also has skyscrapers, six-lane highways, factories and shopping centres. It is home to millions of people, including you.

This book looks at Canada and Canadians. As you might have guessed from the picture on the front cover, it describes people in the past as well as people today. It even gives you a glimpse into the future.

In this book you will be reading about change. The world is constantly changing, and Canada is no exception. There have been many changes in the past. There will be more changes in the future.

As an example of change, think about your own life. As you grow older, you keep changing. You grow taller, of course, but you also

learn new skills, gain experience and change the way you think about some things. How have you changed over the last six years? How do you think you might change over the next three years or the next ten years?

A country such as Canada is also changing a bit every year. For instance, somebody builds a fast-food restaurant where there was once an empty lot. A new family moves into your neighbourhood. A new mine opens and hires many workers. In small ways, these things change Canada.

Not everything changes, though. You can probably think of things about yourself that will never change, no matter how old you are. For instance, if your parents came to Canada from Italy, you have an Italian background. Even if you don't speak Italian at home, you probably eat Italian food and know some Italian customs. When you are older, you will still have that Italian **heritage**. It will always be part of you. Maybe you will want to visit Italy. Maybe you will teach your children some Italian songs.

These photographs show Canadian children in the 1800s and 1900s. What do the photos tell you about how children's lives have changed?

Canada, too, has a heritage. Some things have been part of Canada's growth and development for many years. In this book you will learn about four factors that have been important in Canada's past, are important today and will be important in the future. They will be part of *your* life in the future. These are the four factors:

1. *The Forest Resource.* Forests are Canada's most important **natural resource**. You will learn why forests are important and how Canadians use them.
2. *Communications.* Canada is a large country with communities scattered from coast to coast. It has always been important for Canadians to find ways of sending messages—or **communicating**—across these large distances.
3. *Government.* Canada is one country with different kinds of government. Canadians work together through their governments to get some of the things they need.
4. *Immigration.* People from around the world have made Canada their home. You will learn about the challenges newcomers face in this country and the contributions they make to Canada.

Now that you know the four themes, let's see how they are presented in this book. After this Introduction, the book contains four units. Each unit explores one of the themes. The units are called "Exploring the Forest Resource," "Exploring Communications," "Exploring Government" and "Exploring Immigration."

Students learn about Canada's forest industry. Why is it important to learn about forests?

Right: Two students whisper to each other. Speaking is just one form of sending messages. What other ways might these students communicate?

Each of these four units is divided into five chapters. Look at the chapter titles in the table of contents on pages 4 and 5. Each of the five chapters in each unit tells you something about the theme of the unit.

- Chapter 1 of each unit tells a story about a child your age. For instance, in "Exploring the Forest Resource" you will meet a girl called Michelle. While you are reading the story about Michelle, you will also be learning some important things about Canada's natural resources.
- Chapter 2 of each unit takes you back into the past. You will see how the theme of each unit was important in Canada's past. You will be looking at some of the ways things have changed since the early days.
- Chapter 3 of each unit takes place in the present. You will get a close-up look at one aspect of the theme.
- Chapter 4 of each unit takes you into the past and the present. You will look at examples that show how important the theme is to Canadians.
- Chapter 5 of each unit takes the theme into the future. You will think about changes that might take place in Canada during your lifetime.

The Conclusion reviews what you have learned in the four units. The book ends with a glossary to help you understand new vocabulary words and an index to help you look up information.

Above: Police services in Canada are provided by government. What might this police officer be saying to the boy?

Above right: This Indo-Canadian girl is wearing traditional clothing and jewellery. Why might she decide to keep her Indian customs after settling in Canada?

You will notice that the word "exploring" is used in the title of this book. It is also used in the title of each unit. "Exploring" is a good word to describe what you will be doing when you read this book. In fact, you will be exploring in two different ways.

First, as you read this book you will be exploring Canada. By learning about each of the four themes, you will find out what your country is like, how it got that way and what it might be like in the future. By taking you back in time, forward in time, and into all sorts of different situations, this book will give you an opportunity to explore Canada in new ways.

There is another way that you are an explorer. Your whole life, from the time you are born to the time you die, is like a voyage of exploration. Each morning you wake up to a new day and you never know for sure what is going to happen. You don't know what the school year will be like when you step into the classroom on the first day. Do you know what Canada will be like when you are finished school and earning a living? Nobody knows for sure what the future will bring. Almost certainly, though, it will bring changes.

Through the years, Canadians have been making changes in their country. Often they have been looking for ways to improve life in Canada. Sometimes they have made mistakes. Those Canadians living long ago were exploring an unknown time, just as we are today. When you are exploring through the unknown, you are bound to make some mistakes.

It is easier to look back to the past than it is to look ahead to the future. When we do look back, we can see how Canada has changed over the years and what Canadians have learned along the way. That is why this book could be important to you. It can help you understand your country a little better today. When you understand your country's past, you will be better prepared to meet the challenges Canada faces in the future. As you head off on your voyage of exploration, you can build on the experience of the people who went before you.

Bon voyage!

This map shows the provinces, territories and capital cities of Canada. Where do you live? Which provinces or territories are your neighbours?

ARCTIC OCEAN
N
E
W
S
GREENLAND
ICELAND
Arctic Circle
ellowknife
NORTHWEST
TERRITORIES
Hudson Bay
NEWFOUNDLAND
SASKATCHEWAN
MANITOBA
James Bay
QUEBEC
St. John's
St. Lawrence River
Regina
ONTARIO
P.E.I.
Charlottetown
Winnipeg
N.B.
NOVA SCOTIA
Quebec
Fredericton
Halifax
Ottawa
Lake Superior
Lake Michigan
Lake Huron
Toronto
Lake Ontario
UNITED STATES
ATLANTIC OCEAN
Lake Erie

UNIT I

Exploring the Forest Resource

1

What Is a Natural Resource?

All Aboard!

With a lurch and a rattle the train started moving. Slowly at first, then picking up speed, it clattered along the tracks. Michelle waved wildly to her mother on the station platform. She waved and waved until her mother shrank into a dot and disappeared.

"One kilometre gone, 6250 to go!" said a voice behind her. Michelle turned from the window and smiled at the small, grey-haired woman sitting in the next seat.

Michelle was taking the train from Halifax to visit her uncle in British Columbia. Louise had agreed to travel with her as far as Vancouver, where Louise's grandchildren lived. Louise was also writing a travel article about the trip.

"Where exactly does your uncle live?" asked Louise.

"He lives in Woss on Vancouver Island," answered Michelle. "I have to take a ferry from Vancouver to get there."

"Vancouver Island! You really are travelling from one end of the country to the other, aren't you? You could have had an even longer trip, though. Instead of starting in Halifax, you could have started in some place farther east, like Bonavista."

"Where's Bonavista?" asked Michelle.

"Bonavista is my home town," said Louise. She explained that Bonavista is a fishing village in Newfoundland, right on the Atlantic Ocean. Some of the best fishing grounds in the world are off the Atlantic coast. Fish are important to the people living there. Many work on fishing boats or in fish plants. Louise worked on a boat with her father when she was younger.

"I used to take the wheel while my father checked the fishing lines," she said. "I was pretty good at cleaning fish, too."

Michelle wrinkled her nose and Louise laughed. "What does your uncle do in Woss?" asked Louise.

"He works for a forest company," said Michelle. "He's a **faller**."

"He falls down a lot?"

Michelle and Louise begin their trip. What might each person be looking forward to?

Michelle grinned. "A faller is someone who cuts down trees."

"Ah," said Louise. "Just make sure you're not in the way. There are some big trees in British Columbia."

"I'll watch out for them," Michelle promised.

Louise told Michelle about the giant Douglas fir trees on the west coast. The heavy rainfall and mild climate help the trees grow tall. She said that forests are the most important **natural resource** in British Columbia.

"You'll see some of Canada's natural resources as we travel across the country," said Louise. "Maybe you should make a list of them. That way you'll have a record of your trip."

Michelle had a better idea. She decided to use the map of Canada she had been given with her ticket. She would mark the natural resources on it.

Michelle unfolded her map. She found Halifax on the Atlantic coast. Michelle was taking the train to Vancouver, at the other end of Canada, on the Pacific coast. It was Sunday and she would not reach the west coast until Friday. Michelle thought about her long journey. Five days travelling across the country! The train was a great way to explore Canada.

- If you were exploring Canada, where would you go?

This map shows some of the places that Michelle will learn about as she and Louise travel across Canada. Where does their train trip end?

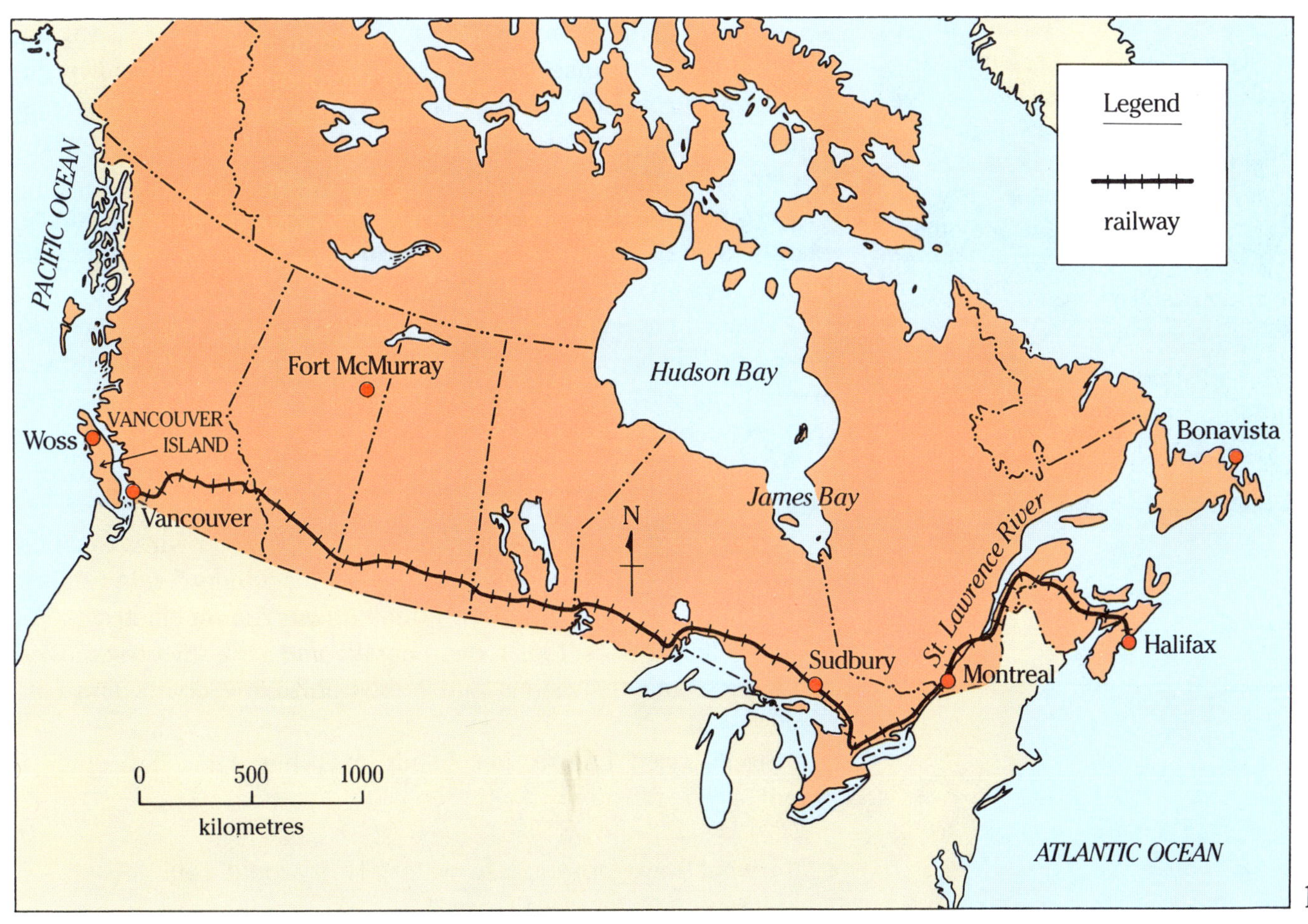

Natural Resources

A natural resource is something found in nature, some natural thing, that people can use. Forests, for instance, are a natural resource. We use the wood for building houses. Fish are a natural resource, too. We eat them.

You can probably think of many other natural resources that are found in Canada. We are lucky to have so many. Some other countries do not have as many natural resources. They have to buy wood, fish and other resource **products** from countries like Canada.

Rivers: A Natural Resource

That night the train crossed New Brunswick and followed the St. Lawrence River into Quebec. Michelle's seat became a bed at night. When Michelle woke up Monday morning the train was just entering the city of Montreal.

Louise and Michelle had time for a whirlwind tour during their stopover in Montreal. Late in the afternoon, they continued their train journey west. Michelle watched from the dome car as they crossed the St. Lawrence River.

Michelle showed Louise the map of Canada. She had written "FISH" in the water off the Atlantic coast. At the other end of the country, in British Columbia, she had written "FORESTS." Louise explained that these are both **renewable** resources. New fish can replace the fish that are caught, and new trees can replace the trees that are cut down.

"What natural resource should I put down for the province of Quebec?" asked Michelle.

"Quebec has lots of different resources, but why don't you choose rivers?"

"Are rivers a natural resource?" asked Michelle.

"Sure. Rivers are made of water, and water is used for lots of things," said Louise. "People travel on water and drink it. They water dry land for growing crops. Some rivers are used to make electricity, too." Louise explained how the water rushing down the river turns the wheels of a big machine called a turbine. The moving wheels then make electric power. It's called **hydro-electric power**—electric power made from water.

"Hydro-electric power," said Michelle. She wondered where, exactly, she should write that down on her map. The province of Quebec was so big.

"Quebec has some of the largest hydro-electric power plants in the world," explained Louise. "There are some enormous power plants built on a river that runs into James Bay." She pointed to a spot on Michelle's map.

Michelle marked the river that Louise pointed to and wrote "RIVERS." Next to it she added "HYDRO-ELECTRIC POWER."

"The electricity made by the turbines is sent over wires to cities and factories where it runs the lights and machinery," said Louise. "How many other things can you think of that run on electricity?"

Michelle sat back, took a deep breath, and said, "Electric stoves and fridges and televisions and radios and blow dryers and can openers and . . ."

"Stop!" cried Louise, her hands over her ears. "I'm sorry I asked!"

- In what ways do you use water? How would your life be different if water were scarce?

Above: This is a hydro-electric plant in Quebec near James Bay. How might the people of Quebec use the power produced by this plant?

Quebec has many fast-flowing rivers that produce hydro-electric power. Can you name another province that has many fast-flowing rivers?

Nickel: A Non-renewable Resource

Tuesday morning Michelle was up early, but Louise was in the dome car before her. Michelle took the seat across from Louise and looked out the window. She saw trees and lakes speeding by, but most of the land looked rocky. They were travelling through the Canadian Shield. Long ago, glaciers covered this region. The moving ice scraped away the soil and left bare rock in many places.

According to Michelle's timetable, the train would soon be arriving at Sudbury, Ontario. Michelle looked at her map. Louise suggested she add another natural resource to it.

Michelle looked puzzled. "All I can see are rocks."

"The natural resource I'm thinking of is found in the rock. It's called nickel."

"Like the nickel in a five-cent piece?" asked Michelle.

"That's right, although nickel is mostly used for other things, such as making steel. Nickel is a **mineral**. There's a lot of it in the rocks around here. Nickel is a **non-renewable** natural resource. You can't grow more nickel."

Louise explained how nickel had been discovered near Sudbury. About a hundred years ago workers were blasting rock to build the railway. Somebody noticed rusty marks on the rock, a sign that the rock contained minerals. A mine was built to get the minerals out of the ground. Today, Sudbury produces most of the nickel mined in Canada. There are many other kinds of mines in this part of Ontario, such as copper mines and gold mines.

Louise looked out at the rocky ground. "This area is not very good for growing crops or big trees," she said. "But it is rich in minerals."

"And minerals are a non-renewable resource," added Michelle. She took out her map and wrote "NICKEL (NON-RENEWABLE RESOURCE)" next to Sudbury.

Louise picked up her camera. "Michelle, could you please look out the window for a moment. I want to get a picture of you looking at the scenery."

"I'll look for rusty marks on the rocks," said Michelle, putting her nose to the glass. "Maybe I'll discover more minerals."

- Some early miners became rich, but many more went broke. Why do you think mining is such a risk?

Most of Canada's nickel is mined around Sudbury. What do you think it would be like to work underground?

Renewable and Non-renewable Resources

Some natural resources are renewable and some are non-renewable. A renewable resource is one that can be replaced. Fish, forests and farmland are renewable resources. People can keep catching fish for years and years, because new fish are hatching all the time. After people cut down trees, they can replace them by planting new ones in the same place. And farmers can grow new crops on their farmland every year.

A non-renewable resource is one that can't be renewed. It cannot be replaced. The minerals underground, such as oil, coal, gold and silver, are non-renewable. When people run out of minerals in one place, they have to look for more somewhere else.

New Towns and Ghost Towns

The train rolled westward past the Great Lakes. By Wednesday it had left the rocky land behind and had reached the prairies. Now the countryside was flat, and as far as Michelle could see it was covered with fields of grain. It was like riding through a huge, yellow ocean.

Michelle could see that farmland was the most important natural resource on the prairies. In the distance she noticed a tall wooden tower that she knew was called a grain elevator. It was used to store grain.

When Michelle woke up Thursday morning and raised the blind, the train was still clattering through the yellow ocean of grain fields. But wait! There was something new in the middle of one field, a strange machine with a long bar that moved up and down like a teeter-totter. After they passed the machine Michelle saw another. And another.

She got up and pulled on her clothes. She found Louise in the dining car, scribbling in her notebook and eating breakfast at the same time. Michelle asked her about the strange machines.

"Oh those," said Louise. "You mean the horseheads?"

"They do look a bit like horse heads," agreed Michelle. "But they bob up and down."

"They are horsehead pumps," Louise explained. "Some people call them nodding donkeys or grasshoppers. When they move up and down, they pump oil out of the ground. There's a lot of oil trapped underground here in Alberta. Those pumps bring it to the surface." She laid down her pencil while she put some jam on her toast.

"Are they pumping oil like the oil I use on my bicycle?" asked Michelle, sitting down across the table.

"When it comes out of the ground it's called **crude oil**. Then it's turned into a number of different products, including the oil you use and gasoline that cars use."

Michelle and Louise enjoy their train ride. If you were to travel across Canada, would you like to go by train?

Horsehead pumps are common in Alberta. Can you see how they got their name?

Louise explained that oil is a very valuable non-renewable resource. Some people call it black gold. Oil companies spend lots of money searching for new oil fields under the ground. If an oil field is found far from any town, the company will bring in workers and build houses for them and their families.

Louise told Michelle about a town in northern Alberta called Fort McMurray. Before oil was discovered near Fort McMurray, it was just a village. About 1200 people lived there. Now there are over 30 000 people in Fort McMurray, many of them working for the oil company.

Louise took a sip of coffee and then continued. "In fact, a lot of the towns in Canada grew up because there were natural resources nearby. Do you remember Sudbury?"

"That's where the nickel mine is, in Ontario," said Michelle.

"Right. Sudbury grew up because of the minerals there. Many of the people in Sudbury live there because they can work in the mine and make money. If nobody had built that mine, there would probably be no town there."

"Did all towns in Canada grow up near natural resources?" asked Michelle.

"A lot of them did," said Louise. "The French, the English and other Europeans first came to Canada for the resources. They came because they heard that the country was rich in natural resources. Some bought furs from the Indians; some came to catch fish. Some came to cut the tall trees, and others went looking for minerals, like gold. Some **settlers** began farming. Towns started to grow up near the resources."

"What happens if a town grows up near a non-renewable resource and then the resource runs out?" asked Michelle. "What might happen to Fort McMurray if the oil runs out?"

"Well, if the people in Fort McMurray couldn't find another way to earn a living there, they would probably move. If everyone moved away, Fort McMurray would become a **ghost town**."

"Is that really what they call them—ghost towns?" asked Michelle.

"Sure. There are lots of ghost towns in British Columbia left from a time called the **gold rush**. During the gold rush thousands of people went to British Columbia to look for gold. **Boom towns** were quickly built for the miners and their families. There were stores, banks, restaurants, schools—just like any town. Then the gold ran out and everyone moved away. Now there is nothing left but empty buildings. Those are ghost towns."

Michelle thought about this for a moment. "So when someone discovers a new resource, people move there to find work and they start a new town. If a resource runs out, people have to move away. If *everyone* leaves, the town turns into a ghost town."

"Right. Now, maybe you should order something to eat before *you* turn into a ghost," suggested Louise, picking up her pencil. "That might stop you asking questions long enough for me to get some work done."

"I've got work to do, too," said Michelle, getting out her map. "Have you got a pencil I could borrow?"

- Why would a ghost town be an interesting place to explore?

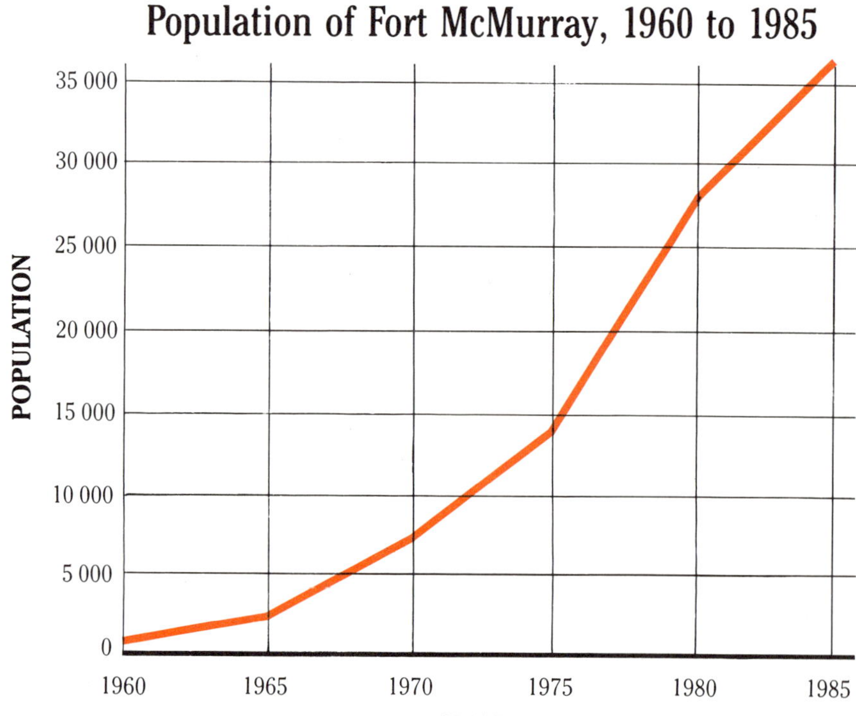

This graph shows how Fort McMurray's population has grown since 1960. In what year did the town have a population of 7500?

Above: In the 1860s, during the gold rush in British Columbia, Barkerville was a boom town. What things can you tell about the town by looking at this picture?

By the early 1900s, Barkerville was a ghost town. Today many tourists visit it during the summer to see how people in British Columbia once lived. What might tourists see there?

End of the Line

The next morning, five days after she had waved goodbye to her mother, Michelle arrived in Vancouver. It was time to meet her uncle for the ferry ride to Vancouver Island. Then they would drive up the island to Woss. As the train rolled slowly into the station, Michelle and Louise stood together, looking out the window for the last time. There was a crowd on the platform, waiting for the train.

"Can you see your uncle yet?" asked Louise.

Michelle looked nervously at all the strange faces. Just what did her uncle look like? Suddenly she saw a familiar face sticking out above the crowd. "That's my uncle!" she cried, pointing. "That's Uncle Joe!"

"And there are Kate and the kids waiting for me," said Louise. She picked up her suitcase.

Michelle grabbed her case and followed Louise down the aisle to the doorway. "Say, Louise! Maybe we could take a trip to Bonavista someday," she suggested.

"You bet. And remember," said Louise, climbing down the steps to the platform, "while you're visiting your uncle on Vancouver Island . . ."

"Yes?" asked Michelle, following her down the steps with her suitcase bumping behind her.

". . . remember to watch out for those big trees."

Michelle and Louise arrive in Vancouver, British Columbia. What do you think they enjoyed most about their trip?

Forests: An Important Resource

"Big trees?" shouted Uncle Joe over the noise of the engine. "Sure we've got big trees. There's one up here at the site I've been saving for you to look at."

Michelle and her uncle were bouncing and bumping up a gravel road in a crummy. A crummy is a truck used to carry loggers to work. Michelle was not used to this kind of road. She hung on tightly to her seat belt.

The road climbed up a forested hillside, past large open slopes where the trees had been cut and the logs lay on the ground. Finally Uncle Joe pulled into one of these logged areas, called **clearcuts**. He turned off the engine.

"There it is," said Uncle Joe, pointing to a tree at the edge of the clearing. "Isn't that some tree?"

It certainly was. It was a gigantic tree, taller than any other ones nearby.

"Let's take a closer look," he suggested, opening his door. Uncle Joe helped Michelle put on a hard hat. Then he put on his own hard hat and grabbed his chain saw from the back of the crummy. Balancing the saw on his shoulder, he strode off towards the tree. Michelle tried to keep up, scrambling over fallen logs and getting caught on the branches.

Close up, the trunk of the big tree was enormous. Michelle stood on one side of it and her uncle stood on the other side, and they tried to grab hands. Impossible. Michelle ran her fingers over the bumpy bark. She looked up the trunk to the top of the tree. The top branches looked as if they were in the clouds. The tree was about 75 m (metres) high.

Looking up like that made Michelle dizzy, so she sat down. Uncle Joe patted the trunk and said, "There are not many trees that are as old as this Douglas fir. Take a guess. How old do you think it is?"

Michelle took a wild guess. "A hundred years old?"

Uncle Joe shook his head. "It's probably four or five hundred years old. This giant has been around a long time."

"Do you have to cut it down?" asked Michelle.

"Don't you think it will make a good telephone pole?"

"Or a flagpole," suggested Michelle.

"Or a lot of matchsticks," added Uncle Joe. "There's probably enough wood in this tree to build a couple of houses. I'll tell you what. Let's see how much you know about the forest resource. How many other ways could you use this tree?"

Michelle named all the things she could think of that were made of wood, like chairs and pencils. Then she remembered that paper was made from trees, too, so she added comics and candy bar wrappers.

Forests: A Renewable Resource

Trees are the largest plants on earth. To grow, trees need light from the sun, and water and nutrients from the soil. The nutrients come from dead plants that have decayed on the forest floor.

Left to themselves, trees will eventually grow old, die and fall to the ground. Each tree produces millions of seeds for future trees. Decaying trees return nutrients to the soil for these new trees. In this way, the forest continually renews itself.

People who **harvest** trees must make sure they do not disrupt this cycle of renewal. There must always be soil and nutrients for future trees. **Foresters** may leave healthy trees nearby to **reseed** the logged area. Sometimes they plant new trees instead. They may also add extra nutrients to the soil.

"Well, you've made a start," said Uncle Joe, "though there are many other products that can be made from wood, everything from cellophane to shoe polish. Now what would happen if we didn't cut this tree down? How would it be used then?"

Michelle was puzzled. "We can't make anything out of the tree if we don't cut it down," she said.

"But the tree can be used in other ways," suggested Uncle Joe. "Think how a squirrel uses it. It lives in the tree, sometimes in an old woodpecker hole. It eats seeds and buds from the tree. It escapes from enemies by running up the tree trunk and jumping from tree to tree."

"I could use the tree myself to climb up," said Michelle. "The view must be great from the top."

"And lots of people enjoy going for walks through the trees in the forest," said Uncle Joe. He told Michelle about other valuable uses of trees. Their roots help keep the soil in place so that it doesn't wash away in heavy rain. Trees shade the creeks so that the water doesn't get too hot for the fish. Trees produce oxygen, which is an important part of the air we breathe.

"This tree is valuable both standing up and cut down," Uncle Joe explained. "Have you any idea what a tree like this is worth after it's sawn into **lumber**? It's worth at least $3000."

Michelle looks up toward the top of a tall tree. What words might Michelle use to describe how tall it is?

Above: Only part of this forest has been logged. Why might it be important to leave some of the forest standing?

Michelle looked up the huge trunk again, with new respect. "When are you going to cut it down?"

"As soon as I see you back in the crummy. You can watch from there. It can be tricky cutting a tree this size. I don't want you to get in the way and become a squashed banana."

"Me neither," agreed Michelle, jumping up and scrambling across the clearcut to the crummy. She hopped in and watched her uncle put on gloves, ear protectors and a face mask. He lifted the chain saw onto a stump. The saw had a motor with a big handle on it, and a long saw bar. Around the edge of the bar was the cutting chain.

Uncle Joe first checked that it was safe to fell the tree. Other people were working near the clearcut, but nobody was close enough to the giant tree to get hurt. Then Uncle Joe yanked the starter cord and Michelle heard the motor buzzing like an enormous, angry bee. He put one edge of the bar against the tree trunk. The chain whirled around the bar, cutting into the wood and spewing out sawdust. Uncle Joe made two straight cuts part way into the trunk and knocked out a big V-shaped wedge. The tree was still standing, but it looked as if someone had taken a big bite out of it.

Now Uncle Joe moved around to the back of the tree for the final cut. As the saw sliced into the trunk, he kept looking up at the top of the tree, waiting for the moment when it would start moving. When he saw the top branches begin to sway he quickly pulled out the saw and ran back several metres.

"Here it goes, Michelle," he yelled.

Michelle clenched her fists and kept her eyes glued to the tree. There was a loud cracking and the huge trunk started pitching forward—first slowly, then faster and faster. It crashed onto the ground with an enormous thump, branches cracking and twigs flying. Only when it was quite still did Michelle let out her breath.

A faller cuts down a tree. What safety equipment is he wearing?

- Why is felling trees dangerous work? How did Uncle Joe protect himself and others?

Canada's Natural Resources

Before we leave Michelle, let's review some of the things she learned on her trip across Canada.

Michelle learned that natural resources are important to Canada. She saw only a few of the country's many resources. Some of these resources are renewable. If used carefully, they can be replaced. Other resources, especially the ones found underground, are non-renewable. They cannot be replaced.

- Name a natural resource near your community. Is the resource renewable or non-renewable?

The rich natural resources drew explorers and settlers to Canada. People came to use the natural resources. Then towns sprang up nearby. Some boom towns became ghost towns after the resource ran out and people moved away. Other towns grew to become today's cities.

Many Canadians today still work in resource **industries** such as fishing, **forestry**, mining and farming. Of all the resources in Canada, forests are the most valuable. Forests are a source of wood, and they have many other important uses, too.

You'll find out much more about the forest resource in the next few chapters.

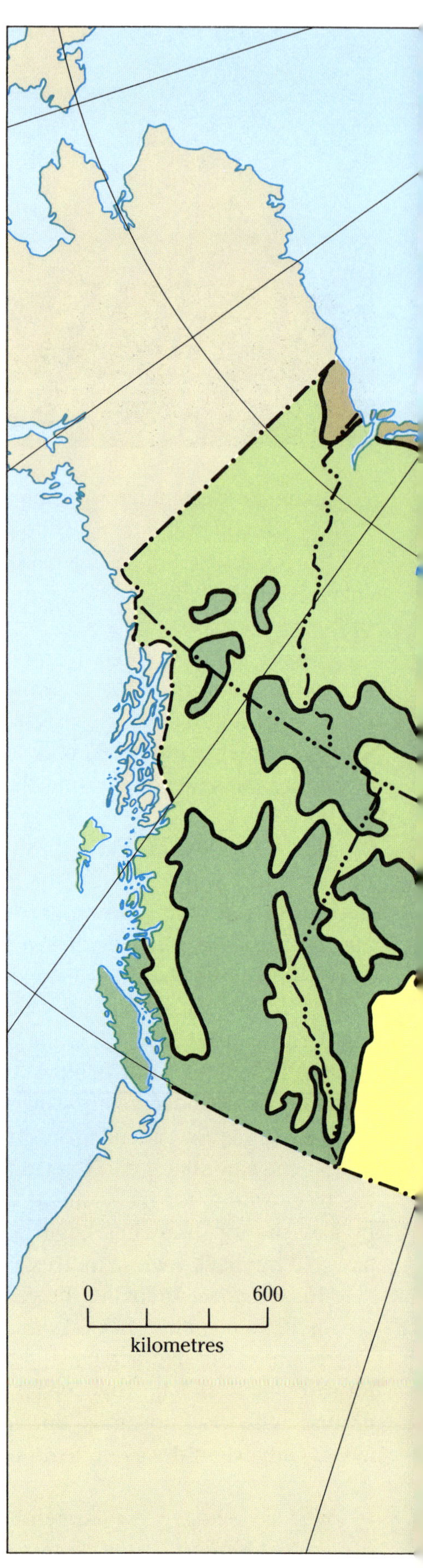

Forests cover about half of the land in Canada. The forest industry uses the trees from the productive forest land. The other forest land includes trees that are too small to use and forests that are too remote. According to the map, what provinces have the greatest amount of productive forest land?

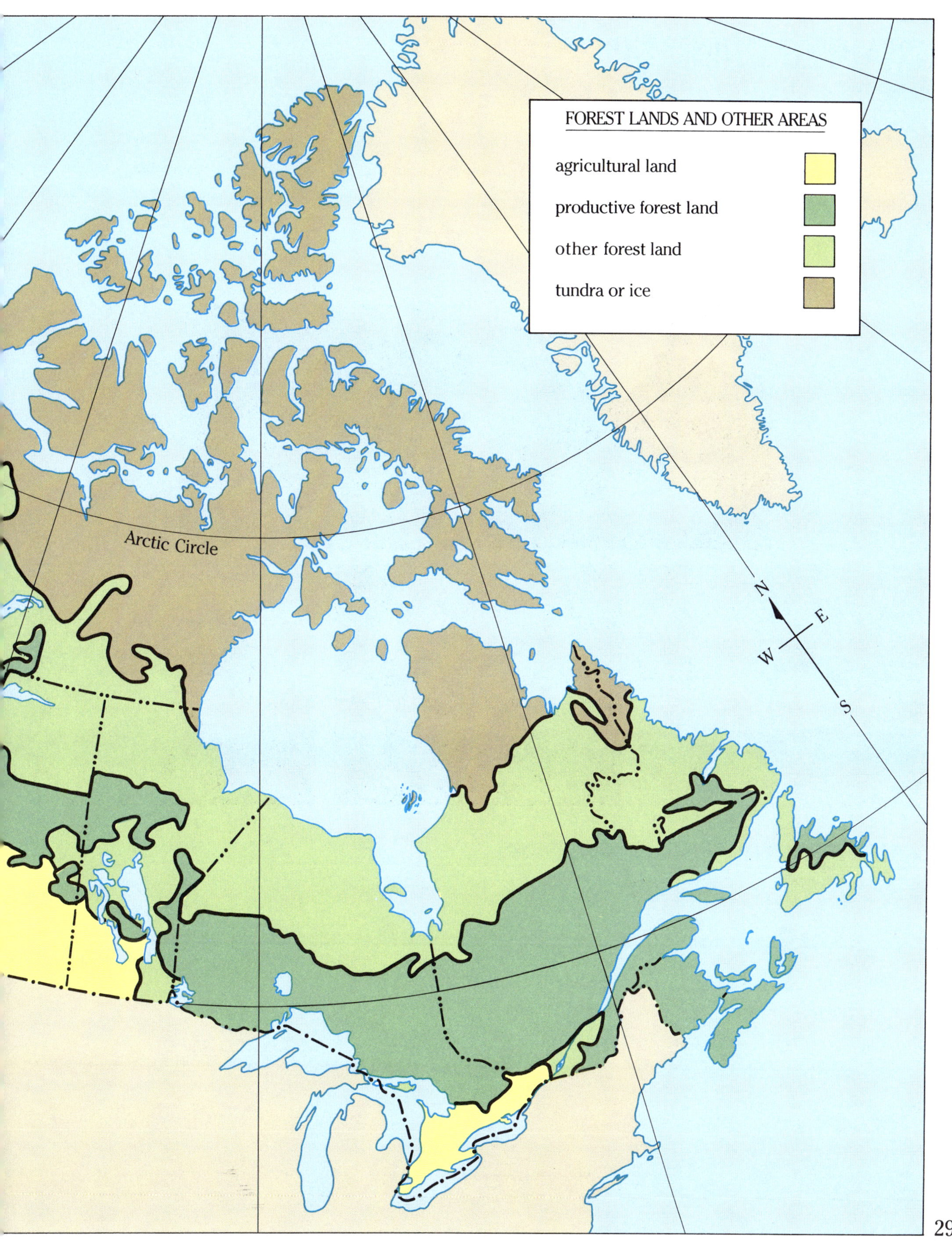
FOREST LANDS AND OTHER AREAS
agricultural land
productive forest land
other forest land
tundra or ice
Arctic Circle
N
E
W
S

CHAPTER CHECKUP

Recalling the Main Ideas

Each picture shows one of the natural resources Michelle learned about on her trip. For each picture, write down

1. the name of the natural resource,
2. whether it is a renewable or non-renewable resource,
3. at least three ways you could use that resource.

Using What You Have Learned

There are many other natural resources that people use. Make a list of as many natural resources as you can. Try to include some of the resources found near your own community. For each one, write down

1. the name of the resource,
2. whether it is a renewable or non-renewable resource,
3. at least one way you could use that resource.

2

How Were Forests Used in the Past?

In the last chapter, you read about Michelle's train ride across Canada. During her trip from Halifax to Vancouver, Michelle learned a lot about Canada's natural resources. These resources include the fish off the Atlantic provinces and the rivers of Quebec. Michelle also learned about the nickel mined in Sudbury, Ontario, and about the oil that is pumped out of the ground in Alberta.

When Michelle arrived on the west coast, she learned about another important natural resource—forests. Forests are the most valuable natural resource in Canada.

You will be learning more about the forest resource in the next few chapters. This chapter explores the past. You will get a glimpse of how Canadians used the forests long ago, and you will be able to see the changes that have taken place over the years. The events that took place before you were born have shaped the way Canadians use the forest resource today. So by learning about the past, you can better understand the present.

Talking about things that happened long ago can sometimes be confusing. To help you keep track of when different events took place, we'll use the **growth rings** of a tree.

Loggers in the early 1920s use a long pole to drive logs to the sawmill. What skills might they need for this work?

Counting the Tree Rings

You can tell how old a tree is by counting its growth rings. In what year did this tree begin to grow?

Have you ever counted the growth rings of a tree? You probably know that after a tree is cut down, you can look closely at the cut end of the trunk and see a pattern of brown rings, one inside the other. These are the tree's growth rings. Trees don't just grow upwards; they also grow outwards. Just under the bark there's a soft part of the tree called the **cambium**. Each year the cambium produces a new layer of wood, making the tree trunk a little fatter.

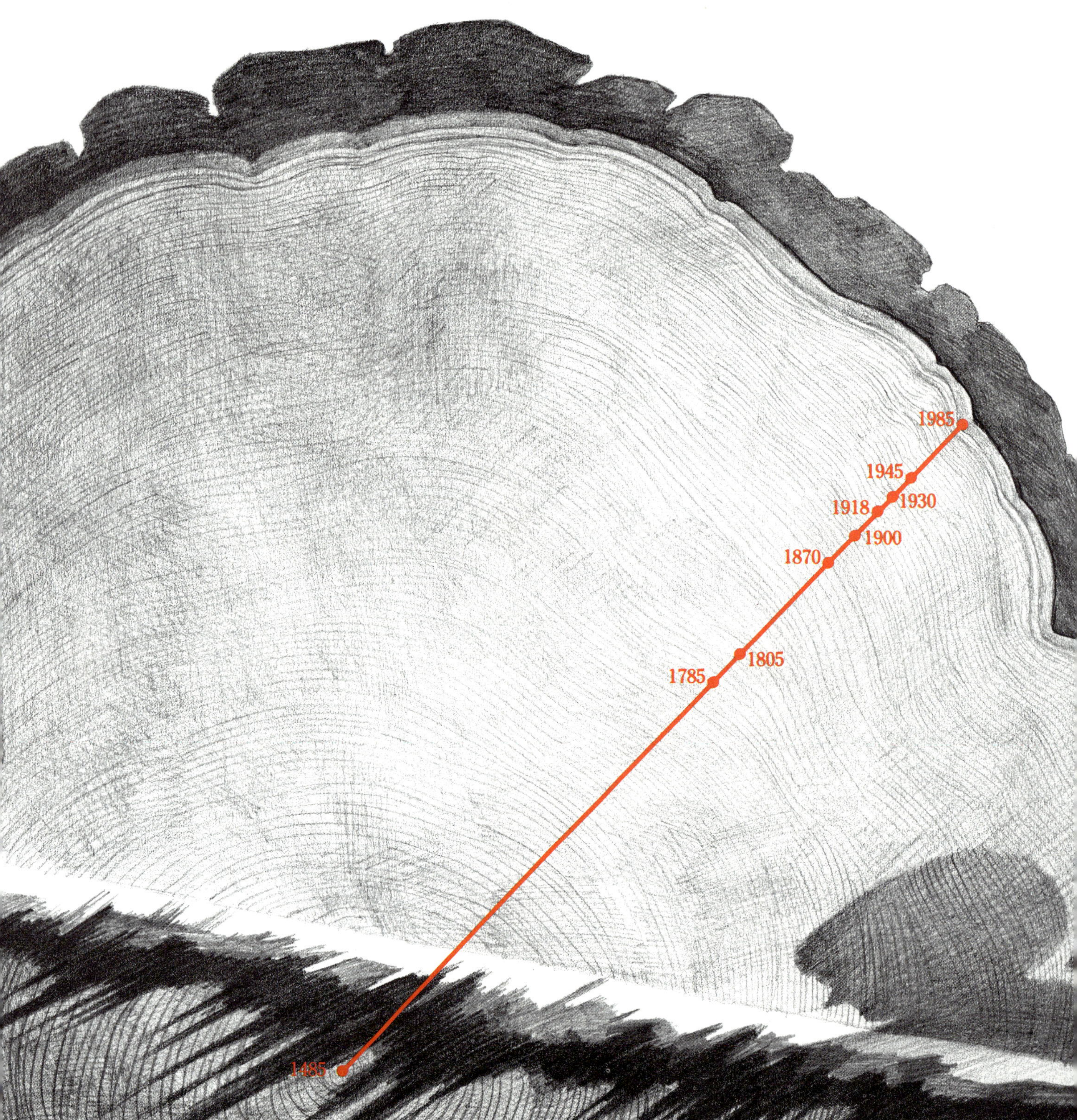

When you look at the **cross-section** of the trunk you can see the layers of wood made by the cambium. They look like rings, one inside the other. Each ring is one year's wood. The smallest rings in the centre are the layers of wood that were made when the tree was young. As the tree got older and fatter, the rings got larger. By counting the rings on a tree, you can tell how old the tree was when it was cut. For instance, a tree with 100 rings will be about 100 years old.

- How many rings would a tree have if it started growing the year you were born?

In the last chapter, Michelle's uncle cut down a gigantic Douglas fir tree that was 500 years old. Imagine what the cut end of that tree would look like. It would be almost 2 m across and covered with 500 rings, one inside the other.

We'll use a picture of these rings as a time line to help us explore the past. This time line covers 500 years. The first date on the time line is 500 years ago, shown by the smallest ring in the centre of the trunk.

That's where we'll start. Think back, and imagine what the forest was like 500 years ago.

Tree Rings

Tree rings can tell you more than just the age of the tree. They can tell you how well the tree was growing each year.

A thick ring means the tree was healthy and producing lots of new wood that year. A thin ring means the tree was not growing very much that year. Maybe it was crowded by other trees, or it didn't get enough water. Diseases and harmful insects can slow down a tree's growth, too.

Some scientists study tree rings to learn about what happened in the past. Differences in the rings can tell them about changes in climate. They can also tell if there were fires or floods in the forest, or if the tree was bent over by a landslide.

How the Indians Used the Forests

Five hundred years ago, before Europeans settled in Canada, the native people were using the forests. The Indian tribes on the west coast hollowed out big cedar trees to make dugout canoes. In eastern Canada the Indians made canoes from bark. These birch-bark canoes were not as strong as dugout canoes, but they were much lighter to carry. If they got torn they could be easily patched up with another piece of bark.

The Indians also used the forests for making homes. On the west coast they built sturdy houses, some big enough for several families to live in. Some tribes in eastern Canada moved around much more. They lived in wigwams made of poles and bark.

Other things were also made from wood. Indians shaped wood into bowls and spoons, paddles and harpoons, snowshoes and toboggans. On the west coast they carved totem poles and wove bark into ropes, baskets and clothing.

Indians used other living things in the forests besides the trees. They got food from the forests—nuts, berries, animals and fish. They made medicines from forest plants. In the east the Indians also collected sap from maple trees.

Even though the Indians used the forests for hundreds of years, they did not use up any of the resource. There were not very many Indians compared to the number of people living in Canada today. They used only what they needed, and the forest could easily replace that small amount. So when explorers from Europe arrived in Canada, the forests looked about the same as they always had.

This photograph from the late 1800s shows an Indian woman weaving cedar bark. What might she be making?

These Indians hollow out a cedar log to make a dugout canoe around 1880. Why do you think they used cedar instead of some other kind of wood?

Settlers clear land for farming in Ontario in the early 1800s. How might they have used the wood they cut?

Clearing the Land

Now let's go back to the time line. We'll move forward 300 years by skipping 300 rings from the centre of the trunk towards the outside edge. We'll come to a growth ring made about 200 years ago, during the late 1700s.

At that time settlers in eastern Canada were clearing land for farms. To get rid of the trees, they burned down huge areas of forest. The settlers did not think the trees were valuable. Of course, they used some for building their houses and fences, and they burned wood for heat. But most trees were just a nuisance to settlers. The forests were in the way of the plows. So the settlers burned down the trees and started farms on the cleared land. This was the fastest way to settle a new land.

Canadians today spend a great deal of money protecting forests from fires. We look back at what the early settlers did, and today we think it was a terrible waste of good forest land. But we can understand why the early settlers had a different attitude towards the forest. They were in a new land that had more trees than they had ever seen. They could not imagine they would ever run out of trees. But they could imagine going hungry in the winter if they did not plant enough crops! And the forests were in the way.

- Why would clearing land be more difficult for early settlers than it is today?

Logging in Eastern Canada

We'll jump forward another 20 rings on the time line. The growth ring we'll look at would have been made in 1805.

There was a boom in Canada's forest industry in the early 1800s. Many people worked in **logging**, cutting down the trees. Canada started to sell a lot of **timber** to other countries. Timber from eastern Canada was shipped to Great Britain for making masts and spars.

Lumber is loaded onto ships to be sent to other countries around 1900. What might this lumber be used for?

Masts and spars were used on sailing ships. Before engines were invented, all ships used sails. The sails were held up by tall poles called masts. The poles that went across the top and bottom of the sails were called spars. Eastern Canada had tall, straight trees that were excellent for masts and spars. White pine trees were especially good.

Eventually, sailing ships were replaced by ships with steam engines, and there was no longer a need for Canadian masts and spars. By then, Canada had started selling wood for other uses. For instance, big tree trunks were cut with an axe on all four sides to make them square. These squared timbers were shipped to Great Britain to make buildings.

Without the modern machines used today, logging and **hauling** were a real test of skill and strength. The most dangerous part was floating the logs down the fast-flowing rivers in the spring. Many men died during these **log drives**.

In those days, customers wanted only the best wood—tall, straight timbers that were free of **knots** or cracks. As a result, early loggers took only the best pine trees, and wasted a great deal of other wood. When they made squared timbers, they sometimes discarded more than half the tree on the forest floor. The leftover wood was not worth selling.

- Can you think of any resources that we waste today?

Bit by bit, the best pine forests in eastern Canada disappeared. They were logged faster than they could grow back. Loggers were forced to switch to smaller pines and other kinds of trees. Yet few people thought of planting new trees to replace the ones that were cut. With so much forest in Canada, it was difficult to imagine running out of trees for logging.

Logging in British Columbia

We'll move forward another 65 tree rings on the time line. Let's look at what was happening in British Columbia around 1870.

By 1870, loggers had started felling the huge trees of the west coast. Some wood was loaded onto sailing ships and sent to other countries. A lot of wood was needed in Canada, too. The government of Canada was building a railway across the country. Wood was needed for railway ties, stations and bridges, and for bunkhouses for the workers to sleep in.

When the railway was finished, settlers from eastern Canada and from other countries moved to the prairies to start farming. They needed wood for fences and buildings. Wood was also needed to build new towns in British Columbia. Miners moved there to look for gold and other minerals.

Forest workers in those days worked long and hard. There were no machines, so all the cutting, hauling and sawing had to be done by hand or with animals. There were no logging trucks, so sometimes the logs were floated down rivers or along the coast to the sawmill. In some places, the logs were chained together and dragged from the forest by teams of oxen.

The person in charge of the bulls was the bull puncher. He was an important man. Usually he was a big fellow with a loud voice. His job was to keep the bulls working. If they moved too slowly, he gave them a prod with a sharp stick called a goad.

The first sawmills in British Columbia were built along the coast. Towns began to grow up around the mills. Some towns continued growing long after the sawmills shut down. They have become modern cities. Vancouver, the largest city in British Columbia, was once a logging town.

In the early days of logging, all work was done by hand. What do you think these loggers are doing?

Teams of oxen, such as this team photographed in the 1890s, were used to haul logs from the forest. Why do you think loggers used oxen instead of some other kind of animal?

Pulp and Paper

Now we'll skip another 30 growth rings on the time line. By 1900, Canada was using the forests for making paper.

For years, paper had been made from rags. Rags were soaked and pounded into a watery **pulp**, which was then poured onto a screen to dry into paper. During the 1800s, rags became scarce. Then it was discovered that paper could be made out of wood instead of rags. The first Canadian mill to make paper out of wood was built in Quebec in 1864. By 1900, there were more than 50 pulp and paper mills across Canada.

Have you ever seen pulp? It is wood that has been ground up and mashed or else cooked in **chemicals** until it looks a bit like soggy oatmeal. It is then rolled out and dried to make sheets of paper. Pulp is used to make all kinds of paper, from cardboard to candy bar wrappers to **newsprint**.

Pulp and paper mills like this one make newsprint and many other kinds of paper. What different kinds of paper do you use every day?

Today Canada makes more newsprint than any other country in the world. Imagine how many newspapers are read every day in all the cities of the world. About one third of that paper comes from Canada.

The pulp and paper industry is now the largest single industry in Canada. It provides work for many Canadians. The industry needs a huge amount of wood to keep all the mills supplied. Two hundred trees a day may be needed to make enough newsprint for just one city newspaper. Fortunately, pulp mills use wood that is not suitable for lumber, mainly wood chips left over from sawmills.

Growing New Forests

We'll count over another 18 rings on the tree trunk, to the year 1918. That is the year the government set up the first forestry **research** station.

When Canadians started using the forests for lumber and pulp, most people were not careful about how many trees they cut or how much wood was wasted. In those days, people didn't think about treating the forest with care. Most people were just happy that forestry was providing jobs and wealth. They thought that Canada would never run out of its huge forests. There would always be more trees over the next hill.

As more and more wood was cut, some people became concerned. John A. Macdonald, the first prime minister of Canada, warned, "We are recklessly destroying the timber of Canada."

Some people believed it was important to learn how to grow new forests to replace the ones that were burned or cut. Finally, in 1918, the Canadian government set up a research station in Petawawa, Ontario. There, scientists could learn how to make trees grow better and faster. They divided the land into sections and tried different ways of growing trees in each section. That way, they began to learn which growing methods worked best.

Today there are forest research stations across the country. People working there have learned a lot about how trees grow and how to make them grow faster. They are developing new kinds of trees that produce better wood in less time. And every year they learn a little bit more.

Canada needs this knowledge. Without new forests, the forest industry will eventually run out of wood. The government and the forest companies today realize the importance of learning how to grow trees. Canadians have learned from the past. We know we cannot afford to treat the forest resource the way the early loggers did.

- Why does it take a long time to learn about growing trees?

Silviculture: Farming the Forest

Silviculture means growing crops of trees. It is farming in the forest instead of farming in the field.

There is more to growing a crop than just planting seeds in the ground. Plants need the right amount of sun and the right kind of soil. They should not be too crowded. They need to be protected from harmful insects and diseases. In some ways, a crop of trees is just the same as a crop of vegetables. If the crop is planted carefully and looked after while it grows, better trees will be produced.

A crop of vegetables will be ready to harvest after a summer, but a crop of trees takes about 80 years to grow. People who work in silviculture have to think far ahead. They are growing trees for the future.

Junior Forest Wardens

Junior Forest Wardens attend camp to learn about the care and protection of forests. What do you think they might be learning here?

Now we'll hop over another 12 years on the time line. That will bring us to 1930.

A club was formed in British Columbia where children could learn about the importance of protecting forests. The members were called Junior Forest Wardens.

At first, they spent most of their time helping to prevent forest fires. A great deal of forest was being burned by fires, many started by careless people. Junior Forest Wardens put up posters telling people to be careful about starting fires. They spoke to other children at school assemblies. They watched for signs of forest fires. Sometimes they even helped put out a blaze. Their motto was "Watch and Warn."

Those first Junior Forest Wardens are grown up now, but new ones have taken their place. Today there are Junior Forest Wardens in most provinces of Canada. They do much more than help prevent fires. Some clubs run Christmas tree farms, plant trees, build forest trails or clean up forest creeks so that fish can live in them.

The idea behind Junior Forest Wardens has not changed, though. It is still important that children learn to care for the forests. They will be responsible for protecting the resource in the future.

Managing the Forests

We'll move forward about 15 rings on the time line to the 1940s. We'll look at how the forests were **managed** then.

In the early days of logging, there were not many rules about where loggers could cut trees or how they did it. Logging companies just took the wood they wanted. They paid the government for the trees they took. The more wood that was cut, the more money the government got. This money was used for roads, railways and other things needed by the new country.

By the 1940s, the government was becoming concerned. The forests were bringing in lots of money, but they were being cut down faster and faster. A lot of wood was wasted.

The government started making rules to protect the forest resource. It set limits on the amount of wood that could be cut. The government wanted to be sure there would always be enough new trees growing up to replace the ones the logging companies cut down.

Most of Canada's forests are on what we call **public** land—land that belongs to all Canadians. Parks and highways are on public land, too. The provincial government usually manages public land, including forests, for the people.

Workers plant a new forest as part of their company's forest management plan. Why might this be hard work?

When the government manages forests, it hires forest managers to decide which areas of the forest should be cut and which areas should be left standing for other uses. Logging companies must get permits from the government to cut trees. Sometimes the government asks the forest companies to hire their own forest managers and make their own decisions about how to protect public forests for the future. But the government has the final say.

Over the years, forest management has become more and more important. Today it includes planting new forests and protecting them from fires and harmful insects. People today realize that the forest resource must be used wisely or it will run out. The work that forest managers do now will benefit Canadians in the future.

- If you didn't like the way the government was managing the forest, what could you do?

New Technology

We're now close to the outside edge of the time line. **Technology** has changed the forest industry over the past 40 years.

Forest workers have been using more machines and less muscle. Gone are the bull punchers and the teams of oxen. In the 1950s, chain saws replaced the old cross-cut saws used by two people. The first chain saws were so heavy that two fallers were needed to hold them, but they were still a big improvement over hand sawing.

In parts of Canada where the trees are smaller and the land is flatter, workers started using mechanical tree harvesters. These enormous machines roll up to a group of trees, snip through the trunks and strip off the branches. The machines then load the logs onto their carriers before lumbering over to the next group of trees.

Moving the logs is easier, too. The teams of oxen that dragged the logs from the forest have been replaced by mechanical skidders. These vehicles have huge tires that bounce over rocks and stumps. They use a winch to pull in whole trees. On steep slopes, logs are attached to high cables strung across the logging site, and an engine pulls the logs along this cable. Logging trucks make the job of getting the logs to mills much easier.

The mills themselves are mechanized. They are sometimes equipped with **computers**. When a log comes in, the computer measures it in a fraction of a second and shows the **sawyer** exactly how it could be cut with the saw. The sawyer uses this information to decide how to cut the log. Then the computer runs the saw. The finished boards are sorted by a machine and dumped into piles. It is

The mill's computer measures the log and shows the sawyer where to cut. How do you think the red lines in the picture help the sawyer?

The skidder can drag logs over very rough ground. What might it be like to ride in a machine like this?

all very fast, and the new sawmills waste much less wood than the old ones did. That means there is more good lumber produced from each tree.

Many of these new machines do the work that people used to do. This makes the forest industry much more efficient. It is possible to harvest trees and run the mills with fewer workers. However, more people are now needed for replanting and silviculture jobs. In general, forest workers today need more training than they did in the past. It takes skill, not just muscle, to operate the machines used in the forest industry today.

- How has the forest industry changed over the past 40 years?

Changes in the Forest Industry

We've reached the outside bark of the tree trunk. We've covered 500 years of forest history.

During those years Canadians have changed the way they harvest and use wood. Machines have changed the work of loggers in the forest and sawyers in the mills. New forest products have replaced masts and spars. As methods of forestry have changed, new jobs have replaced the old ones.

During those years Canadians have learned that it is important to take care of the forest resource—to manage it so that there will be enough trees for future **generations**. Today there are limits on the amount of wood that can be cut. Pulp and other products use wood that was once wasted. New trees are planted for the future. People working in silviculture are developing better, faster ways of growing forests.

Canadians have learned a lot from the past, but we don't always use that knowledge. Not enough new trees are planted to replace all the trees that are cut. The forests of the future often seem less important than the jobs and forest products today. What will future Canadians think when they look back at the way we use our forest resource today? Will they think we manage our forests wisely?

During the past 500 years, many changes have taken place. Even the forests themselves have changed. Those gigantic, 500-year-old trees, such as the one we used for our time line, are nearly all gone. They have been replaced by newer forests with trees that will be harvested long before they grow that big or that old.

Some of the old trees have been preserved in parks, though. You can walk through the cool, quiet shade beneath these trees. They remind us of what the forest used to be like long ago when only the native people lived in this land we now call Canada. They remind us of all the things that have happened since. Trees are the oldest living things on this earth. They have lived through a lot of changes. What changes does the future hold?

Some of Canada's oldest trees are preserved in parks. What do you think the land around your school was like 500 years ago?

Ottawa
From Forest to City

You have read about how Canadians have used the forests. There have been many changes over the years. Canada has also changed in other ways.

Once, Canada was all wilderness. Today there are cities with skyscrapers and streets crowded with people. How did these cities start? Why are they located where they are?

In many cases, today's cities started as small settlements that grew up near natural resources. Ottawa, the capital city of Canada, began that way.

At first, the only people living in the Ottawa Valley were the Algonquin Indians. The Indians hunted moose and caribou in the tall forest. They travelled along the rivers in light birch-bark canoes.

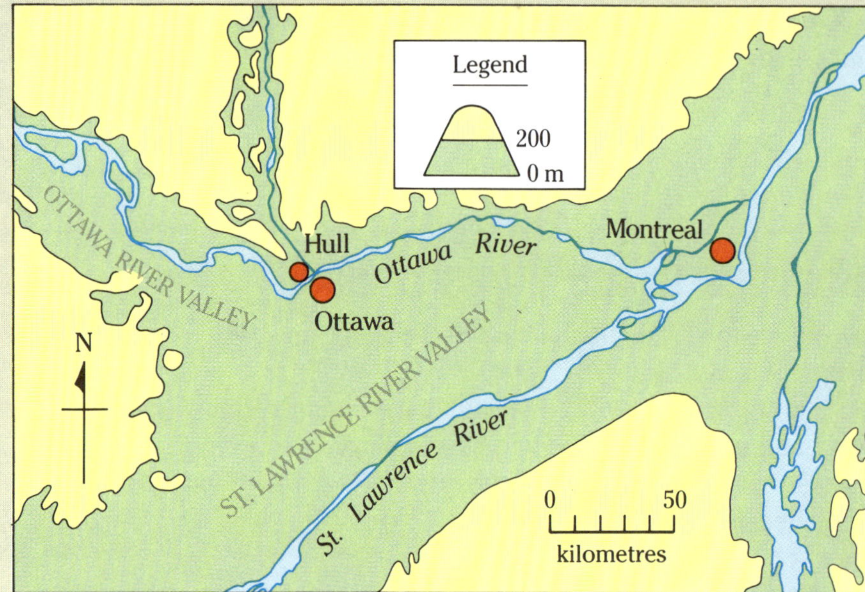

This map shows the Ottawa Valley as it is today.

The Algonquin Indians were the first people to live in the Ottawa Valley.

This picture from the late 1800s shows people working in a mill built by E.B. Eddy along the Ottawa River.

In 1800, a family with seven children moved to the Ottawa Valley. The Wrights saw that the area had good forests and good soil for farming. The waterfall on the river could be used to make power to run a sawmill.

The Wright family started clearing land to plant crops and build log cabins. The children worked alongside their parents. Year by year, more families came and the settlement grew.

People built mills on both sides of the river. They built timber chutes — like water slides — to float logs around the waterfall.

One man attracted to the area was E.B. Eddy. In 1852, he started manufacturing hand-made matches and wooden washboards. His company became larger and larger. By 1890, Eddy was also making pulp and paper.

The mills drew workers to the small community. They worked long hours, six days a week, in the noisy, crowded mills.

The communities beside the river grew. The town on the north side of the river, where the Wright family had settled, was named Hull. The milltown on the south side of the Ottawa River had become a larger city named Ottawa.

Today Ottawa is a city of over 500 000 people. Many work for the government, but the forest resource is still very important to this area. Sawmills and pulp mills dot the valley. The E.B. Eddy pulp and paper mill alone employs 2000 people.

Today Ottawa is the capital of Canada.

What Could You Do during National Forest Week?

On the board, the teacher wrote, "May 4–10 is National Forest Week." Turning to face the class, he explained further. "During National Forest Week, students across Canada will be taking part in different projects. Some will plan an activity to help them learn more about forests. They might visit a tree nursery, for instance. Other students will do something to improve an area of forest. They might clear garbage out of a forest creek. Some students will draw posters that teach other students about preventing forest fires."

The teacher looked around the class. "What do you think we should do during National Forest Week?"

During the class discussion, many ideas were suggested. One student wrote them all down on the board. After a vote, the class decided on two projects for the week.

One project was to make up a play. The class would perform this play for the rest of the school. It would be about a group of children who go camping in the forest. The children in the play would choose a safe place to camp so that their campfire would not accidently start a forest fire. The play would include a scene that takes place the next morning when the children make sure the fire is out before they leave the campsite. The play would teach other students how to prevent forest fires.

Drawing a poster is one way of showing other students how to protect the forest. What might students learn from this poster?

The other project was a long-term one. The students would begin growing Christmas trees for the school. During National Forest Week, the class would plant one tree in the school yard. Every year after that, students at the school would plant another tree. After about 10 years, the first tree would be big enough to cut down for a school Christmas tree. If the students kept planting one tree a year, there would always be one tree ready to cut down at Christmas and nine more growing up. The students would also learn something about growing trees. They would be able to measure the growth of the trees and watch for insects. Although the students in this class would graduate and leave the school, the growing trees would be left as a gift for future students.

- What project would you like to do during National Forest Week?

Each year students plant a tree in the school yard. What might they learn about the forests from this project?

CHAPTER CHECKUP

Recalling the Main Ideas

In this chapter you have read about changes that have taken place in forestry over the years. Imagine that a settler who cleared land in the 1780s falls asleep for 200 years and wakes up in the 1980s. The settler asks you to explain some of the changes that have taken place during the time he or she has been asleep. Write down five sentences to describe five different things you will tell the early settler. (Make sure your sentences give examples of changes in forestry jobs, changes in the technology used in the forest and changes in the way we manage the forest.)

Using What You Have Learned

Look at this photograph of two early loggers on the British Columbia coast. Use the picture to help you answer the following questions.

1. Why is this tree so much bigger than most trees cut today?
2. The early loggers wasted a lot of each tree. What part of this tree will not be used?
3. How do you think the workers will haul this tree out of the forest to the sawmill? If this tree were close to a river or ocean, how might it be taken to the mill?
4. How are the clothing and equipment of today's loggers different from those of the early loggers?
5. The fallers in the photograph would have taken several hours to cut this one tree. Today two people can cut hundreds of trees in the same time. Over the years, foresters have learned how to cut down forests much faster. What effect do you think this change has had on our forest resource?

3

How Can Forests Be Used Today?

In this chapter we're going to take a close-up look at a small town called Spruceville. We'll watch a **public meeting** to find out why the forest is important to the people of Spruceville.

Spruceville is not a real town, but the people you'll meet there are typical of real people across Canada. Like other Canadians, they have different ideas about why the forest is important and how it should be used. They do not always agree.

If Canada had unlimited good forest land, there would be plenty of forest for everyone. There would be enough for logging, for wildlife, for parks and for all the other possible uses. Unfortunately, that is not the case. Especially near towns, good forest land is limited. Areas of forest have already been logged or covered by roads, houses and farms. Some forests have been flooded by reservoirs—lakes that store water for hydro-electric power plants. Other forests have been set aside for parks, and no logging is allowed there.

There is a great demand for the forest that is left. Some people want to log it. Others want to leave it the way it is. With these different points of view, it can be difficult to decide the best use for an area of forest.

- Are there forests near your community? How are they used?

Who finally decides how the forest will be used? That's usually the provincial government's job. Forest managers working for the government have to decide what's best for everyone. It's not easy to make these decisions. Let's take a look at how a decision was made in Spruceville.

Workers and machines build a new highway through forest land. What do you think the government should consider before it builds a new road?

A Public Meeting in Spruceville

Spruceville is built on the banks of a river with rolling hills all around. There are offices, stores, banks and a gas station on the main street of town. Just down the river is the sawmill, where about 60 people in Spruceville have jobs.

Peter LeBlanc owns LeBlanc's Logging Company. About 30 people in Spruceville work for him. His logging company cuts wood and trucks it to the sawmill.

Through the years, most of the forest near Spruceville has been logged. New trees are growing, but it will be years before they will be ready to be cut down. LeBlanc's Logging Company now has to drive farther and farther to find wood. Then it has to truck the heavy logs all the way back to the mill. Hauling logs a long distance gets expensive.

There is one area of good forest close to Spruceville that has not been logged. That forest is on the hillside right above town. Peter LeBlanc wants to get permission from the government to log that forest.

Linda Gill is the district forest manager for the government. Her job is to manage the forests around Spruceville. She decides how the forest should be used and how much can be cut each year.

Peter LeBlanc went to Linda Gill's office with his **cutting plan** for the hillside above Spruceville. The plan showed which areas he wanted to log. It explained where he would build logging roads and what methods he would use to harvest the trees.

Linda Gill knew she had a difficult decision to make. Some people had already phoned her office saying they did not want logging on that hillside. Ms. Gill decided to get the opinion of other people in Spruceville. She wanted to hear how they felt about the forest. So she called a public meeting.

The school gymnasium was packed on the evening of the public meeting. There were people standing at the back. Ms. Gill called the meeting to order.

"I'm here to listen," she said. "I want to hear how you think we should use the forest above town. I have to make a decision, and there are many different choices I could make. I could allow Peter LeBlanc to log the whole forest, or I could let him log just some of the forest, or I could refuse him permission to log any of it. No matter what decision I make, I'm not going to please everybody. To make the best possible decision, I need to hear your views."

- Do you think a public meeting is a good way to help a forest manager make a decision?

Forest manager Linda Gill asks the people of Spruceville how they want to use their forest. Why does she need to listen to their views?

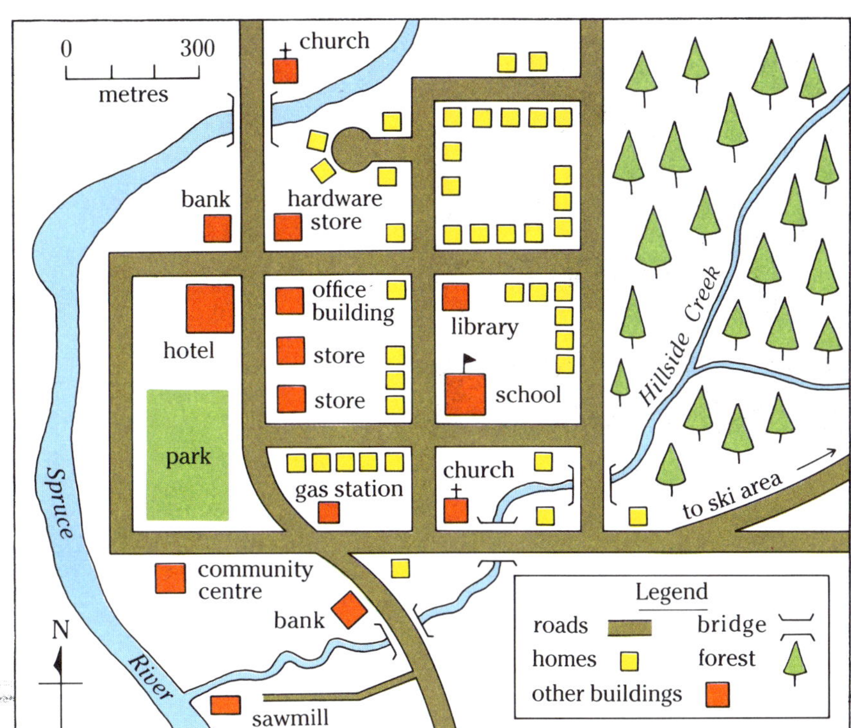

Right: This map shows Spruceville. In what direction is the forest from the town?

Peter LeBlanc

Peter LeBlanc was the first to stand up and speak. He explained why he wanted to log the hillside.

"I'm running out of wood close to the mill," he said. "That hillside has enough trees on it to keep my workers busy for several years. I need that wood."

He looked around the audience. "You need that wood, too. All of you use wood products. In fact, right now Spruceville is using lots of wood to build the new community centre. Where will that wood come from if logging companies like mine aren't allowed to harvest the forest? If we have to drive farther to get wood, the lumber you buy will cost more. We can't just let those good trees on the hill sit there. We need to use them."

- Why will lumber cost more if truck drivers have to haul it a long way?

Jane Anderson

After Peter LeBlanc was finished speaking, someone in the back called out: "Mr. LeBlanc's right! Let's use those trees." A few people clapped.

"I don't think he's right at all!" shouted another voice from the front. Linda Gill called for quiet and asked the person at the front to speak.

Jane Anderson stood up. "I am representing the Spruceville Outdoors Club," she said. "The members of our club use the forest above town for hiking in the summer and cross-country skiing in the winter. The forest is one of the last unspoiled areas around Spruceville. It's a beautiful place—quiet and peaceful. Sometimes we see animals and birds. We take our children there to learn about nature. Logging would change all that."

She turned to face the audience. "Are logging companies going to be allowed to cut every last bit of forest around Spruceville? Surely we can afford to save some forests for the future, for our children. I don't care if I have to pay a bit more for wood products. There are some things that are more important than money. I think the hillside should be kept as a park area. I say NO LOGGING!"

Ms. Anderson sat down and the people in her corner of the gym clapped and nodded. Other members of the audience shook their heads.

Jim Charlie

Jim Charlie asked to speak. "I work for Mr. LeBlanc," he said. "If he doesn't log that hillside, I could be out of a job."

Mr. Charlie continued, "I'm not the only one that would be hurt. Mr. LeBlanc has about 30 workers, and he hires extra students in the summer. Where will they work if there are not enough logging jobs? Also, the sawmill needs wood to keep running. If Mr. LeBlanc can't supply the mill with enough wood, workers there could lose their jobs."

He turned to look at Ms. Anderson. "I like parks, too, but those forestry jobs are more important to Spruceville. We can't afford to lose them. What's the use of a park if people have to leave town because there aren't enough jobs?" Jim Charlie sat down.

Fritz Müller

Then Fritz Müller, owner of the Spruceville hardware store, stood up. "I don't want people to lose their jobs," he said. "I want them to keep spending money in my store!" There were some chuckles at this.

Mr. Müller continued, "When I'm not in the store, I like to go fishing. My favourite fishing spots are on one of the creeks that flows down through the forest. I'm afraid that dirt will be dumped into the creeks if Peter LeBlanc builds logging roads on the hillside. Dirty water will hurt the fish, especially when they are laying eggs."

Mr. Müller explained the importance of fishing to the community. "I'm not the only one around here that likes fishing. I sell fishing licences to lots of tourists that come into my store. I tell them to go up the creek in the forest and catch trout. If the fishing is good, those tourists usually stay around town for an extra day or two. That's good, because they spend money in our hotels and restaurants."

Mr. Müller summed up. "So if Mr. LeBlanc is allowed to log the forest, I want to see some strict rules about how he does it. Make sure he protects that creek."

Pauline Yuen

Pauline Yuen stood up. She was a biologist working for the government. She explained that Mr. LeBlanc had already made some changes to his plan to protect the fish. He had changed the route of a logging road so that it wouldn't cross the creeks as often. He had agreed not to drop any trees into the creeks.

Ms. Yuen continued, "I'm satisfied that we can protect the fish. Now I'm more concerned about the wildlife in the forest. Many animals depend on that forest for food and shelter. Logging can destroy their **habitat**."

Ms. Yuen explained a bit more about the wildlife. "There is a herd of elk that uses that forest during the winter. I would like to do a study to see exactly where the elk go and what they need to survive. Then we may be able to take steps to protect them. I'm not saying there should not be any logging on the hillside. But it must be carefully planned so that the animals are not wiped out."

- Do you think people should care about animals that live in the forest? Tell why.

Angela Rosso

Angela Rosso, owner of the Spruceville Real Estate Company, waved a hand from the back of the gym.

"Go ahead, Ms. Rosso," said Linda Gill.

"I'm representing the Spruceville Chamber of Commerce," said Ms. Rosso. "That includes most of the businesses in town. The Chamber of Commerce thinks we should let Mr. LeBlanc log the hill because the jobs he provides are important."

She explained, "The loggers spend money at Mr. Müller's hardware store and at other stores in town. That's good for the stores and for the people who work in them. Mr. LeBlanc's company and his workers also pay **taxes** to the town. We use their tax money to hire garbage collectors and people to run the public library."

Ms. Rosso looked at Mr. LeBlanc. "We need businesses like LeBlanc's Logging Company to keep the town running. If there are no jobs, a town soon goes downhill. We should find ways to help Mr. LeBlanc make jobs; we certainly shouldn't stand in his way. I say that we should let Mr. LeBlanc log the hillside." Angela Rosso sat down.

The Forest Habitat

When you think of the forest, you probably think of the trees. Yet the forest is also a habitat—a home for other living things.

Each animal has a special place in the forest habitat. Each has a job to do. Insects chew and tunnel their way through the rotting wood on the forest floor, turning it into a spongy new layer of soil. Birds feed on harmful insects that damage the trees. Wolves prey on deer, keeping their numbers down. (Since deer nibble on the tender tops of young trees, too many of them could be harmful to the forest.)

When people cut trees, clear land or build roads or trails in the forest, they disturb the forest habitat. For instance, people may disturb birds nesting in certain areas of the forest. Many animals are hit by vehicles driving along roads built through the forest. Some animals can adapt to changes to their habitat, but others cannot. These animals move elsewhere or die.

Logging greatly changes the forest habitat, so it can have a disastrous effect on some of the animals that live in the woods. Forest managers must learn which animals live in each area of the forest. They may be able to plan the logging so that it does less damage to the animals. They may even decide not to log at all.

Deer run through forest land that has been logged. How has the forest habitat been affected by logging?

Jeremy Goldberg

Jeremy Goldberg spoke next at the public meeting. He was the science teacher at the Spruceville high school.

"I'm worried about logging on that hillside," he said. "If we allow any logging up there, we'll have to be very, very careful. That forest is important to Spruceville. Our water comes from the creeks that flow down from the forest. If people build logging roads and drive machinery around on that hill, they will disturb the soil. It could be washed into the creeks. Then our tap water would get dirty."

Mr. Goldberg paused and looked around the gymnasium. "There's another reason we need to be careful about logging. Logging can change the way water flows down the hill. For instance, after an area is logged, the soil may be flattened. This hard soil doesn't soak up as much water. If we get a heavy rainstorm, a lot of water may flow into the creeks at once. Or if we get a hot spell in March and all the snow melts at once, that water could fill the creeks. The creeks might even overflow, come rushing down the hill and flood parts of Spruceville."

Jeremy Goldberg looked serious. "I know that logging will give our town jobs, but most people don't realize how valuable that forest is to Spruceville in other ways. It helps keep our water clean and it may prevent flooding." Mr. Goldberg sat down. A group of students at the back cheered.

This landslide was caused by an increase in the flow of water down the hill. How might the landslide affect people who live in this area?

Peter LeBlanc Replies

Peter LeBlanc jumped up. "Good heavens, Mr. Goldberg! I don't want my logging to cause flooding or dirty water any more than you do. Nor do I want to spoil the forest for fish and wildlife, or for people who like hiking. I'm not going to cut all the trees and leave the whole hillside bare. For one thing, Ms. Gill would never let me!"

Mr. LeBlanc explained that there are many ways of logging a forest. A forester would look at the forest near Spruceville and decide which logging methods would work best there.

Mr. LeBlanc told about some of the new logging methods he could use that would do less harm to the forest environment. These methods would cost more, but they would protect the forest for other uses. He admitted that the forest would look different after it was logged. He said that it would be replanted immediately.

This forest worker is studying the fish in a forest stream. How might logging damage a fish habitat?

The Forest Floor: A Giant Sponge

The forest floor is soft and spongy. Soil is mixed with dead leaves, needles, rotting wood, twigs, moss and other plants.

When it rains, the forest floor acts like a giant sponge. The water is soaked up by the soil. Then it very slowly drains through the soil into the creeks.

The forest also helps keep the water in the creeks clean. The roots of the trees and other plants hold the soil in place and keep it from washing into the creeks. On steep slopes, trees are especially important. If all the trees are removed from a steep slope, there is a greater chance that the soil will wash away.

Mr. LeBlanc explained some of the logging methods that might help to protect the environment:

- Loggers might not cut all the trees at once. They would take only patches of trees. Other trees would be left to prevent the soil from washing away.
- A strip of trees might be left along the creek.
- Parts of the forest that are important to wildlife might not be logged.
- Trees around trails and campsites might not be logged.
- Machines with huge rubber tires might pull the logs to the loading zone. The huge rubber tires do less damage to the soil than vehicles with metal treads.
- Loggers might work only in the winter. When the ground is frozen it is less easily damaged.
- On steep slopes, logs might be pulled to the loading zone along cables high above the ground. Then the logs would not disturb the soil.
- Helicopters or huge balloons might be used for lifting logs from steep slopes. However, this method is very expensive.

"There is a big difference between careless logging and careful logging," said Mr. LeBlanc. "I can promise you I will do a careful job." He sat down.

Linda Gill looked around the gym. "Anyone else?" she asked.

- If you spoke at the meeting, what would you say?

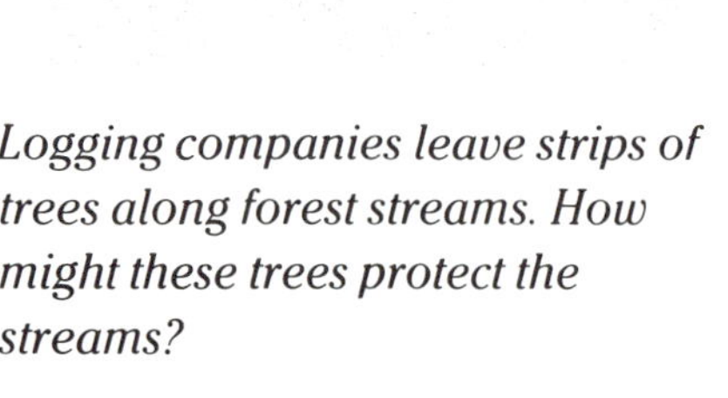

Logging companies leave strips of trees along forest streams. How might these trees protect the streams?

Logging for Long-Term Benefits

What would happen if Canadians decided to log all their forests now? There would be many forest jobs. Forest towns would boom. Canadians would make a lot of money.

But once the forest was gone, the jobs and benefits would end. There would be a long wait until new forests grew up.

Instead, Canadians could decide to log more slowly. We would make less money now, but the benefits would last longer. By the time forest companies finish logging the older forests, new forests would have had time to grow. While logging is taking place in one area of forest, other areas could be used by wildlife and people.

That way, Canadians can benefit from our forests today, tomorrow and maybe forever.

A new forest of young trees has been planted where another forest once stood. How might this forest management practice protect the environment?

The End of the Public Meeting

Fritz Müller stood up again. "Lots of folks here have different points of view," he said. "It would suit me fine if there was no logging, but some people are worried about forestry jobs. Somehow we've all got to live together in Spruceville. So I think we should work together. Let's come up with a plan for the hillside that most of us can agree on."

Fritz Müller suggests that the people of Spruceville work together on a plan for the forest. Why is it important for people with different opinions to work together?

There was a great deal of clapping at this. Linda Gill stood up. "We've certainly heard lots of different opinions. Now I'd like to form a **committee** to help me decide on a plan for the hillside. I want people on the committee who represent all these different points of view."

Right: Spruceville is located on the eastern bank of the Spruce River. How does the land change as you move east from the river?

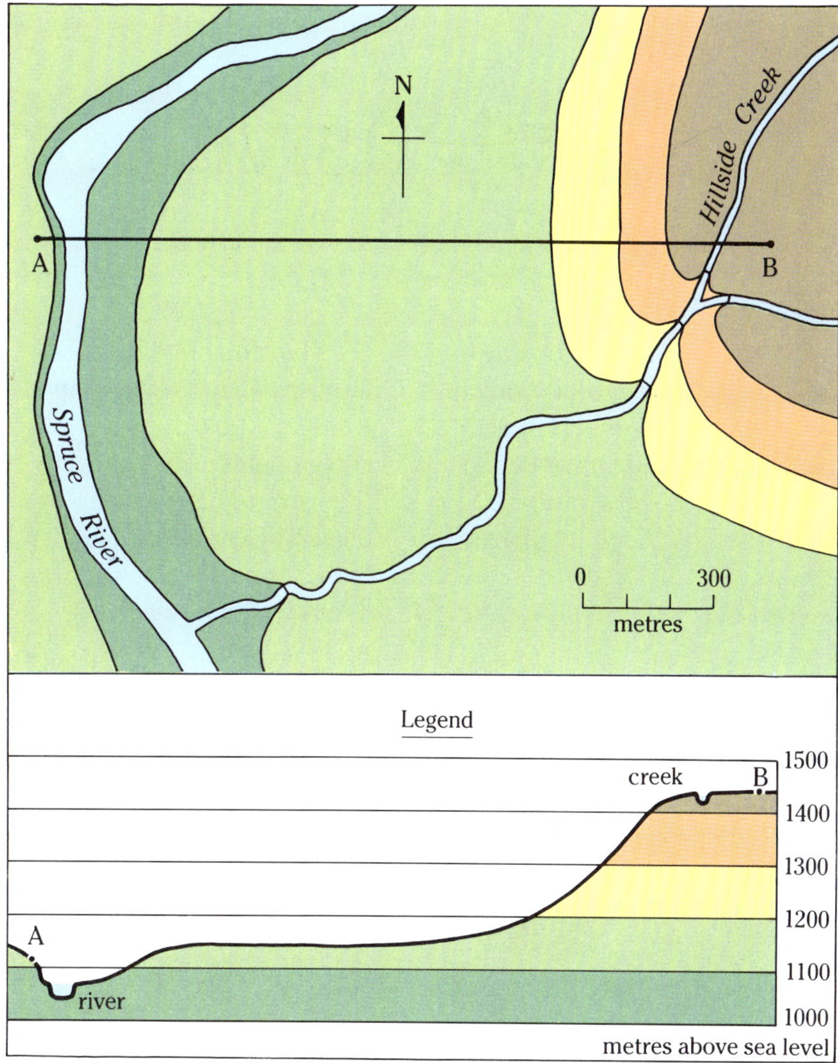

A committee was formed. It included Peter LeBlanc, Jane Anderson, Pauline Yuen, Angela Rosso and Jeremy Goldberg. With the forest manager's help, they would collect information about the forest.

They would make a map showing all the creeks and the steep slopes in the forest. They would find out where the trails were. They would learn what animals lived in the forest and what kind of habitat the wildlife needed. They would find out where the best wood was and what logging roads would be needed to get to that part of the forest.

When the committee had all this information, it would decide on a plan for using the forest. There would be another public meeting so that the committee could explain the plan to the people in Spruceville.

"Thank you all for coming," said Linda Gill. "I'm glad we heard all your ideas. The meeting is now over."

You have heard the different opinions in Spruceville. The people there must decide how to use the forest resource. What would you decide?

Intensive Forestry

Intensive forestry is a way of getting more wood from an area of land. The first step is to study the land to find out what kinds of trees will grow best there. That depends on many things, such as the climate, the soil and the slope of the land.

Then foresters become farmers. They plant a crop of trees and look after their crop to keep it healthy and growing. Intensive forestry produces bigger, better trees in less time than it takes for trees to grow on their own in the forest.

Intensive forestry is the way of the future. There are no more forests to discover, so we have to get more wood from the forest land we have now. In some parts of Canada this is already happening. We need to do much more.

1 *Developing better trees in seed orchards. Seeds from these trees will be used to grow* ***seedlings*** *for future forests.*

2 *Preparing the ground and planting carefully selected seedlings on the site.*

3 *Thinning the young trees to prevent crowding, and* ***fertilizing*** *to improve growth.*

4 *Protecting the forest from fire, disease and pests.*

5 *Collecting seeds from the best trees.*

Sharing the Forests

Think of Canada's forest land as a gigantic pie. This pie must be shared by many people. Everyone would like to have a bigger piece. Unfortunately, the pie is only so big. It can't get any bigger.

In fact, bites have already been taken from this forest pie. It has been eaten away by parking lots, cities, roads and farms. The pie that is left is smaller than it once was. Yet there are many different ways it could be used.

In Canada today, forests are very important for providing wood. As you saw in Spruceville, that is not the only reason people think forests are important. Canadians must decide how much of their forests should be used for one thing and how much should be used for another. The **politicians** and the people of Canada must decide how to divide up the pie.

How big a slice should be used for logging? After all, logging provides jobs and forest products. How big a slice should be used for parks? Parks allow people to enjoy nature and escape from the noise of the city. Should areas of forest be set aside just for drinking water? How much forest should be preserved for wildlife habitat? Can a forest be used for several purposes at once? These are difficult questions, and there are no easy answers.

Just the same, forest managers need these answers. They need them so that they can decide the best way to manage our forests. Forest managers are not just making decisions for Canadians today. The decisions they make now will affect Canadians in the future. So forest managers must think far ahead. They need to balance the needs of people today (like those in Spruceville) with the needs of people in the future.

This family is using the forest as a source of relaxation and enjoyment. Do you visit the forest in your spare time?

- Why should people today care about the needs of people in the future?

The people in Spruceville had different opinions about the forest. Yet they all agreed on one thing. They all thought the forest was valuable, for one reason or another.

You don't live in Spruceville, but the forest is valuable to you, too. Canada's forests are important to all Canadians, even those who live far from the forest. You'll find out more about that in the next chapter.

Since the forest is so valuable, it should not be wasted or used recklessly. We all use the forest and we share it with many other people. Everyone who uses the forest must protect the resource and treat it with care.

Becoming Involved

Some Canadians are particularly concerned about the future of our forests. They are willing to volunteer their time and energy to do what they think is important for our forests. Here are two such people.

Dave Mattern

Dave Mattern of Edmonton, Alberta, spends weekends helping young people learn about the forest. He takes them camping or skiing in the woods. He teaches them what to eat and how to dress to be warm, dry and safe in the outdoors. "I want them to feel that the forest is a comfortable, natural place to be," Mattern says. While having fun and adventure, the children learn a great deal about forests and how people should treat them.

The boys and girls Mattern works with are members of the Junior Forest Warden program. Children in the club take part in many different forest activities. For instance, Mattern's group is learning to manage an area of public forest for timber. The children study the forest and decide which trees to cut, where to build trails and how to protect the soil.

Mattern spends many hours each week with his Junior Forest Wardens. It's worth it when he sees the children using information and skills they have learned. Mattern believes that children who have fun and learn about the forest will continue to care about forests when they grow up. They will insist that the government and forest companies do a good job of managing the forest.

Junior Forest Wardens at a summer camp learn to handle a fire hose.

Valhalla Provincial Park attracts many tourists each year.

Colleen McCrory

Colleen McCrory grew up in the small village of New Denver, in the mountains of British Columbia. As a child, she went hiking and fishing in the woods with her brother. Today she has a family of her own to take care of. She also runs a store in New Denver.

In 1974, logging companies asked the provincial government for a permit to cut trees on the mountainside near New Denver. McCrory joined with others in her community to persuade the government to make those mountains part of a park. "I didn't want that great wilderness area to be destroyed," she said. "I felt it was worth preserving for future generations." Though logging jobs might be lost, McCrory believed that a park would attract tourists and create new jobs in the community. She believed that jobs in tourism would last longer than jobs in logging.

It took 10 years to persuade the government to preserve the area. McCrory learned to talk to politicians and to newspaper and TV reporters. There were many things she didn't know how to do, but she was willing to get help from others and to learn from her mistakes. After 10 years, McCrory was exhausted but successful. The government made the mountain area into Valhalla Provincial Park. For her hard work, McCrory received an award from the Governor General of Canada.

CHAPTER CHECKUP

Recalling the Main Ideas

The article below might have appeared in the Spruceville newspaper the morning after the public meeting. Fill in the words that are missing. (You will need several words for most of the blanks.)

Views Aired at Forestry Meeting

There was standing room only at the public meeting yesterday evening. The discussion was lively. As hardware store owner Fritz Müller said, "Lots of folks here have different points of view."

At the start of the meeting, logging company president Peter LeBlanc gave his reasons for logging the hillside. LeBlanc said he needs the wood because ____(1)____. LeBlanc reminded the audience that the lumber they buy will cost more if ____(2)____.

Other speakers in favour of logging included Jim Charlie and Angela Rosso. Charlie, who works for LeBlanc's Logging Company, was worried that people would ____(3)____ if LeBlanc is not allowed to log the hill. Rosso, president of the Chamber of Commerce, said Spruceville needs the ____(4)____ and ____(5)____ that LeBlanc's business will provide.

Some speakers were worried about how logging would affect the forest environment. Biologist Pauline Yuen was concerned that logging might destroy wildlife that needs the forest for ____(6)____. High school teacher Jeremy Goldberg said that forests are important because they ____(7)____ and ____(8)____.

Jane Anderson spoke for the Spruceville Outdoors Club. "Are logging companies going to be allowed to cut every last bit of forest around Spruceville?" she asked. She wants the forest used for ____(9)____.

LeBlanc promised he would use logging methods that would ____(10)____. At the close of the meeting, a committee was formed. The committee will help forest manager Linda Gill prepare a ____(11)____.

Using What You Have Learned

In this chapter, you heard people suggest several different uses for the forest near Spruceville. Here are some other ways that people in the meeting could have suggested the land be used:

1. to build new houses
2. to build a ski hill with lifts
3. to start an outdoor adventure camp for children
4. to build a hydro-electric dam on the creek
5. to build dirt bike trails

Choose two of these uses. For each one, write down two opinions that people might give. One opinion should be in favour of that use of the forest and should explain why. The other opinion should be against that use of the forest and should explain why.

Example:

LAND USE—to build new houses.

OPINIONS—For: "I think we should use that forest land for new houses because —."

Against: "We should not use that land for houses because —."

4

Why Is the Forest Industry Important to Canadians?

In the last chapter, we visited a public meeting in Spruceville. We found that the forest has many important uses. It provides clean water, prevents flooding and is a home for wildlife. The forest is a pleasant place for fishing and hiking. It is also a source of wood for the forest industry.

This chapter explores that last use of the forest. We'll look at the forest industry and see why it is important to every Canadian. We'll see why it is important to you.

Do you live in a town like Spruceville where many people work in logging or at a sawmill? If so, it's easy to understand why the forest industry is important to people in your town. Do you live in a city far from the forest? In that case, it might not be so obvious that the forest industry is important to you. You may not even think about the forest. Instead of living in a wooden house, you may live in an apartment building made of concrete. You may not know anyone who works in the forest industry. So why is the forest important to you?

This chapter will explain why. You'll discover that all Canadians benefit from our forest industry, even people who rarely see a forest. We'll look at three ways the forest industry is important. First, it provides many jobs for Canadians across the country. We'll meet some of the people **employed** in forestry—from tree planters to chemical engineers. Second, the forest industry makes wood products that we all use. We'll look at the variety of products that are made from wood. Finally, we'll see how the money made by the forest industry helps all Canadians. You'll discover that the forest industry benefits *you* in many ways.

What exactly is the forest industry? The industry is made up of people who grow forests, harvest the trees, turn the wood into products and sell those products. The chart on the next page will give you an overall look at this process. Start by imagining a young, growing forest. Now think of all the steps that must be taken before that forest is turned into a product we can use, such as the paper this book is printed on.

Paper, a forest product, can be folded to make animal shapes. In what other ways do you use paper?

From the Forest to You

1 Growing the Forest

The forest may have been seeded naturally, or seedlings may have been planted. Foresters can improve the forest's growth by thinning out the weaker trees or adding fertilizer to the soil. The forest needs to be protected from fire, disease and insect pests.

2 Harvesting the Forest

The trees are cut by machines or by fallers with chain saws. The logs are loaded onto trucks or barges for the trip to the mill. Sometimes logs are floated down rivers or along the coast.

3 Making Wood Products

At a sawmill, the best logs may be peeled into thin sheets for **plywood**. Other logs are sawn into lumber, which may later be used to make furniture or houses. At a pulp mill, logs are ground into chips for pulp. Pulp can be used to make paper and many other products.

4 Selling Wood Products

The wood products are shipped overseas or they are sent by train to customers throughout North America. Forest companies earn money from the products they sell. Some of the money is used to pay the workers and the people who own the forest companies. Some money is paid to the government for the trees that were cut. Some money is used to buy equipment, to do research and to grow new forests.

Women's Work

At one time there were almost no women working in forestry. Today there are still seven times more men than women in the forest industry, but women are doing almost every kind of job. Women are forest managers, truck drivers, mechanics, mill workers and scientists.

Most jobs in the forest industry today require skills rather than strength. More and more women are taking the special training needed for these jobs. Jobs in the forest industry often pay well. They can be challenging and interesting.

As women gain experience in the forest industry, you will see more of them in the top jobs. Women will be chief foresters and forest company presidents.

A Variety of Jobs

At every step of the way, the forest industry provides jobs for a variety of people. Some of these people work right in the forest. Others work in mills, offices and factories. Some jobs require workers who are strong and physically fit. Others need workers with special training or university education.

It would be impossible to tell you about all the jobs in the forest industry. Instead, you'll read about a few sample jobs, just to give you an idea of the many different kinds. You'll see people with many different interests and skills. They all earn a living by working for the forest industry. Maybe you know people who do some of these jobs. Or maybe you'll read about a job you would like to try when you are older.

- Why are jobs important to Canadians?

Growing the Forest

The first two workers you'll meet help to grow healthy forests. Growing new forests is becoming more and more important as the older forests are cut. Growing a healthy forest depends on many things. People must choose the right kinds of trees, know about the soil and make sure the trees are not crowded. There are people working in all these areas. Together they help to grow our forests.

Tree Planters

Above: *Tree planters replant logged areas. What kind of tool is this tree planter using?*

In one hand they carry pointed shovels. Heavy bags of tree seedlings hang from their belts. The tree planters move slowly across the logged hillside, stopping every two or three metres to plant another tiny tree in a patch of bare soil.

It is hard work. The weather is often cold and wet. Tree planters may plant a thousand trees in one long day. Each seedling is delicate. It must be placed in the ground with care or it won't survive.

Some logged areas don't need replanting. Seeds from nearby trees will start a new forest and reseed the area. However, most new forests grow more quickly when new seedlings are planted. Planting also means foresters can choose the kind of trees they want for the site. Scientists are developing better, faster-growing seedlings for tree planters to use.

- Have you ever planted a tree?

Entomologists

An entomologist looks for ways to control insect pests. What is he looking at here?

An entomologist is a scientist who studies insects. Entomologists help keep the forest healthy. They find ways to protect the trees from harmful insects.

It's hard to imagine that little caterpillars and beetles could be such a gigantic problem. Yet every year, they damage huge areas of forest. Some insects nibble young buds and needles, causing the trees to grow small and crooked. Others kill the trees by eating the cambium under the bark.

Some forest insects can be killed by spraying the forests with chemicals from airplanes. However, some chemical sprays are also harmful to other things that live in the forest, and even to people. So entomologists look for better ways to control harmful insects. For instance, they might find another insect that attacks the pests without hurting the trees or anything else in the forest. This useful insect could be let loose in the forest to kill off the harmful insects.

- Why don't entomologists just kill *all* the insects in the forest?

Entomologists must be good at thinking up new solutions to pest problems. They need patience. It can take years before they win the battle against even a tiny enemy like a caterpillar.

Harvesting the Forest

Tree planters and entomologists help forests to grow. Then, when the trees are about 80 years old, forest managers decide which areas should be logged and how the logging should be done.

Once forest managers have decided on a cutting plan for the forest, the harvesting can begin. The trees must be logged and transported to the mill. There are many different ways to log a forest, depending on such things as the kind of trees, the size of the trees, the steepness of the slope, and how the site will be reseeded afterwards. There are also different ways of transporting wood—by road, by water or by rail. So there are many different kinds of jobs in this part of the industry. Here are two examples.

Computer Operators

How much forest is there? How big are the trees? How fast are they growing? Are they damaged by insects or disease? What is the soil like? How steep is the slope? Where are the creeks?

Before forest managers can plan how to harvest the trees, they need information to answer questions like these. This information is called a **forest inventory**; it is a list of everything that is in the forest. Computers can keep track of all this information. Keeping the forest inventory up to date is a job for computer operators.

They use information collected from many sources, including photographs taken from **satellites** in space. Computer operators store this information in the computer's memory. Whenever a forest manager needs to know about an area of forest, the computer operator can display a map of that area on the computer screen, showing all the information.

- Why is it important to keep the forest inventory up to date?

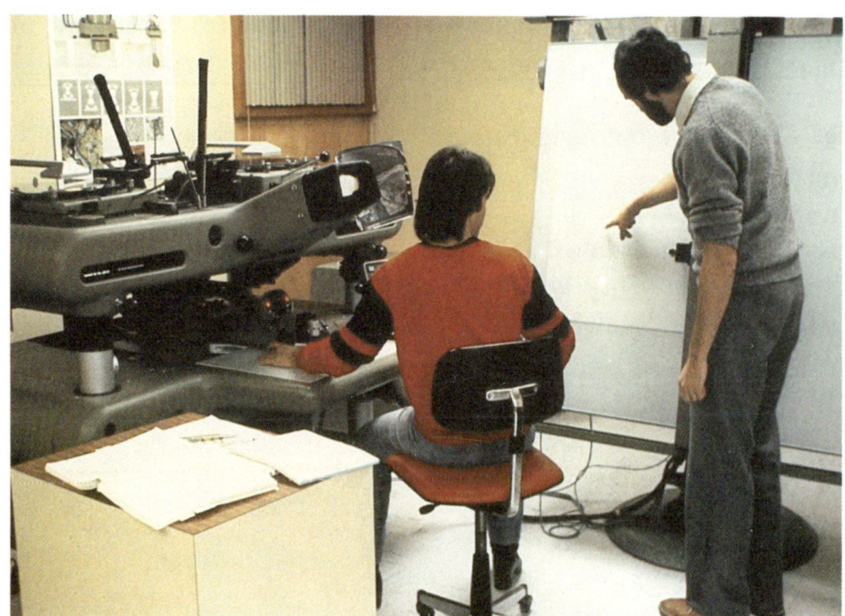

Forest workers store information about a forest area in their computer. How might a forest manager use this information?

Chokermen

A chokerman is part of the woods crew, the people who actually work in the forest harvesting the trees. Chokermen can be men or women. The chokerman attaches the chokers (loops of heavy wire rope) around the felled trees. Then machines can pull them to the loading area.

Like the rest of the woods crew, chokermen work outside in the rain and mud. The work is hard and dangerous, and sometimes the hours are long. Chokermen work near heavy equipment in a tangle of fallen logs and brush. They must be careful and quick on their feet. They must follow safety rules and regulations so that they don't get hurt.

Above: A chokerman attaches a choker to a log. Would you like to work as a chokerman?

Making Wood Products

Once at the mill, the bark is taken off the logs. Then the logs are sawn, ground up, chipped or peeled. Eventually they will be turned into useful forest products. Later in this chapter you'll learn more about these products. Right now, meet two kinds of workers who help make them.

Sawyers

You might imagine that a sawmill would be a noisy, unpleasant place to work, with huge saws whining and sawdust flying. Some sawmills are certainly like that, but these days many sawyers do their jobs from comfortable, padded chairs. They sit in soundproof booths made of safety glass.

- Why are sawyers protected from the noise of the saws?

On closed-circuit television screens, sawyers check the cutting pattern that the computer has suggested for each log. They watch the saw rip through the log at over 100 km/h (kilometres per hour). They use a telephone to talk to workers in the other booths.

Many of the sawmill jobs that used to be done by people, such as sorting the sawn lumber into different piles, are now done by machines. There are fewer jobs in modern mills, and these jobs require more skill and less muscle. A sawmill worker may need to be able to operate computers and other modern machines.

From a booth above the saw, the sawyer watches each log as it is cut. Why might this work be lonely sometimes?

Chemical engineers test out new paper products. Why might they develop new products?

Chemical Engineers

How was the paper in this book made? What makes it different from the paper in newspapers or wax paper or postcards or cardboard boxes?

Each kind of paper has its own recipe. The recipes are developed by chemical engineers. They start with wood pulp and then add other ingredients. Some papers are coated to make them shiny or waterproof. Some have bleach to make them whiter or dyes to give them different colours.

Chemical engineers in a pulp mill are a bit like cooks. They try out new recipes to see if they can make better paper products. Sometimes they discover easier, cheaper ways to make the old products.

- What kind of new paper product would you like to make?

Selling Wood Products

The sawyer and the chemical engineer are just two of the many people who help make useful wood products. Many more people help sell these products to customers in Canada and other countries. The people who sell wood products have very important jobs. Everyone else in the forest industry depends on these workers. Here is one of those jobs.

The lumber trader finds buyers for the lumber produced by the sawmills. Who might buy lumber from the trader?

Lumber Traders

"How much wood do you want? What size? Okay, I'll have it in Chicago in two weeks."

Lumber traders spend most of their working day on the phone, making deals. They sell lumber from the mills to customers throughout North America. Usually the lumber is shipped by train, so it is sold by the railcar load. For instance, a customer in Edmonton might need nine railcars of lumber by next Friday. Another in the eastern United States might need three railcars by the end of the month.

Lumber trading can be a hectic job. The trader must keep track of hundreds of orders travelling on different railways to different cities all over North America. It is important that the lumber arrive when it is promised so that the customers are satisfied. Otherwise they will probably ask a different lumber trader next time they need to buy wood.

- What might happen to the jobs of other forestry workers if the lumber trader cannot sell enough wood?

Helping the Workers

You've just read about a number of different jobs in the forest industry. This final example is a bit different. A person with this job does not actually work with wood at all. This person helps the other workers in the forest industry.

Union Leaders

Most forest workers belong to an organization called a **union**. The workers pay money, called union dues, to the union. In return, the union makes sure the workers get fair treatment.

The union leaders meet with the companies that hire the workers. Together, the union and the companies try to work out a contract. The contract is an agreement between the company and the workers. It says how much the workers will be paid, how many hours a day they will work, and how much time off they will have when they are sick or on holiday. It also sets safety standards for the workers. Good union leaders care about getting a fair contract for the workers.

A forest worker talks to a worker from the union. How might the union help him?

You have read about just a few of the jobs in the forest industry. You can see that the industry is important because it provides many jobs for people. In all, it employs about 260 000 Canadians from coast to coast.

Forestry is the country's largest industry, bigger than fishing or farming or anything else. It employs more people than any other industry. One day you will be looking for a job. The forest industry might have just the job you want.

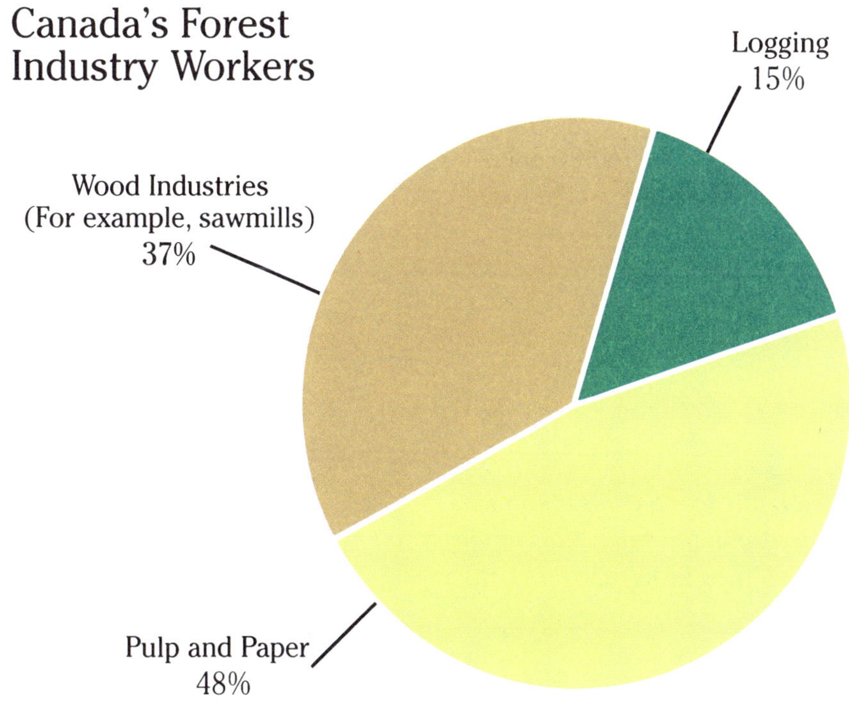

This circle graph shows the percentage of people who work in the three divisions of Canada's forest industry. Which division has the fewest workers?

This construction worker in Japan is using Canadian lumber to build a home. What province might have shipped this lumber to Japan?

A Variety of Forest Products

Let's look at another reason the forest industry is important to Canadians. The industry produces an amazing variety of forest products. In fact, trees provide us with enough different products to fill a department store! Step inside this imaginary store and take a look around. You'll discover many products that Canadians use every day.

Do you pour real maple syrup on your pancakes, for example? That syrup is made from the sap of maple trees, so it is a forest product. However, this imaginary store doesn't just contain things you can eat. You'll find forest products you can use for building boats, pushing mops, playing ping-pong, polishing shoes, blowing noses and wrapping sandwiches.

Let's take them one at a time.

Lumber

Trees are sawn into boards of all shapes and sizes. Then the lumber is usually dried. Dried lumber is not as heavy to transport and is less likely to warp out of shape. Lumber is also graded, which means it is marked to show its strength and quality.

These boards are used for building boats, houses, bridges, furniture, musical instruments and more things than we could possibly name.

- What other materials can be used to build bridges, boats or houses?

Leftover Wood

Small pieces of wood are left over after a round log is sawn into rectangular boards. These pieces were once wasted, but now they can be used for mop handles or door handles or the strips of wood around windows. Waste wood can even be turned into pressed logs for the fireplace. The main use of waste wood is to make chips for pulp mills.

Even tiny wood chips are made into useful products. How might these chips be used?

Left: This mill worker is making plywood. What skills might he need for this job?

Plywood and Other Panel Boards

Have you ever wondered how large, flat boards, like the ones you use for ping-pong tables, are made out of tall, round trees?

Plywood is made by peeling long, very thin sheets off a spinning log. These thin sheets are coated with glue and pressed together to make a flat board. The many layers of wood glued together make plywood very strong.

Plywood is gradually being replaced by cheaper kinds of panel boards. These boards are made by pressing small bits of wood together with glue into flat sheets. Like plywood, these boards can be used for doors, walls, floors, furniture—and ping-pong tables.

Chemical Products

Wood contains certain chemicals. These can be removed by cooking the wood or treating it in other ways. The chemicals can then be used in products such as tar, turpentine, paint, cleaning solvent, enamel and shoe polish.

Many people use shoe polish to protect their shoes. Did you know that shoe polish is made from chemicals contained in wood?

Right: This picture shows the inside of a pulp and paper mill. The pulp is spread on a mesh screen and drained of all water. Why do you think the water is being removed?

Pulp and Paper Products

How does wood become paper, such as the paper tissues we blow our noses with, or the paper in comic books, or cardboard boxes?

Wood is made of **cellulose fibres**, tiny strands that can be seen under a microscope. These cellulose fibres are held together with a glue-like substance called lignin.

When the wood is ground up or cooked, it becomes mushy cellulose pulp. The pulp can then be spread out and dried into thin sheets of paper.

- Newsprint is much cheaper than the paper in this book. What is the difference between the two? Why would newspapers use newsprint instead of this paper?

Cellophane is sometimes made from cellulose pulp. What uses might you have for cellophane?

Other Cellulose Products

Cellulose pulp can be treated with chemicals and turned into other useful products. One is the cellophane used for wrapping sandwiches. Other cellulose products include record albums, camera film, artificial leather wallets, sponges and car dashboards. Most of these products are made from oil today, but they could be made from cellulose instead.

You have read about some of the different products that can be made from trees. Those round, uneven logs can be turned into useful objects of all shapes and sizes. Some early settlers thought forests were a nuisance, but Canadians today know they are a treasure. As scientists discover more about the uses of wood, the forest becomes even more valuable.

Look around you and see how many things you can find that are made of wood. Imagine how different your life would be if you lived in a country of grasslands and deserts that had no forest. There would be no forest industry and no forest products made in Canada. Fortunately, that's not the case. Canada has some of the best forest land in the world. As a result, Canadians can make many different forest products. These products are used by all Canadians.

Benefits for All Canadians

So far in this chapter we have seen that the forest industry provides many jobs. These jobs are an important benefit to Canadians. We have also seen that the industry supplies people with a variety of forest products. You use some of these every day. Everyone benefits from having many forest products. Now we'll see how the money earned by the forest industry benefits all Canadians. You may not think you see any of that money, but you do. Here's how it happens.

Wages

People who work in forestry receive **wages** for their work. These wages are spent on food, clothing, houses, piano lessons, cars, babysitters—all the things that people need.

When money is spent on food, it keeps jobs in supermarkets. When it is spent on piano lessons, it keeps piano teachers working. When it is spent on houses, it gives builders, plumbers and electricians work. When it is spent on babysitters, it provides some teenagers with extra money.

You can see that the wages paid by the forest industry do not just help the forest workers. These wages also help people in other jobs to earn money.

- Do you earn money? How do you spend it? Who benefits from your wages?

We all benefit from the forest industry. How might the people shown in this picture benefit from forestry?

Taxes

Both the forest workers and the forest companies pay taxes. Part of the money they earn goes to the government. The more money they earn, the more taxes they pay.

Tax money is used by the government for many **services**, such as roads, bridges, schools and hospitals. The government hires people to provide these services.

Just think of all the people who work to keep schools running, for example. There are teachers, principals and custodians. There are also people who sell school sports equipment, people who write textbooks, people who drive school buses, and many others.

Without the taxes paid by forest workers and companies, the government would have less money for schools and other services. The government would not be able to hire as many people or buy as much equipment. Some people would lose jobs, and Canadians would all receive fewer government services. Everyone benefits from forestry taxes.

- How do you benefit from forestry taxes?

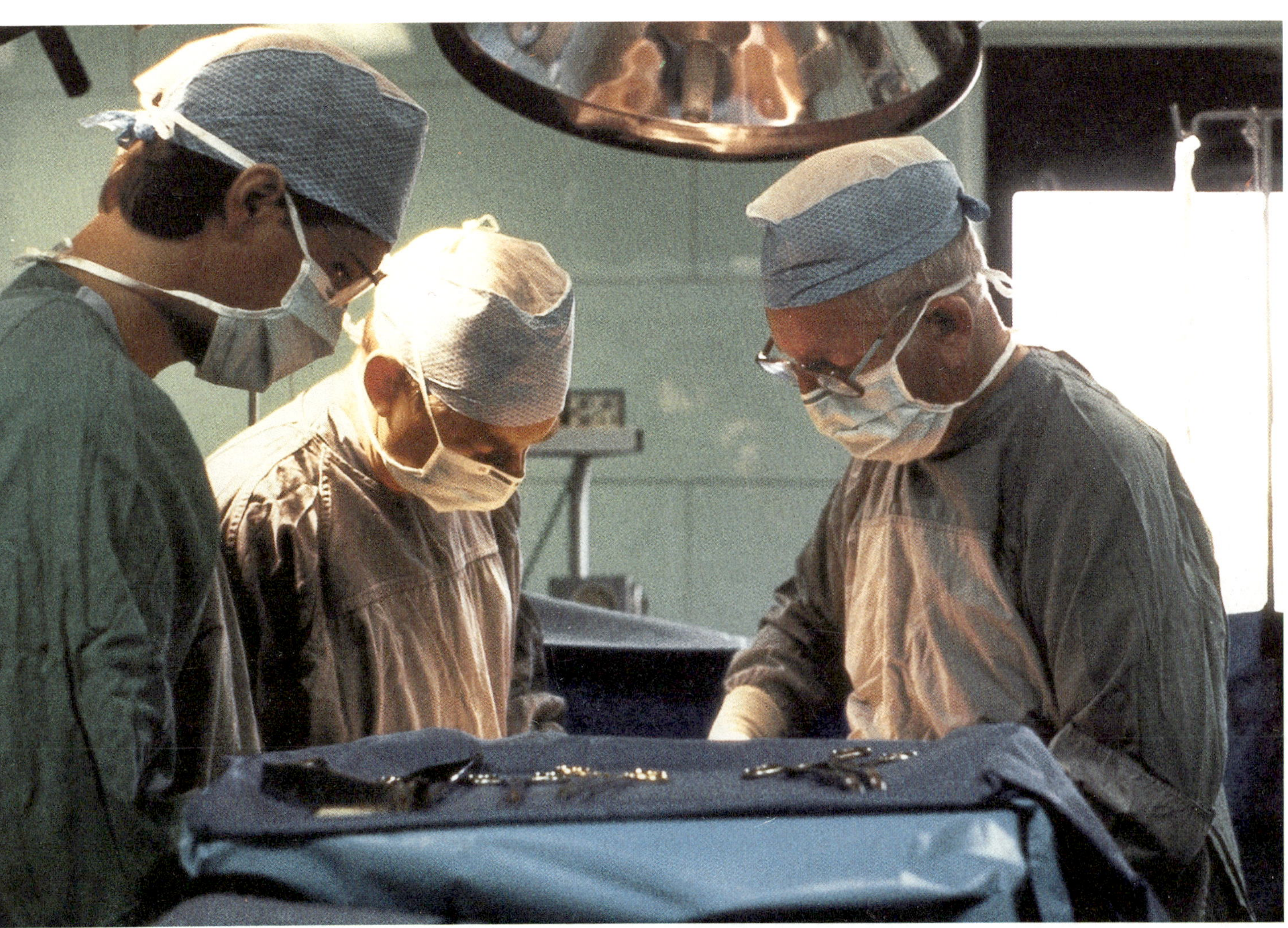

The government uses forestry taxes to provide public services such as hospital care. What might happen to such services if the forest industry has a bad year?

Exports

Many forest products made in Canada are **exported**, which means these **goods** are sold to other countries. Each year Canada exports a large amount of wood, pulp, paper and other forest products.

In return, Canadians are able to buy things from other countries. Canada **imports** Japanese televisions and American grapefruit, for example. If you've ever looked at the labels on clothing and toys in a store, you'll know that many things we use are made in other countries. Canada would not be able to import as many of these **foreign** goods if it did not have forest products to trade for them. All Canadians benefit from forest exports.

This lumber is being sent to other countries. How does selling this lumber benefit Canadians?

Good Times and Bad Times in the Forest Industry

The forest industry provides wages, taxes and exports. Every Canadian benefits from them. Other industries, such as fishing, farming and mining, also pay wages and taxes. Because forestry is the biggest industry in Canada, it provides the most benefits.

Bad Times

Very few new houses are built in the United States. People there stop buying wood from Canada.

Our forest industry makes less money.

Our forest industry employs fewer workers.

The forest industry pays less tax money to the government. Fewer workers pay taxes.

Good Times

Canadian forest companies sell a large amount of lumber to the United States. It is used to build new houses there.

Our forest industry makes lots of money.

Our forest industry employs many workers.

The forest industry pays more tax money to the government. More workers pay taxes.

Yet the forest industry goes through good times and bad times. During good times, when the industry is selling lots of forest products, it makes more money. It can pay more wages and taxes. During bad times, when the industry has trouble selling its products, it makes less money. It pays fewer wages and taxes. And all Canadians feel the effects.

Here are two charts to show how good and bad times in the forest industry might affect you.

'he government eceives less tax noney. It cannot pend as much noney on chools.

Your school receives less money from the government. Your school cannot afford to buy any new equipment. It cannot buy a new computer or improve the soccer field.

If you like computers or soccer, the bad times affect you. How will you feel?

'he government eceives more tax noney. It can afford o spend more noney on schools.

Your school receives more money from the government. Your school can afford to buy new equipment. It might buy a new computer or improve the soccer field.

If you like computers or soccer, the good times affect you. How will you feel?

Good Times and Bad Times in Chemainus

The town of Chemainus is on Vancouver Island, in British Columbia. For over a century, people in Chemainus have worked at a sawmill located on the waterfront. Like most towns that depend on the forest industry, Chemainus has been through good times and bad times.

The first mill in Chemainus was built in 1862.

The years 1892 to 1895 were a bad time for many people in British Columbia. The Chemainus mill shut down for three and a half years.

During the early 1900s, there was a mining boom near Chemainus. Towns grew up near the mines. People needed to buy lumber, so the mill did well.

In 1914, World War I started in Europe. Almost all shipping stopped during the war, so the mill was forced to shut down.

After the war, the Chemainus mill started up again. Then, in 1923, a big fire destroyed the mill and many workers left town.

In 1927, a new mill opened and times were good for the people of Chemainus. Most people had jobs and plenty of money.

Above: In 1981 the people of Chemainus decided to paint the history of their town on the walls of several town buildings. Artists came from as far away as Great Britain to help. Many of them painted murals of Chemainus's early logging industry. This mural shows the steam train used by a local lumber company to carry logs to Victoria.

Everyone in Chemainus thought the murals were a great success. This mural shows a team of oxen pulling a log from the forest.

Today many tourists visit Chemainus just to see the wall murals and, as a result of the tourists, many people in the community have new jobs. This mural shows two loggers cutting down a large fir tree.

Below: One artist painted a mural of the native Indians who used to live in the Chemainus area. They, too, played an important part in the growth of the town. This mural shows several Indians who were well known as local Indian leaders.

In the early 1930s, times were bad all over North America. Many people were without jobs. Unsold lumber piled up on the wharf at Chemainus. The mill was forced to cut back wages to 25¢ an hour, and to lay off many workers.

In 1939, World War II started. Although many men left Chemainus to fight in the war, the mill continued to operate. After the war, when the men returned, there was a big need for new houses. The mill boomed. Good times continued during the 1950s and 1960s.

By the early 1980s, the lumber industry hit bad times again. Many mills shut down.

In 1983, the Chemainus mill closed for good. The mill, built in 1927 after the big fire, was old and out of date.

In 1984, the forest company decided to build a new mill. It was smaller and more efficient than the old mill and needed fewer workers.

People in Chemainus were glad to have the new mill, but they realized that their town could no longer rely on the forest industry to provide jobs for everyone. They decided that Chemainus would be a good place for tourists. To attract tourists to Chemainus, they painted murals on the walls of the buildings in town. The murals show the history of Chemainus and the early days of the forest industry.

The Forest Industry and You

In this chapter you discovered what the forest industry means to Canadians. You met many of the people who work in the industry. Jobs in forestry benefit the workers and all Canadians. Everyone benefits from the money paid in wages and taxes. You also saw some of the forest products the industry produces. You use many of these products in your daily life. Some of Canada's forest products are exported. In return, Canadians can buy goods from other countries.

The forest industry needs wood to make its products. This wood comes from the forest. Since the industry is so important to all Canadians, we all should care about our forest resource. Those shady green forests that blanket our hills and valleys are a great source of wealth for all of us.

The forest industry has played an important role in the lives of Canadians since the days when our trees were cut down for masts and spars. However, some people working in the industry and the government in the past did not treat the forest resource with enough care. They cut down more trees than the forest could replace. They did not ask themselves what would happen when the best forests ran out.

Today we are learning from mistakes made in the past. We know that if we want to have healthy forests in the future, we need to do a better job of managing our forests now. We know how important our forests are.

If our forests are used wisely, all Canadians—including you—will continue to benefit from the forest industry.

Many of the products we work and play with are made of wood. What wood products do you use?

Fire!

It takes 50 to 80 years to grow a tree, but just moments to burn it down. Each year forest fires destroy an area about twice the size of Prince Edward Island. The trees that are destroyed would provide enough wood to keep 78 pulp mills supplied for a year. Some years, fires burn more wood than people harvest.

It makes no sense to spend money planting and growing new forests if they will be destroyed by fire. Three quarters of all fires are started by careless people. It is important that you, your family, your friends and all Canadians prevent fires in the forest. When good timber burns, we all lose.

MAKING A DECISION

How Can We Reduce Paper Packaging?

It was near the end of the school day. The teacher walked to the table at the front of the classroom with a large paper bag. After spreading out sheets of newspaper on the table, the teacher dumped out the contents of the paper bag.

The students gathered around the table for a better look. The table was littered with candy bar wrappers, raisin boxes, lunch bags and other paper boxes, wrappers and packages.

The teacher explained, "This is just some of the packaging we've thrown out today. It adds up to quite a pile, doesn't it? It makes up a large part of our daily garbage. Here's what I want you to decide. Is all this packaging material necessary, or is some of it a waste of paper? Is there any way we can reduce the amount of packaging we throw out?"

The class took a closer look at the objects on the table. "You have to use packaging," said Tim. He pointed to a potato chip bag. "You couldn't buy potato chips without a package. And sandwiches would dry out if they weren't wrapped."

Shaheen picked up a cardboard juice carton. "This was mine. I like using these small cartons for juice. It's more convenient than bringing a thermos every day."

Anne was looking at the garbage left over from lunches. "But some of these things could be used again," she said. "We could be taking our paper lunch bags home to use again. And look at this small box that held raisins. Why not take it home and fill it up with more raisins for the next day?"

Aaron pulled out a cardboard and cellophane package that had contained a new pen. "What about this package?" he asked. "Why do you need to wrap up a pen?"

Eventually the class decided that some packaging was useful but some was not really necessary. Some packaging was used to make products look more attractive or to make products look bigger than they actually were. That way, more people might buy them. The students decided they could try to buy products that did not have extra packaging. They could use some packages more than once. That way, they would reduce the amount of packaging they needed to throw out.

- What kinds of packaging do you throw out?
- How could you reduce the amount of packaging you drop in the garbage can?

The students in this picture have brought paper packages to class. How many different kinds can you see?

CHAPTER CHECKUP

Recalling the Main Ideas

Imagine you are showing a visitor around Canada. The visitor is thrilled by the scenery. But the visitor thinks the logged areas look ugly and cannot understand why Canadians cut down trees. Below is your explanation. Fill in the missing words.

If we didn't cut down any trees, we wouldn't have a forest industry. The forest industry is very important to Canadians.

For one thing, we use the wood to make many different ____(1)____. For instance, ____(2)____ and ____(3)____ are made from wood. These products are useful to Canadians, and useful to people in other countries, too.

The forest industry is also important because it provides many Canadians with ____(4)____. Two examples of people who work in the industry are ____(5)____ and ____(6)____.

People working in the industry pay ____(7)____ to the government. This money benefits all Canadians. For instance, it can be used for ____(8)____.

Forestry has always been an important industry in Canada. Gradually we have logged most of the good forest land. To make sure we have forests to harvest in the future, Canadians must ____(9)____.

Using What You Have Learned

The pictures below show four different Canadians. Explain how each one benefits from the forest industry.

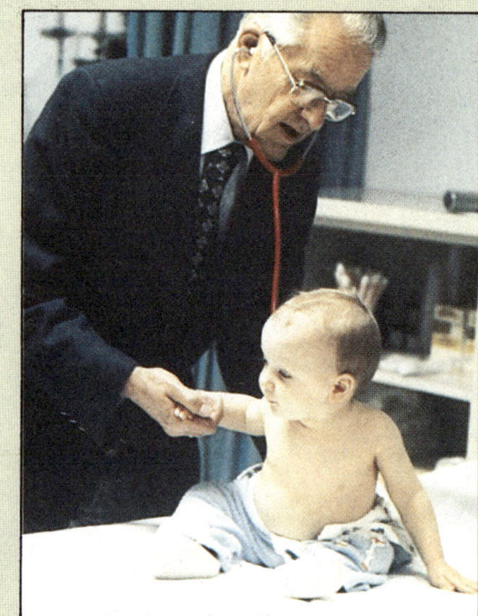

5

How Might Forests Be Used in the Future?

Friday, September 23, 2039

The sign over the door said "Welcome to High River Community Learning Centre."

"They were called schools in my day," thought Ms. Rogers as the automatic doors swung open.

Once inside, she looked around with interest. She hadn't visited a classroom for a long time. Computer **terminals** were grouped in clusters around the room. Ms. Rogers looked over the shoulder of one boy as he worked on a math problem. Next to him, another student was using the computer to find information for her social studies report. Ms. Rogers wandered over to a third student who seemed very intent on her work. She watched the girl type, "Do you want to come over to my house after . . ." Suddenly the girl realized she was being watched. Blushing, she tapped the erase button and the typed message disappeared. Ms. Rogers smiled and turned away. She was glad to know some things never changed.

"Ms. Rogers! I'm so glad you could come," said a voice behind her. Turning around, Ms. Rogers saw the teacher, Mr. Lee. "Sorry I didn't see you when you walked in," Mr. Lee said. "I was busy working with one of my at-home pupils."

Mr. Lee explained that some of the students worked at home, using their **videophones** to talk to the teacher. "Once I decide which programs they will use, the students can learn on their own with the help of the computer," he said. "I just give the students an extra push when I think they could be working harder."

Mr. Lee led Ms. Rogers to a comfortable chair in the corner of the room. There were cushions all around. A television **monitor** stood to one side. Speaking into a small microphone on his wrist watch, Mr. Lee said, "Students, it's time for our guest speaker. Please finish what you are doing and come to the discussion corner." All around the room, heads popped up as the students heard the message on their headphones or over the intercom.

The students settled themselves around Ms. Rogers. Mr. Lee addressed the group. "We have been learning about different jobs," he reminded them. "Last week we had a visit from a shuttle pilot who flies passengers between the earth and the moon. This week we have a forester to talk to us. Ms. Rogers has agreed to answer any questions you might have about forestry."

Ms. Rogers watches a student using a computer. What might Ms. Rogers learn from visiting a classroom?

For a moment the students looked at each other shyly and squirmed in their places, waiting for someone else to ask the first question. Then a hand shot up. Ms. Rogers nodded to the small girl in the front row. The girl asked Ms. Rogers why she decided to become a forester.

Ms. Rogers looked down at the serious face. "The first time I really became interested in forestry was when I was about your age," she said. She told the students about her visit, years ago, to her uncle who worked in the forest. "He was a faller, someone who used to cut down trees with a chain saw. You've seen old pictures of chain saws, haven't you? My uncle cut down a gigantic tree while I was there. I was quite small at the time, so the tree seemed enormous as it came crashing down."

Ms. Rogers paused to remember that summer long ago. "My uncle gave me a hard hat to wear. It was at least three sizes too big. I probably looked ridiculous, but I felt very important. And I loved being in the forest. I loved tramping around in the bush and smelling the freshly sawn wood."

Ms. Rogers smiled at her audience. "That was my introduction to the forest," she concluded. "From then on, I was hooked."

A small red light started flashing on the box beside Ms. Rogers. Mr. Lee explained that one of the students at home had a question. Ms. Rogers pressed the button on the box and a picture of a boy appeared on the television monitor.

"Ms. Rogers," the at-home student began, "I once saw a tree stump that had over 400 rings on it. My dad said that tree must have been as tall as a rocket ship when it was cut down. Is that what all the trees were like back then, when you were my age?"

Ms. Rogers shook her head. "There weren't many of those really big trees left even back then," she said. She explained that most of the biggest trees, the ones growing on the best forest land, had been logged long before. Most of the **old growth** forests were gone. The 1980s and 1990s were a time of change in the forest industry in Canada. The industry was starting to harvest younger, **second growth** forests.

Ms. Rogers continued, "Those new forests are the ones we have today. The trees are smaller because they haven't been growing for 400 years. We make up for the smaller size by using them differently. Today we use much more of the wood from each log. Almost no wood is wasted."

Another student raised his hand. "What else has changed since those days?" he asked. "How are things different now?"

Ms. Rogers sat back and thought for a moment. Then she began, "A lot of things have changed. . . ."

By now you've probably guessed that Ms. Rogers is Michelle, the girl you met in Chapter 1. This chapter takes place in the future, about 50 years later. Michelle is now grown up.

In 50 years, many changes can take place. Ms. Rogers is explaining some of those changes to students living in 2039. What do you think she will tell them? How do you think the forests will change in the next 50 years?

The next few pages will give you some ideas about the future. You'll read about a number of things that *could* happen in the future. Probably you'll be able to think of other possibilities. Of course, no one knows for sure what changes will take place. However, by looking back at what has happened in the past, and looking at what is happening at present, we can make guesses about the future.

In 50 years, you'll know if any of your guesses were right.

Ms. Rogers discusses forestry with students. What might the students learn from her?

What Might the Forests of the Future Look Like?

Canada's forests look very different today from when the native people first lived here. Most of the tall trees are gone, replaced by cities, farms and smaller, second growth forests.

Today people continue to make changes to the forest. Their activities affect the way our forests will look in the future.

Can you imagine yourself walking through a forest 50 years from now? What do you see?

Above: Will forests look like orchards, with trees planted in straight rows? Perhaps radio-controlled robots will go up and down the rows, mowing the weeds, fertilizing the trees and spraying to control pests.

Right: Will there be much less forest for logging than there is today? Will Canadians use up most of the old growth forests and then decide it costs too much to plant new forests? Will it be cheaper to buy wood from other countries than to grow and harvest our own?

Will Canada be one of the few countries in the world to keep some old growth forests? Will tourists pay to see these forests that have never been logged? Will film companies use these forests to shoot movies about life long ago?

Will scientists find ways to make trees grow much faster? What other qualities might these "supertrees" have? Will people of the future grow trees that are free of knots, crooked sections or disease?

What Might Forest Technology Be Like in the Future?

How often have you thought, "There's got to be an easier way!" People are always looking for tools and machines that will help them do their work faster and better. It's the same in the forest industry. The industry hires scientists to develop new technology. This technology makes the industry more efficient and helps Canada compete with other countries that grow wood.

The early loggers who cut down trees with axes and huge handsaws would be amazed at today's computer-operated machinery. Today's loggers would probably be amazed at what forest technology will be like 50 years from now.

Will modern mills be completely run by computers and robots? Can you imagine a mill where logs go in one end, finished paper comes out the other end, and no workers are needed?

Right: Will forest managers make all their decisions without ever seeing a real forest? Will they look at models of the forest on a computer screen instead?

Will forest companies use logging methods that do less damage to the environment? For instance, will loggers use huge balloons and other "lighter than air" machines to lift trees off steep hillsides?

Right: Will there be a forestry retraining centre for workers whose jobs have been taken over by machines? Will robots do most of today's jobs in the forest while people do research and develop new technology?

How Might We Use Wood in the Future?

We use different products today from the products people used in the past. A hundred years ago, school children did their work on slates, which are small blackboards. Today's students use paper. Future students may do most of their work on computer monitors. As consumers find new products that do a better job than the old ones, they switch.

People in the forest industry know this. They are always developing new products they think people will find useful. They are finding more and more uses for wood, especially waste wood. What products do you think people will be buying 50 years from now?

Will people of the future use different forest products from what we use today? Will they wear disposable paper clothing and eat high protein woodburgers?

Will there be laws forcing people to recycle forest products? Will there be a ban on paper plates and other paper products that are only used once and then thrown away?

Above: Will cars, jets and rockets run on fuel made from wood instead of gasoline? Will wood products replace other things, such as plastic, that are now made from oil? Will factories now running on hydro-electric power switch to power made by burning fast-growing wood?

Below: Will people read newspapers on their home computer screens instead of on paper? Will Canada stop making newsprint?

How Might Canadians Use Forests in the Future?

In the past, Canadians have used forests for wood. They have used forests for hiking, fishing and other activities. They have cleared forest land for farms and cities. How will we use forests in the future? It depends on how they are most valuable to us. Will we make the most money and provide the most jobs by using forests for wood? Or will there be other uses that are more valuable to us, even though they may not provide as much money? How do you think you will use the forests 50 years from now?

Above: Will all forests, even parks, be used for logging? Will people who want to see old growth forests watch ***videotapes*** *of forest scenes on their giant wall screen at home? Will forests disappear as cities, roads and hydro-electric reservoirs cover more and more land?*

Above: Will tourism become a more important industry than forestry? Will there be many more forest parks, and a ban on any logging that might spoil the view from the highway? Will forest recreation become so popular that people will have to make reservations if they want to spend an afternoon walking in a local forest park?

Below: Will Canadians change their attitude towards the forest? Will they think a natural forest looks messy, and prefer to walk in planned forests with neatly spaced trees?

Above: Will clean drinking water become more valuable than wood? Will Canada export drinking water to other countries? Will some areas of forest be closed to logging, hiking and all other uses in order to protect our water?

Looking to Your Future

In this chapter we have been talking about the future of Canada's forests. Now let's think about your future. What will you be doing in 50 years? What does the future hold for you?

Will you be like Michelle and choose to work in forestry? Even if you don't, the forest will probably be important to you in other ways. You may take your children camping in the forest. You may use forest products. Your drinking water may come from the forest. You may be on a committee to decide how the forest near your community should be used. In one way or another, forests will likely be as important to Canadians in the future as they have been in the past.

Forests have always been a source of wood and wealth. More recently, people have learned that forests are important in other ways. We couldn't get along without forests. They contribute to the air we breathe, the clean water we drink and the food we eat. While people can harvest some of this renewable forest resource, they cannot cut down trees as if there is no tomorrow. There *is* a tomorrow. People in the future deserve to benefit from the forest resource, too.

Decisions about forests in the past were made by people who lived long ago. Decisions about today's forests are being made by adults living today, such as your parents and grandparents. As for the future, it belongs to you and your generation. You will be making the decisions about forests in the future.

Right now, across Canada, there are young trees that started growing the year you were born. Their roots are spreading through the soil, sucking up water and nutrients. Their leaves and branches are reaching towards the sun. If they are properly cared for, these trees will grow to become the forests of the future. These trees will become *your* trees—and part of your future.

Forests are an important renewable resource for all Canadians. Why must forests be protected?

Above: Bears depend on the forest for food and shelter. What might happen to bears and other animals if the forests are cut down?

UNIT CHECKUP

Learning from the Past

The pictures on the left below show how the forest was used in the past. The pictures on the right show forest use today.

1. Write a caption for each picture that describes the activity shown.
2. Describe some of the main differences between forest use in the past and today.

Looking to the Future

Look at this picture of the forest. People might change this forest habitat in different ways. Here are some examples of how the forest land might be used:

1. for a campground
2. for a sawmill
3. for farmland
4. for forest research

Pick one of these uses and write a paragraph explaining how the forest might change if this activity takes place. Draw a picture showing what the land might look like 50 years from now.

Getting Involved

Imagine that the forest near your community is being destroyed by forest fires started by people camping. What could *you* do to help solve this problem?

Summing Up

Imagine you are taking a group of younger students for a walk through the forest. From what you have learned in this unit, what are five things you would tell them about forests?

UNIT II

Exploring Communications

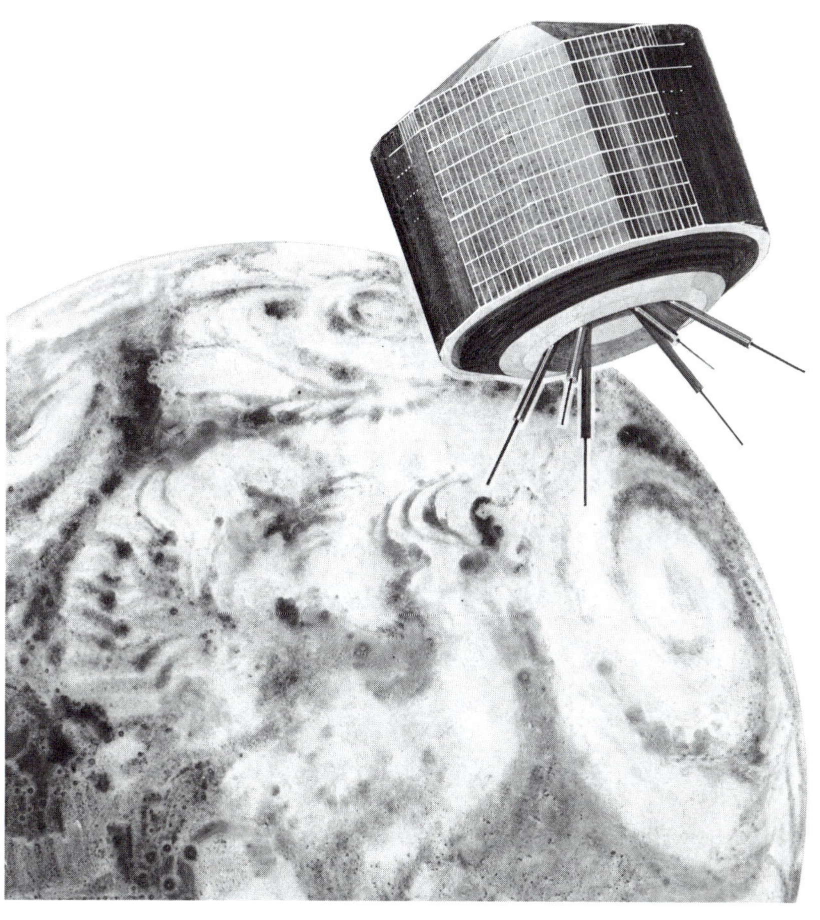

1

What Is Communication?

David's Message

The noise in the room was deafening. David liked it that way. Pounding at the keys of his electric piano, he almost drowned out the sound of the television blaring away in the corner. Almost, but not quite.

"Hundreds of people were killed today in bombing raids . . ."

David looked up when he heard the bombing sounds coming out of the television. He frowned and then went back to his playing. He started to sing some new words he had just written. They didn't sound quite right, so he scribbled a few changes. The television continued in the background.

"Many children were left homeless as the war continues in . . ."

David looked up at the television again with a sigh. He watched for a few moments and then tried to concentrate on the keyboard again. He was hoping to come up with some really good new songs for the school's music festival next month. His band always seemed to play the same old stuff. It was time for something different.

"Rebels opened fire on the town this morning . . ."

David jumped up and turned off the television. Suddenly it was quiet. Returning to his seat, he stared at the blank screen for a few minutes as if he could still see the **newscast**. Then he turned to pick up his pencil and paper. He had an important song to write.

David makes up a new song on his electric piano. Have you ever thought of writing a song?

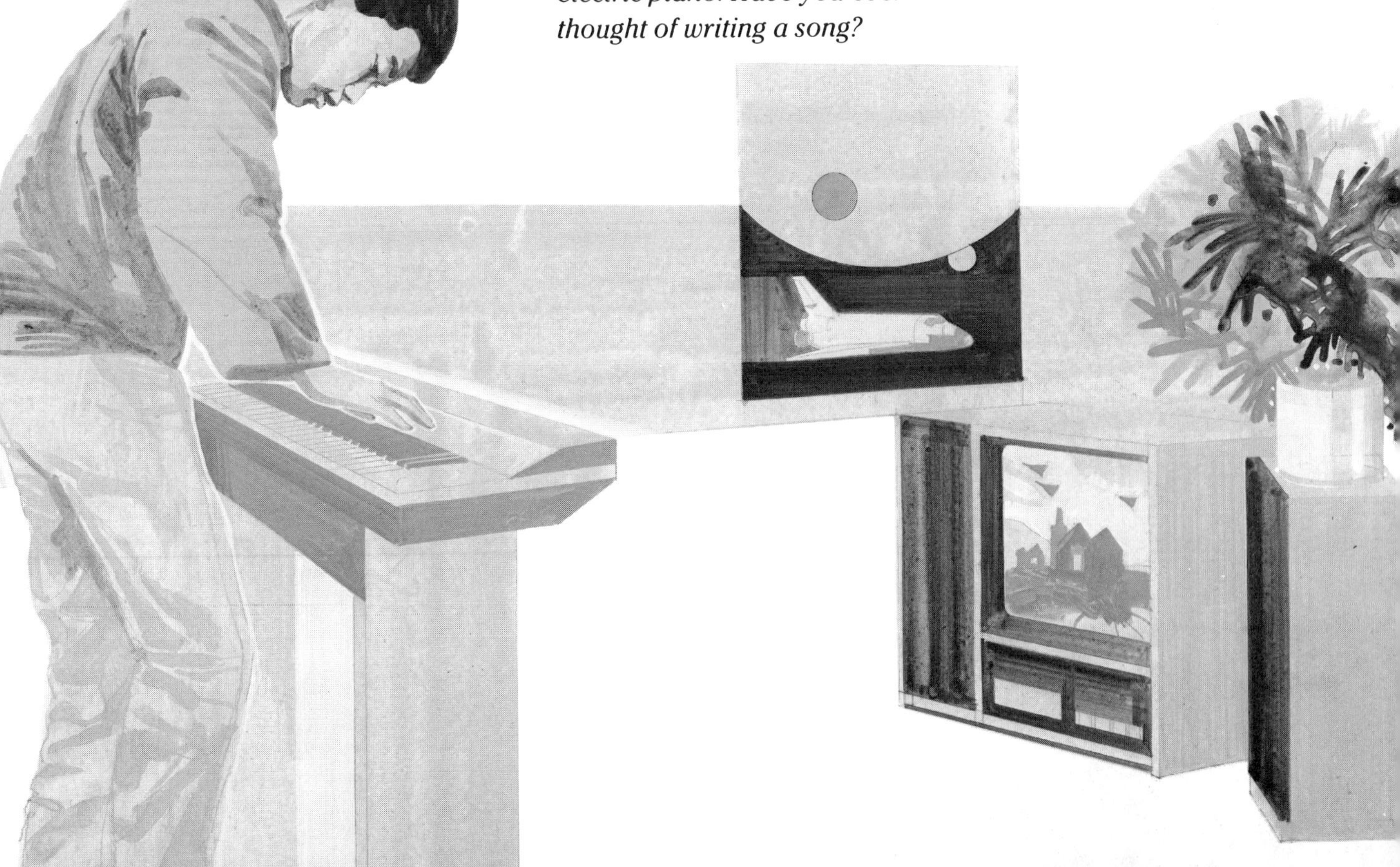

At band practice the next afternoon, David was hopping up and down with excitement. "This is it! This is the most important song I've written in my whole life!"

John, the guitar player, looked doubtful. "But David, you've only written three songs in your life."

"And this is definitely the most important," repeated David. "It's not just the music that's good. The message is really important, too. I'm calling it 'David's Message.'"

David began playing his new song. By the time he was finished, three minutes later, the band was impressed. "What gave you the idea for the words?" asked Sharon.

David explained that he had been listening to the news on TV, which seemed to be mostly about bombing and shooting. Then he had seen a boy on the screen—a boy about his own age, wandering through the bombed streets. The boy looked lost; maybe he was even hurt. David wished he could talk to that boy. In fact, he wished he could talk to children all over the world. "I figured, if we could talk to each other and get to know each other, we could become friends. And maybe, if we could be friends now, then our countries would not fight so much when we grow up."

David knew the children would not be able to visit each other, since they lived so far apart. He thought they could write letters and talk on the telephone. Then he remembered that they would all speak different languages. They wouldn't be able to **communicate**, even if they could call each other on the phone.

"That's when I had my brainwave," he said.

He remembered that there are children all over the world who like music. Even if they do not understand the words to songs, they still enjoy the music. So David decided he would communicate his friendship through music. He would write a song to children all over the world. It would be a song about friendship.

"So that's what I did!" said David.

John grinned. "So now you just have to get this song of yours all over the world."

"Right," agreed David. "How do I do that?"

Sharon leaned forward over her drums. "Let's start with the music festival, okay? There'll be hundreds of kids there from other schools. Let's make sure they like the song first. Worry about the rest of the world later."

- Music can communicate messages without using words. Can you describe music that might communicate a cheerful message? A frightening message? A sad message?

Communication

When you talk or write to your friends, you are communicating. You are sending a message from you to them.

For **communication** to work, the message must get from you to your friends. Speaking is the most common way of sending a message. The telephone, radio and **computer** help us send messages over long distances.

Then your friends have to understand your message. If you spoke to them in a language they did not understand, you would not really be communicating. If you sent them a letter and they could not read your handwriting, you would not be communicating.

When we communicate, we exchange ideas, information, thoughts and feelings. Although we usually use words, we can also send messages with our gestures and expressions, such as waving and smiling.

Sending the Message across Canada

The students at the music festival loved the song. They stood and cheered. They made the band play "David's Message" twice.

A reporter from the local newspaper was at the festival. She noticed how the other students responded to David's music. She wrote a story about the song and the newspaper printed some of the words. By the next day, "David's Message" had reached everyone who read the daily paper.

"Hey, we're famous!" cried John when the band got together that evening.

David shook his head. "Everyone in town knows about my song," he said. "But that's not going to help the world. How do I get my message out to more people?"

John suggested sending the words to the newspapers in a big city, papers that were read by more people. Sharon shook her head. "Forget the newspapers. 'David's Message' is music, so it needs to be heard. It's not very exciting just to read about it."

The band quickly decided the telephone would not be very good for sending "David's Message" either, since that would mean phoning one person at a time. "I'd be an old man before I was finished," said David. "I need to be able to play my song to a lot of people at once."

"In that case, you'd better phone the radio station," said Sharon.

David shook his head. "They won't listen to a kid like me."

"Tell them you're the one who was written up in the paper," suggested John. "Tell them you're famous."

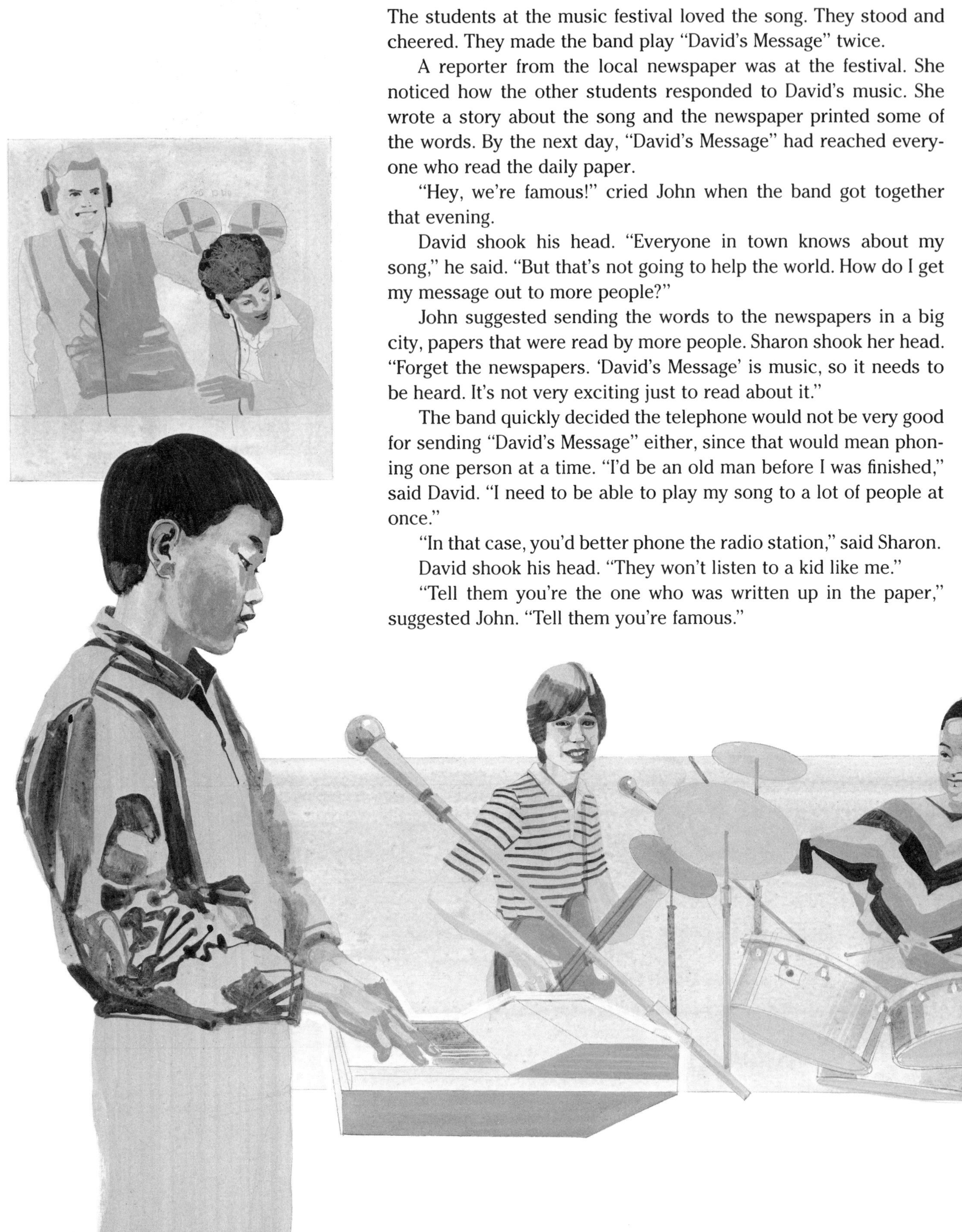

These huge presses print thousands of newspapers every day. Why are newspapers an important method of communication?

Much to David's surprise, the music **director** at the radio station was interested in hearing the song. On Saturday morning Sharon's mother drove the band to meet him. The radio station recorded the song on tape and played it several times over the next few weeks. People in nearby communities heard "David's Message." Then David received a call from the **producer** of a children's television program. She wanted to know if the band could come to Toronto to be on national television.

National television! Of course they could go! The television company paid for the band and Sharon's mother to fly to Toronto.

The show was seen by over one million children across Canada. That night, David was so excited he could hardly sleep. When he closed his eyes he could see radio waves carrying his message through the air all over the country. He could see television signals streaming from **satellites** in space and beaming his message down to every little corner of Canada.

After the television program, the band made lots of friends. Children in every province and territory wrote letters. Some even telephoned.

Sharon tacked up a sign on her bedroom door that said "DAVID'S MESSAGE—COMMUNICATION HEADQUARTERS." She went to work answering all the mail. Soon there were so many letters that she could not possibly answer each one. So instead she made up a **newsletter** and printed lots of copies. She sent copies to all the children who had written.

- What methods of communication did David's band use to send the message to Canadians?

Far left: David and the band record "David's Message" at the local radio station. Why is radio a good way to send a message?

Methods of Communication

You may have heard people talk about "the **media**" or "the news media." The media include radio, television, newspapers and magazines. These methods of communication send information to many people at one time. Each communicates information in a different way.

Radio

Radio communicates using sound. Radio is best for messages that do not need pictures. You can listen to music, interviews and plays on the radio. Radio plays use sound effects, such as the sound of a door closing or rain falling, to help people imagine what is happening.

Television

Television communicates using sound and **video** pictures. You can actually see and hear people and events. Television is best for presenting exciting action, such as an erupting volcano or a hockey game.

Printed Material

Newspapers, magazines and books communicate using print and photographs or drawings. Although you cannot hear music or watch action in a newspaper, you can read detailed information. You can carry this information with you and read it whenever you want.

Other Methods of Communication

There are many other methods of sending a message. Have you ever seen an airplane pulling a message behind it? Below are more ways of sending a message to many people. One day you might use some of these methods yourself. If you lost a pet, how might you let people know?

Put up posters in your community.

Write the message on a sandwich board and walk around your community.

Make up a bumper sticker and put it on your parents' car.

Deliver notices to all the homes in your neighbourhood.

Speak at a school assembly.

Fly a kite with your message hanging from it.

Sending the Message around the World

David was still not satisfied. His message was reaching more and more Canadian children, but it was not getting to children in other countries. He knew that other countries had television and radio. The children would hear his song if he could get the radio stations to play it. How could he ask the people in another country to play his song when he didn't speak their language?

Sharon made a suggestion. "There are lots of children in Canada who come from other countries, or their parents do," she said. "Some of them speak Italian; some speak Japanese; some speak German. And don't forget, lots of kids in Canada speak French. I could put a notice in my newsletter, asking all these kids who speak different languages to write to television and radio stations in other countries."

David looked excited. "It just might work!"

It did work. Soon "David's Message" was being played on radio stations all around the world. Children in many different countries were listening and then learning to play it. The band started getting letters from other countries. Sharon started collecting the **foreign** stamps.

Canadians use the postal system to communicate with people all over the world. What do you think this postal worker is doing?

"Well, now I guess you're satisfied," said John. "Millions of children must have heard your message by now. Maybe even that boy you saw on television wandering through the streets has heard it."

David didn't answer. He stared at the floor. "There's something missing," he muttered.

John looked at Sharon, shaking his head. Sharon looked at David, waiting.

"I know what it is," David cried, jumping to his feet and pacing the room. "We're sending the message out, but we're only sending it one way! I don't hear other kids sending it back!"

Sharon reminded him about all the letters that were pouring in, but receiving letters was not enough for David. "Remember the music festival?" he said. "Remember how good it felt when the crowd was singing along? We were singing the song to the other students, and, at the same time, they were singing it back at us. We really felt like one big, friendly group, all sharing the same message of friendship. We were all clapping to the same beat. We were all caught up in the music and excitement."

David continued talking excitedly. "That's what I want to happen with kids all over the world. I want us all to play the music together, all at the same time. Even if we don't speak the same language we could play my song together."

John shook his head. "You never give up. How are you going to get together to play with all these kids all over the world at once?"

David sighed and sat down. Sharon ran her finger slowly around the edge of her drums. "I wonder . . ." she said softly.

- Do you or your parents know someone who lives in another country? How do you communicate with that person?

People and Language

Some people speak English, some speak French and some speak Chinese. There are many different languages in the world, but all people use some kind of language to communicate with each other.

That makes people different from other living things. Birds can call loudly when they sense danger and dogs can growl when they are unfriendly, but those sounds are a very simple kind of communication. For more complicated messages, you need to use language. For instance, no animal could say, "These turnips taste awful. Do I have to eat them? Couldn't I have chocolate ice cream for supper instead?"

One-Way and Two-Way Communication

Have you ever wanted to talk back to your television? You can't, though, because the television signal only comes *into* your home. You can't use your TV to send a message back *out* to the television station. Your television is a one-way communication system. Your radio is another.

Telephones and two-way radios are different. You can carry on a two-way conversation with them. You can send *and* receive messages. You can talk *and* listen at the same time.

Someday you may be able to use your television for two-way communication. By pressing special buttons on the set, you'll be able to send a message saying what kind of information you want on the screen. Your television will be connected to a computer that will receive the message, find the information you want, and send it back to your TV screen.

Singing Together

Six months later, the band was in the Toronto television studio again. It was five minutes to four. David, John and Sharon were waiting. In another television studio in Tokyo, Japan, a band made up of Japanese children was also waiting. There were bands waiting in television studios in France, Australia, Egypt, Brazil—20 countries in all.

In the **control room** in Toronto, the television director was making last-minute preparations. She looked over the 20 TV screens on the panel in front of her. Each **monitor** showed a different group of children with instruments. On the whole, the television signals coming in by satellite from the other countries looked good.

Three minutes to air time. In the studio, the camera operators were ready. John drummed his fingers nervously on his guitar. Sharon squinted at the bright lights shining in her face. David sat at his keyboard and stared at the blank television screen in front of the room, waiting.

Two minutes to air time. The director was making a final check of the sound and pictures coming in from the 20 studios. Since the director could not show all 20 pictures on the screen at once, she would quickly switch from one to the other. For instance, she could show what was happening in the French studio and then switch to the Japanese studio.

One minute to air time. Thirty seconds. Ten seconds. Five, four, three, two, one...

They were on the air! In the studio, David saw himself on the television monitor with the words "David's Message" written underneath. He smiled, and watched himself smile on the screen. Just a fraction of a second later, when the television signal reached their countries, the bands in Japan, France and all the other countries saw David smile. Then they heard him clear his throat and say, "Hello from Canada!"

In the control room, the director quickly flipped a switch and the French studio appeared on the screen. A girl with long dark hair waved and said, *"En France, les enfants disent bonjour."*

One by one, each country said hello. Then David and his band appeared on the screen again. He nodded at Sharon, who began a steady drum beat. In the other studios around the world, the drums took up the beat.

David took a deep breath. He gave a nod to John, and they started playing the first notes of the song. After David's band had sung one verse, the director flipped a switch and showed the German band belting out the second verse. Then the Japanese children sang the third verse. Then the Egyptian band sang the fourth verse, and then the Israeli group sang the last verse.

Timing is an important part of every television broadcast. Each portion of the broadcast is timed by the script assistant and no portion is allowed to run beyond its time limit. What is the assistant holding here?

Below: David plays the last verse of his song. Can you imagine how he is feeling?

As each country sang a verse of "David's Message," David's smile grew wider and wider. Watching the other bands sing, he could almost forget that they were really far away. It was not quite like the music festival, of course, where all the children were in the same room with him. But David could see the other bands sing. He could hear them sing. It was close enough.

By each singing one verse, the bands played the entire song four times. Then David's band sang the last verse again. Pounding on his keyboard, David played his heart out. He felt surrounded by music, surrounded by friends.

Then, with a final clash of cymbals, it was all over. The sound died away and the television screen went blank. The studio was still.

David turned to Sharon and John. Sharon smiled, and David gave her a tired nod.

- If you could send a message to children all over the world, what would you say?

Communication and You

In this chapter you have read about how David communicated his message to children in his town, children across Canada, and even children around the world. You saw some of the different ways David communicated this message. First he sang at the music festival, and then his words were printed in the newspaper, and then his band played for radio and television. There are many different ways people can get their message out to other people.

Why do people need to communicate? Why do you communicate with others? Probably there are several reasons. Sometimes you want information. You ask someone the time or phone your friend to see if there is a baseball practice on Saturday. Sometimes you want to learn new things. You watch a television program on dinosaurs or ask your art teacher to explain how to do a project. Sometimes you want to tell things to other people. You talk to your parents and friends about your thoughts and feelings.

- What is the first thing you said this morning? Why did you say it?

This worker is repairing communications equipment. What skills might he need for this work?

Also, people communicate in order to become closer to other people. Have you ever walked into a room full of strangers, for example on your first day in a new school? Perhaps you can remember how much better you felt when someone smiled at you or started up a conversation. Communicating with other people can make you feel as if you are part of a group. Instead of feeling cut off from everyone else, you feel as if you belong.

There are many good reasons why people need to communicate with others. It is easy to talk to someone standing next to you. But if you want to talk to someone far away, or to many people at once, you need to use a telephone, a radio, or some other piece of equipment. This equipment is a tool that helps people communicate, and scientists are continually developing new and better tools for the job. However, these tools do not tell us *what* to communicate. That is still up to us.

The need to communicate never changes. What does change, however, is the way we communicate and the kinds of equipment we use. People use the term **communications** when they are speaking of the science that helps us send and receive messages. People working in communications develop **networks** of wires, satellites and towers, for example, that allow us to send and receive messages over great distances.

If used wisely, a good communications network can be very valuable. In a huge country such as Canada, people often live far apart. If we could not communicate across those large distances, it would be impossible to work together as one country. How could

These satellites are part of a communications network for people around the world. How might this network be used to bring different countries together?

we find out what was happening in other parts of the country? How could we tell our government what we want? How could we feel as if we all belonged in this country if we were not able to share information and ideas? Communications equipment helps bring us together.

Communications networks can bring Canadians closer to people in other parts of the world, too. In the story you have just read, David wanted to share his message with children around the world. He felt that the children could become friends if they could communicate with each other. They could get to know each other almost as if they lived in the same neighbourhood. In fact, some people say we live in a "global village" today. That means that we are able to communicate with people all over the globe, just as if we were all neighbours in a small village.

Not all countries can afford expensive communications equipment such as satellites. In many countries, people cannot afford telephones or televisions. So although people have invented ways to make communication easier and faster, not everyone in the world is able to take advantage of these new ways.

In Canada, though, we take modern methods of communication for granted. We expect to be able to phone someone across the country. We expect to see satellite weather pictures on TV. It is hard to imagine what life was like before these things were possible.

- How would your life be different if you did not have a telephone or television set?

In the next chapter, we'll get a glimpse of Canada in the past. We'll go back in time to see how communications has developed over the years and how new inventions have changed the lives of Canadians.

CHAPTER CHECKUP

Recalling the Main Ideas

In this chapter David communicated with many people. To do so, he used the following methods of communication:

1. newspapers
2. telephones
3. letters
4. radio
5. television

Decide which of the above words belong in the blanks in the sentences below. You may use each word more than once.

1. ______ and ______ use printed words to send messages.
2. ______ and ______ use only sound (such as voices and music) to send messages.
3. ______ uses both pictures and sound to send messages.
4. ______, ______ and ______ provide information to many people at once.
5. ______ and ______ are usually used to communicate with one person at a time.
6. Using ______, it may take you several days to send your message.
7. Write down the ways of communicating you use every day.

____

____

____

Using What You Have Learned

We communicate with other people for different reasons. Here are some of these reasons:

1. to get information
2. to learn new things
3. to talk about our thoughts and feelings
4. to bring us closer to others

Think about the times you communicate with other people. From your own experience, write down one example that illustrates each of the reasons given above. In each case, name the person you were communicating with and the message you were giving or receiving.

2

What Was Communications Like in the Past?

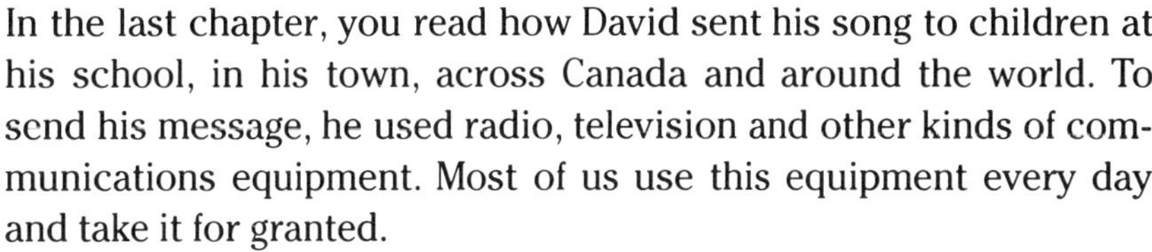

In the last chapter, you read how David sent his song to children at his school, in his town, across Canada and around the world. To send his message, he used radio, television and other kinds of communications equipment. Most of us use this equipment every day and take it for granted.

Stop for a moment and think of the amazing things we can do with today's communications equipment. We can settle back into a comfortable chair, press a few buttons on the telephone and talk to someone hundreds of kilometres away. We can turn a knob on the television set and watch a hockey game in Edmonton. During commercial breaks we can switch channels and watch whales swimming off the coast of Mexico. We can turn on the radio for the latest news from the Parliament Buildings in Ottawa. We can find out what the weather is like in other parts of the country.

All this information is at our fingertips. We can receive information from people across town, across the country and around the world, without leaving our homes. It's easy, and it's fast, but it was not always like that.

Before the modern inventions in communications, most messages were carried from one place to another. Communities were often far apart. Messengers carrying information could travel through hundreds of kilometres of wilderness without seeing anyone. Travel was slow. There were no engines in those days. Messengers travelled by foot, by canoe, by horse, by snowshoe and by dogsled. They climbed over mountains and paddled along rivers.

The first Europeans who arrived in Canada relied on Indian messengers. The Europeans built fur trading posts scattered throughout the wilderness. Indian runners carried messages from one trading post to the next.

- Why would Europeans use Indian messengers instead of other Europeans?

Indians often acted as messengers for the early fur traders in Canada. What kind of messages might have been sent from one trading post to another?

Local Indians brought furs to the trading posts and traded them for European goods. The furs were loaded into canoes for the long trip to the St. Lawrence River. The men who paddled the canoes also carried messages to and from the trading posts. After a long, lonely winter, the people at the trading posts were happy to see the canoes coming down the river.

In Canada, it became very important to find faster ways to communicate. In this big, lonely country, many people felt cut off from other people. Settlers wanted to keep in touch with family and friends back home. Fur trading companies wanted to send instructions to their workers in small trading posts in the wilderness. The government wanted to find out what was happening in the rest of the country. People did not want to wait months for an answer. Messengers travelling by foot, by horse or by canoe were very slow.

At first, communications changed as **transportation** improved. Roads were built, and messengers could travel faster and more easily. Later, new inventions in communications made it possible to send information without messengers travelling from one place to the next.

These new ways of communicating brought isolated people in touch with the rest of the country. They made Canadians feel more like friendly neighbours, even though they still lived far apart.

In this chapter, we'll explore the past. We'll go back in time and see how communication in Canada became faster and easier because of new **technology**. We'll see how new inventions in communications changed the lives of Canadians.

In 1752, the Halifax Gazette *was printed on Canada's first printing press. How might a weekly newspaper have affected the lives of the settlers?*

Mail and Newspapers

Today most Canadians have mail delivered to them every weekday. Many receive a daily newspaper. Imagine what it might have been like to live in Canada in the 1700s. In some parts of the country people might receive mail and newspapers only once or twice a year.

The first Canadian newspapers appeared in Halifax and Quebec City around 1760. The papers were published once a week, and they were only a few pages long. The pages were printed with a hand press—very slow by today's standards. In one day, a printer and his assistant could print 160 copies of a four-page newspaper. Since travel was also slow, newspaper subscribers living outside of town could expect to wait a long time for the "news" to reach them.

Canada's own mail service did not really start until 1851. Before that, decisions about the mail were made in Great Britain. When Canada took charge of its postal service, the first Canadian stamps were printed. More and more post offices were built to handle the mail. As roads improved, the mail moved faster and faster.

Then the "iron horse" arrived! Section by section, railways were built. Suddenly people could expect to receive letters and newspapers in a few days instead of waiting several weeks.

Before 1854, it took ten and a half days to send a letter by horseback from Quebec City to Windsor, Ontario. In 1854, with the new rail line connecting the two cities, it took only two days.

In 1886, trains were travelling from coast to coast on the Canadian Pacific Railway. Mail took five and a half days to get from Montreal to Port Moody, on the Pacific coast.

There were even mail sorters on the trains. They collected mail from stations along the way. If the train didn't stop, they used a long iron bar with a hook to grab the mailbag hanging from a post on the station platform. Cramped in the swaying train car, the mail sorters worked quickly. They sorted the letters and put them into different mailbags to be dropped off at different stations. They would throw the mailbags onto the platform as the train rattled past.

Mail continued to move faster and faster. In the 1920s, airplanes started carrying mail. Today planes can take the mail across the country in a few hours. Most mail sorting is now done by machines instead of people. The sorting machines use the postal code that Canadians started using in 1971.

- How do you think the mail sorters felt when machines started doing much of the work that had been done by hand?

In the early twentieth century, most mail was transported across Canada by train. A train will soon pick up the bag of mail hanging on the post. How would this method save time?

Today, some mail travels across the country in just seconds. Using **electronic** mail, customers can take a letter to a post office in Halifax and order an exact copy of the letter to be printed in the post office in Vancouver, almost instantly. Newspapers can use new technology, too. Instead of printing all the papers in Toronto, publishers can send plans for all the pages electronically to cities across Canada. Printers in those cities use the plans to print newspapers for the readers living in that area. That's much faster than shipping tonnes of newspapers across the country.

Telegraph

"Sending messages over wires? I don't believe it!"

In 1846, many Canadians were amazed to see a new invention called the **telegraph**. They called it the "talk by lightning" machine. It seemed to work by magic. Using **electricity**, people could send messages along wires.

Telegraph operators used a lever to turn the electric current on and off, tapping out a pattern of short and long beeps. These short and long bursts of electricity travelled along a wire many kilometres long. At the other end of the wire, the electricity caused another lever to tap out the same pattern. The short beeps were called dots and the long beeps were called dashes. The dots and dashes spelled out words using Morse code. Every letter of the alphabet has a different combination of dots and dashes. For example, the signal for help is · · · - - - · · · (SOS).

By 1876, telegraph wires hung from a long line of poles stretching across the prairies. When the telegraph worked, it was wonderful. Settlers could call the doctor or order a new part for their farm equipment. The mounted police could send messages to police in other forts to head off escaping criminals. Some prairie settlers even used the telegraph to play checkers and chess with other settlers down the line.

Unfortunately, the telegraph line only worked in fits and starts. The poles would fall down or be burned in prairie fires. Bison would rub up against them and get the wires tangled in their horns. Wet leaves touching the wire would stop the electric current from flowing through the wire. The prairie workers who kept the telegraph working were the heroes of the day. They went out at night and in blizzards to fix the wires and prop up the poles.

Workers string telegraph wires in British Columbia in the early 1900s. Why might it be difficult to repair these lines if they were damaged?

Telegraph machines do not use Morse code today. Instead, they can send and receive written messages. For example, a message can be typed into a **teletypewriter**. The message is carried over wires and then typed out by another machine in a different place.

Although most people do not use the telegraph today, it was a very exciting invention in the past. For the first time, messages could be sent electrically from one place to another. For the first time, no messenger was needed to send a message farther than the distance a person could see or hear. The telegraph drastically changed communications.

- How did the early telegraph machines work? How do they work today? What is the main difference between them?

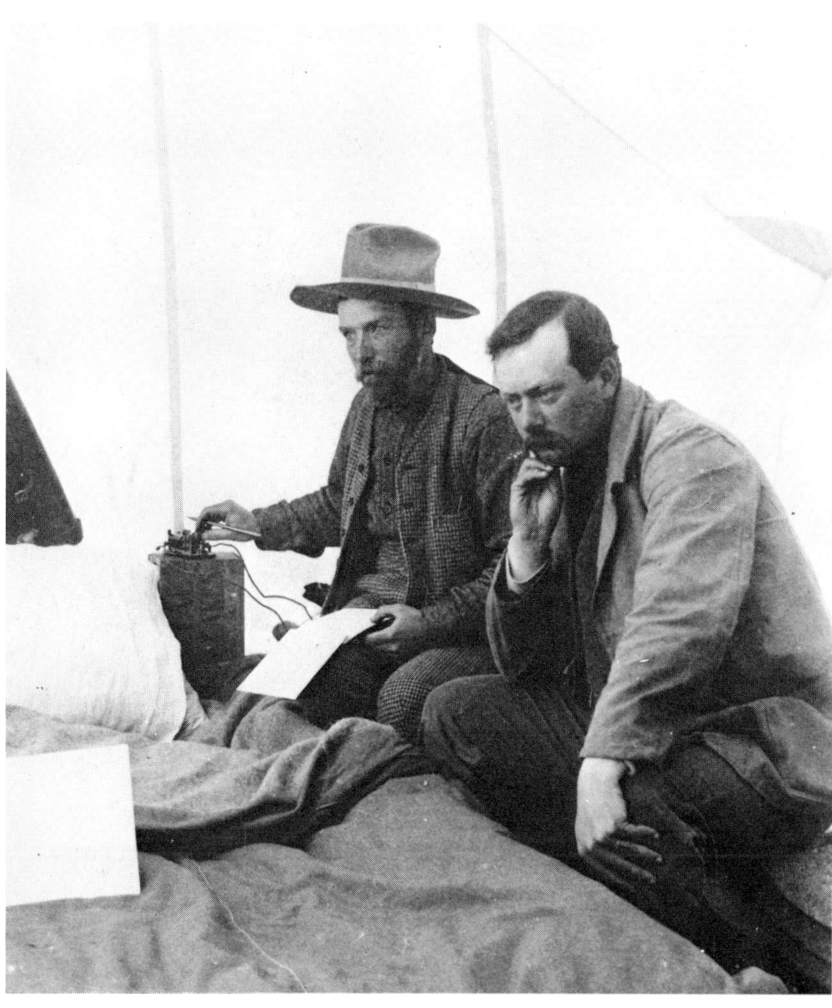

Above: A telegraph operator sends a message on the wire in the early 1900s. How is he sending the message?

Alexander Graham Bell

Alexander Graham Bell was full of energy and imagination. He would wake up friends in the middle of the night to show them something he was inventing. His most famous invention is the telephone.

Bell taught deaf people and was interested in how people hear. He got the idea for his telephone from studying the human ear. In your ear there is an eardrum—a thin sheet of skin like the top of a tightly stretched drum. When sound waves travelling through the air hit the eardrum, it moves back and forth quickly, or vibrates.

Each end of Bell's telephone had a membrane like an eardrum. Sound waves would cause the membrane at one end to vibrate. Electricity travelling through a wire would carry the pattern of this vibration to the other membrane. The other membrane would vibrate in a similar pattern and make the original sounds.

Bell worked with an assistant, Thomas Watson. They set up his invention in two different rooms in a house. On March 10, 1876, Watson picked up his end of the machine. He heard Bell say, "Mr. Watson, come here. I want you!" Bell had just made the world's first telephone call.

Bell was born in Scotland, but he did most of his work in the United States and in Canada. He made the world's first long-distance call in Ontario. While Bell listened on the telephone in the town of Paris, Ontario, he heard his father speaking in Brantford, almost 13 km away.

Bell lived in Nova Scotia for much of his later life. He continued inventing and discovering new things. He was always enthusiastic and curious. He was always thinking in new directions.

Alexander Graham Bell, the inventor of the telephone, was also a teacher of the deaf. Here he is helping a boy who is both deaf and blind.

Telephone

"Cheap and Quick Communication by DIRECT SPEECH," said the ad in the Victoria newspaper. A new invention, the telephone, arrived on the west coast of Canada in 1880. Only a few years earlier, Alexander Graham Bell had invented the telephone. Unlike the telegraph, the telephone could carry voices over wires.

One of the first phone lines in Victoria was less than a kilometre long. It ran from Jeffree's clothing store to Pendray's soap factory. A newspaper reporter explained how it worked: "In the office at each end of the wire there hangs against the wall a small black-walnut box. At the side of the box is a small crank, which a person desirous of communicating with another turns." The reporter then explained that the person in the office at the other end of the wire hears the alarm bell and answers the telephone: "Taking the speaking-tube in his hand, he places it near his mouth and asks what is wanted."

At the beginning, people sometimes shouted into the phone. They thought they had to shout, since they were talking to someone far away.

As telephones became more popular, **telephone exchanges** were built. Callers rang up the exchange and told the switchboard operator who they wanted to call. They did not always use telephone numbers. Instead, they might say, "Give me Arthur's grocery." The switchboard operator would connect the right wires so that the telephone call could take place.

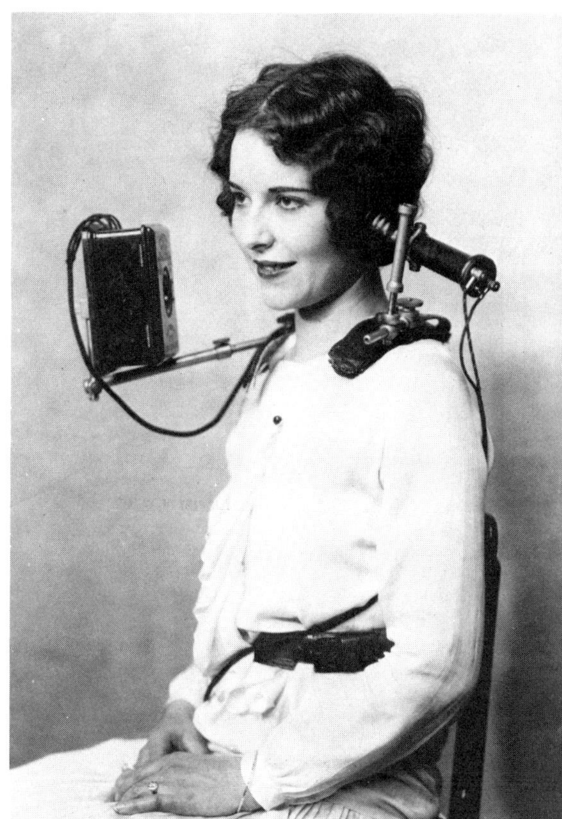

Above: This picture shows the harness worn by telephone operators in the 1880s. How might this harness help the operator do her job?

Telephone operators work in the busy central office of the telephone company in the 1890s. What do you think it was like to work as an operator?

In a small town, the person who looked after the switchboard did more than just connect calls. Telephone operators were the best source of information in town. They would give callers the time or the latest news. They would find doctors when they were not at home, or alert people if there was an emergency. Sometimes they even solved arguments between two callers.

Telephones became more and more popular. Most Canadian homes now have at least one telephone. Canadians make over 22 billion telephone calls a year. Switchboard operators could not handle that many calls. But technology has changed. Telephone connections are now made automatically.

- When might you speak to a telephone operator today?

Radio

"He shoots! He scores!" When you hear that, you know you are listening to a hockey game. Imagine the excitement of people in 1923. They heard the very first play-by-play hockey game ever **broadcast** by radio.

Radio was a wonderful new invention. It could send human voices through the air without using any wires. That's why, at first, it was called a "wireless."

The first radio signal to cross the Atlantic Ocean was received near St. John's, Newfoundland, on a cold, wet December night in 1901. The Newfoundland site, now called Signal Hill, was chosen by the Italian inventor Guglielmo Marconi. At Signal Hill, Marconi attached an **antenna** to a kite that would fly high over the hill. The antenna received a signal sent all the way from England. The signal consisted of three dots, which mean the letter "S" in Morse code. A Toronto newspaper called this new, wireless communication "the most wonderful scientific discovery of modern times." Marconi's experiment proved that radio waves could travel around the curved surface of the earth.

Guglielmo Marconi and his assistants stand on Signal Hill in Newfoundland. Marconi experimented with radio waves. In 1901, here on Signal Hill, he received the first radio signal from England. Why might this be a good place to receive a signal?

The world's first radio broadcast of a human voice, not just a signal, was made by Reginald Fessenden, a Canadian. On Christmas Eve in 1906, he stepped before a microphone and played a Christmas carol on his violin. He signed off by saying "Merry Christmas." People on ships at sea were amazed to hear him.

By the 1920s, there were radio stations all across Canada. The Canadian National Railway used stations to broadcast news and music to its trains as they passed. Each seat in the parlour car was equipped with headphones so that passengers could listen to the radio. Some people bought train tickets just for the fun of listening in.

Above: Passengers on a train in the 1920s listen to the radio as they travel. Why might people have enjoyed this?

An announcer broadcasts from a sound booth at a radio station. A radio operator handles the controls. What kinds of information might you obtain from the radio?

The dish-shaped antennas at the top of this tower receive microwave signals. Why do you think the antennas are located as far from the ground as possible?

Not everyone thought radio was wonderful. Some **politicians** in the government shook their heads over this "radio craze." Others said it was ridiculous to spend so much money "on radios and other frills and fads."

That didn't stop radio. It was here to stay. Soon there were school broadcasts, radio plays, symphony concerts, news and even commercials. The first singing commercial on radio was for Toronto Wet Wash Laundry in 1926. It was sung to the tune of "Three Blind Mice."

- Why do most radio stations broadcast commercials?

Today there are many different radio stations in Canada. One network that can be heard all across the country is the Canadian Broadcasting Corporation (CBC). The CBC was formed by the Canadian government in 1936, and it is owned by all Canadians. It broadcasts programs in English and French. The CBC helps Canadians learn more about Canadian news and culture.

Radio has become an important part of Canadian life. We have radios in our cars. We take portable radios to the beach. We even wear tiny radio headphones as we walk along the street. People all over Canada can listen to the latest news and music wherever they are.

Microwaves

There were some problems with the poles and wires used for telephone calls. In storms and bad weather they fell down. It was also very expensive to take telephone poles and wires to remote communities with few people.

The people on Prince Edward Island had another problem. Their telephones were connected to the rest of Canada by a **cable** running under the water to Nova Scotia. The cable would break when it was rubbed against the rocks by ice or waves.

It was a great day on November 20, 1948, when the **premier** of Prince Edward Island had the first telephone conversation with the premier of New Brunswick without using underwater cables. Instead, they used **microwaves** to carry their voices back and forth across the water.

Microwaves are very short radio waves. They travel through the air in a straight, narrow beam (like a flashlight beam, except that you can't see it). To make sure nothing on the ground blocks their path, microwaves are sent from the top of tall towers. Often these towers are built on the top of buildings or on mountainsides.

Microwaves are beamed from one tower to another. On the top of each tower there is an antenna shaped like a dish or a horn that receives the microwave signal. In 1948, there was a tower in Prince Edward Island and another in Nova Scotia, and microwaves sent the

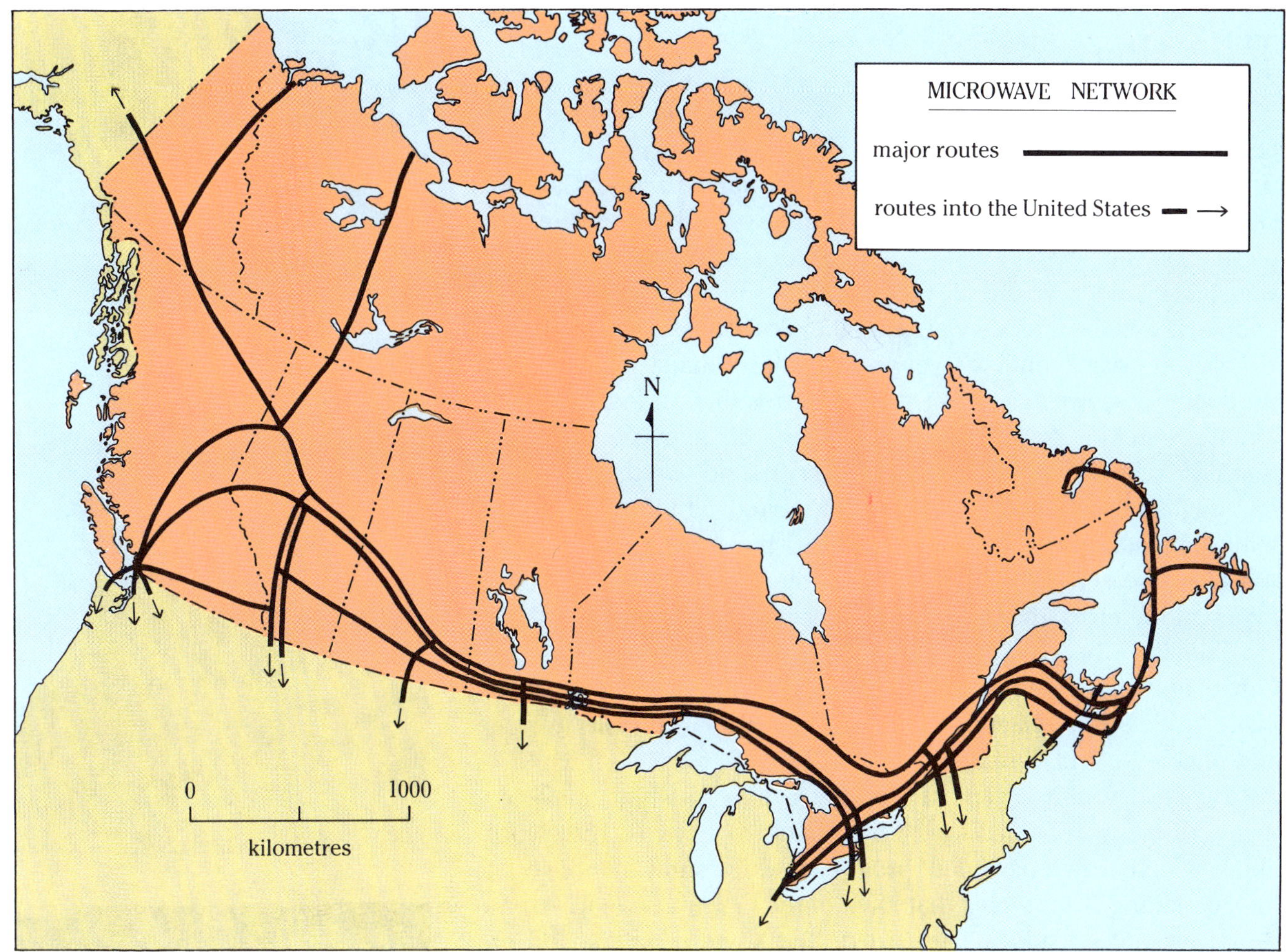

premiers' telephone conversation across the water. Microwaves could also send radio and, later, television signals.

By 1958, Canada's telephone companies had built a line of microwave towers across the country. Each tower received the microwave signals, made them stronger, then passed them on to the next tower. The 139 towers formed a communications highway over 6200 km long. It was the longest line of microwave towers in the world. It sent information across the forests, prairies and mountains, from coast to coast, in one fiftieth of a second. That's faster than you can wink an eye.

- Would it be easier to build a line of microwave towers across the prairies or across the mountains?

This map shows the microwave network that extends across Canada and into the United States. Why do you think that most microwave routes are located along Canada's southern border?

Television

"Get your coat and hat on. Let's go to Ogilvie's Department Store to see the moving pictures."

About 100 000 people visited the Montreal department store in October 1932 for a glimpse of this new marvel—the television. The picture on the screen wasn't in colour, or even black and white. It was black and red. But it was a moving picture. And for most people, it was the first television set they had ever seen.

Still, it wasn't until 20 years later that Canada really started producing its own television programs. By then, Canadians were already watching American programs on their television sets. The first CBC television program was in French, and two days later the first English program was broadcast. It started with the name of the television station: CBLT. Unfortunately, the letters were upside down on the screen! After that error, the program improved, and included the news, the weather forecast and entertainment.

Television became more and more popular. There were some Canadians who were not sure that this new invention was a good idea. "It gives the children bad eyes, makes them unable to sleep and unable to study," said one teacher in 1953.

Even today, although most Canadians enjoy watching television, many people worry about how it has changed our lives. They worry about people watching violent programs, which show lots of shooting and killing. They worry that most of the programs we watch are American, not Canadian. They worry that some people spend too much time watching television and not enough time doing other activities.

Yet television has also changed our lives for the better by bringing us useful information and exciting entertainment from all over the world. We can see people and places we never could have seen without television. In 1969, when a person walked on the moon for the first time, this event was shown on television. Many people were thrilled to be able to watch it.

- How important is television in your life?

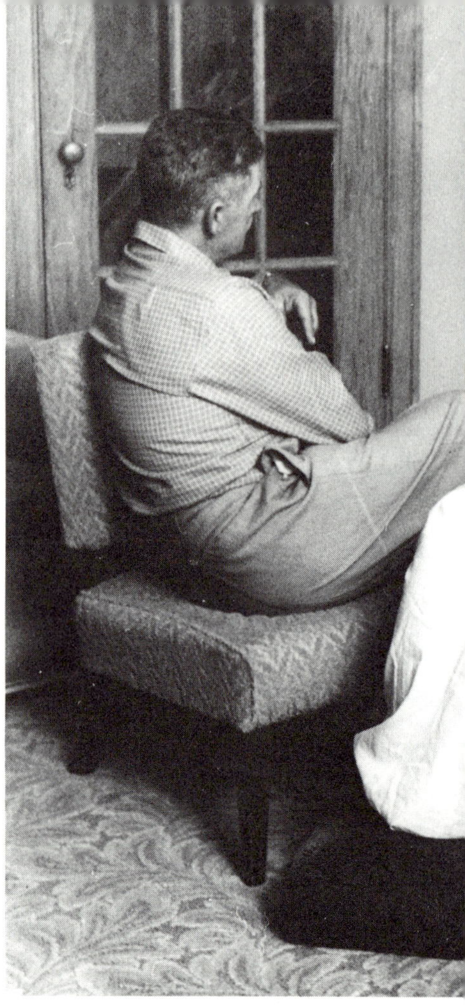

A group of friends watches television today. What kinds of programs do you and your friends like watching?

Left: A family watches television during the 1950s. How do you think they might have felt about this new form of communication?

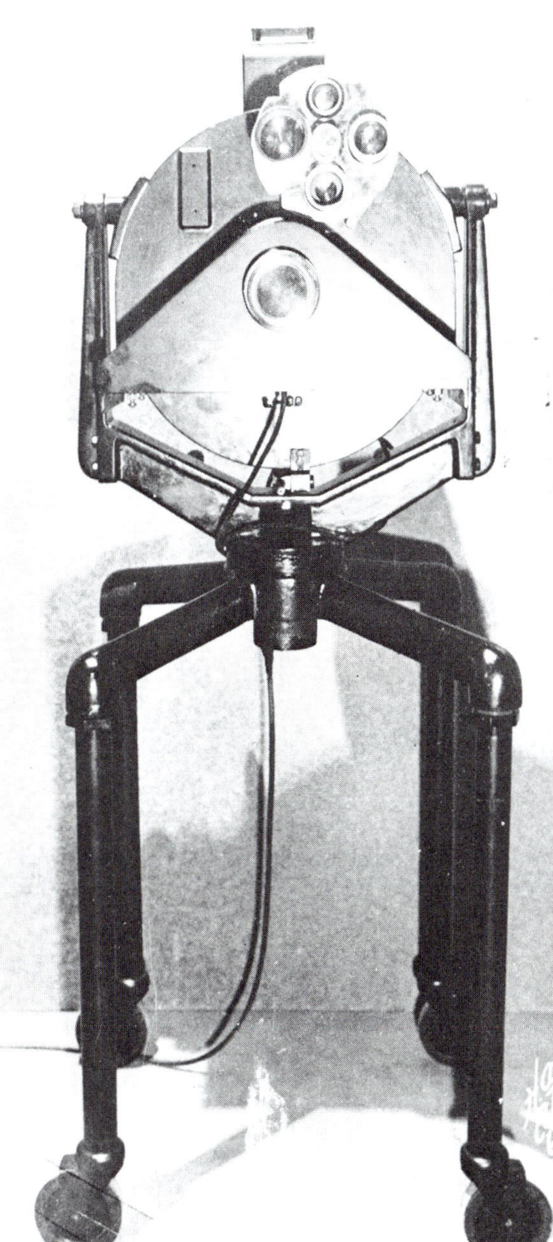

Above: This is the kind of television camera that was used when television was first developed in the 1930s. In what ways might it be different from today's cameras?

Satellites

Pangnirtung is a small Inuit village on Baffin Island in the Northwest Territories. It is a long distance from the nearest city. Pangnirtung is about as close to the North Pole as it is to Ottawa. Yet it is still part of Canada.

In 1972, it was difficult for people in Pangnirtung to find out what was happening in the rest of Canada. There were no telephone wires going there. There were no microwave towers across the northern wilderness. What's more, radios do not work very well in the Arctic.

In November of that year, Canada launched its first communications satellite into space. That satellite was called *Anik A-1*. ("Anik" means "brother" in the language of the Inuit.) Satellites brought great changes to small Arctic villages like Pangnirtung. In a couple of months, the rest of Canada was just a phone call away. By spring, people in the village were able to watch television, live and in colour. By the summer of 1974, people in Pangnirtung had ordered 300 television sets.

Satellites work a bit like microwave antennas, but instead of being built on mountain tops they are placed in orbit 36 000 km above the earth. Telephone and television signals are beamed up to the satellite from an **earth station**. It takes the signals about one eighth of a second to get there. The satellite then strengthens the signals and sends them down to other earth stations thousands of kilometres away from the first one. The station at Pangnirtung could receive these signals.

You can imagine how life in northern communities changed in the 1970s because of satellite communications. The people there could get the latest news and weather forecasts. They could phone another community for help if there was an emergency. They could order new parts for their snowmobiles.

There were other changes, too. Can you imagine how children who had never left Pangnirtung might feel after watching television programs about city life in the south? What might they think after watching commercials for toys they never knew existed?

By the early 1980s, people in the north were producing some of their own television programs. Some of these programs were broadcast in *Inuktitut,* the native language of the Inuit. They let people know what was happening in other northern communities.

Canada was one of the first countries in the world to use satellites. Now there are many communications satellites that belong to Canada and other countries. Satellites have brought television, radio and telephone service to some of the most isolated places in Canada.

- Why do you think Canada was a leader in satellite communications?

An earth station sends signals to a satellite and receives signals as well. Why are satellites important to isolated communities?

Below: This map shows the location of earth stations across Canada. How many cities have more than one earth station?

Recent Inventions in Communications

In the early 1980s, farmers in southern Manitoba took part in an experiment called Project Grassroots. They were trying out two new ideas in communications—**optical fibres** and **videotex**.

Optical fibres are very thin threads of glass, about the thickness of a human hair. In Project Grassroots, these long fibres were used instead of the usual copper wires to carry telephone and television signals to the farmers. Copper wires use electricity to carry signals, but optical fibres use beams of light instead.

Optical fibres can carry many more signals at once than copper wire can. For example, if 24 people are making phone calls at the same time, four copper wires are normally needed to handle those conversations. By contrast, one single optical fibre might carry up to 12 000 phone conversations. There would still be room left over for television or radio signals to travel along the same fibre. So it is cheaper to use cables with optical fibres than cables with copper wires because one cable can carry more signals.

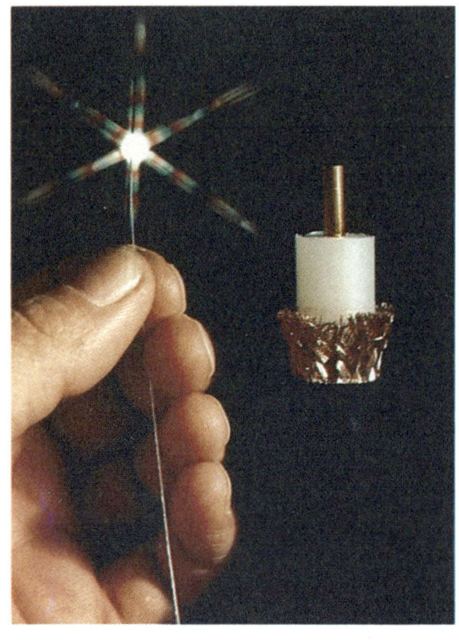

Telephone signals can be carried by optical fibres or copper wire. How does the optical fibre that the person is holding compare with the copper wire on the right?

The other invention tested by Project Grassroots is called videotex. The farmers' televisions were hooked up, through these optical fibre lines, to a computer far away.

Farmers need to know all kinds of information, and in southern Manitoba they were able to see this information on their TV screens. They pressed buttons on a keyboard to indicate the kind of information they wanted. The computer received the request and sent the right page of information over the phone line to the TV screen. (They are called "pages" even though they are on a screen instead of on paper.)

For instance, the farmers could find out the price of cattle at the market. Then the farmers would know if it was a good time to sell their animals. They could find out how much a bag of seed would cost. They could get an up-to-date weather forecast. They could get information on how to run the farm.

With videotex, all this useful information is stored in a computer **information bank**. It is a big library. Computers store the information and bring it out when it's needed. New, fast methods of communication can get that information from the computer to our homes instantly. Someday you, too, will likely use your television to get information from a computer bank.

You're probably not a farmer, so you wouldn't want to know the price of cattle. But you might want to know how much different bicycles cost, for instance. You could ask for that information and the computer would show you pictures of all kinds of bicycles on the TV screen. You could choose the one you wanted and type in your order. It would be delivered and charged to your credit card. You wouldn't have to leave your house.

A young musician reads music off a videotex "page." Why might it be easier to use videotex instead of sheet music?

Videotex can provide up-to-date facts, figures, pictures and other information. Since almost everybody uses information of some kind, there are countless possible uses for videotex. For instance, it is used in employment centres to find out about jobs that are available across Canada. It is used by doctors to get the latest information on diseases. It provides tourists with information on hotels and concerts in town.

The videotex system used by the farmers in Project Grassroots was developed by the Canadian government in 1978. It is called Telidon. Someday people all over Canada and in other parts of the world might use Telidon to get information they need from computer information banks.

- What kind of information would you like to receive on videotex?

Communications and Canadians

Through the years, new and better ways of sending information have been invented. These inventions have helped Canadians send information faster and farther. Now it does not matter how far away people live. With the right equipment, we can still communicate with them. It does not matter if they live on an island or a mountain top. They can still communicate with us.

Sometimes it seems as if we are surrounded by voices and pictures speeding through the air, through wires, and to and from space. We are surrounded by more and more information that travels faster and farther than ever before. No wonder some people are saying that we now live in the "Information Age."

Canada has often been a leader of new inventions in communications. With such a large country, Canadians *had* to find new ways to communicate over long distances. So, in the past, Canadians built railways and telegraph lines, installed microwave antennas and developed satellites. These networks linked Canadians from the Atlantic to the Pacific, from the United States border to the Arctic Ocean. They have also kept Canadians in touch with the rest of the world.

Today Canada continues to find new ways of communicating information. The videotex system called Telidon is an example of one of Canada's recent inventions.

The invention of the telegraph changed the lives of early settlers on the prairies. The invention of the satellite changed life for the Inuit in the Arctic. Changes now taking place, such as the use of Telidon and computers, will affect your life, one way or another. Some people are excited by new technology. Some are frightened by it. They wonder if the changes it brings will be good or bad.

One thing will never change, though. People have always needed to communicate with others, and they always will. We live in a world with other people, and communication is what ties us together. When we communicate, we learn from each other. We help each other. We learn that there are people who think the same as we do and people who think differently. We begin to understand each other. We make each other laugh. We find out we have friends.

We will always need to communicate with other people. New inventions in communications will not change that. What they can do is make this communication much easier and faster.

These astronauts are working with the "Canadarm" outside the space shuttle Discovery. *The arm was developed and built by Canadians. It can be used to work on satellites in space. How do satellites link Canada with other nations?*

MAKING A DECISION

How Much Television Should You Watch?

The teacher was reading a newspaper article to the class. "Today young people spend more time in front of the television than they spend in school," she read.

Turning to the class, the teacher asked, "What do you think about that? Is it bad for children to watch so much television?"

During the discussion that followed, the students mentioned many good things about television. Programs could be interesting, exciting and fun to watch. The students also had some bad things to say about television.

"There's too much violence," said Lam. "After a while, it seems like it's okay to go around hitting people and wrecking cars."

"It's not very real," said Amy. She said that people on television were always beautiful and glamorous, although they aren't in real life. Most programs had happy endings. "In real life," she said, "things aren't always that easy."

Several students complained about the advertisements. "They make you think that if you buy a new kind of shampoo, your life will change," said André. "That's not true."

The teacher broke into the discussion. "You have made some important criticisms about television," she said. "Should we stop watching it altogether?"

Nobody liked that idea. Instead, some students suggested that they could limit the amount of television they watched. They could also choose programs carefully instead of watching whatever was on.

Lara suggested that her family could move the television from the living room to somewhere less comfortable and convenient. "That way," she said, "I would only watch TV when I really want to."

Paul thought that it was important for children to understand advertising gimmicks.

All the children agreed that there were other things to do in their spare time besides watching TV.

- Do you think you watch too much television?
- What do you think about the television you watch?

What messages do you think these advertisements are giving to the viewer?

CHAPTER CHECKUP

Recalling the Main Ideas

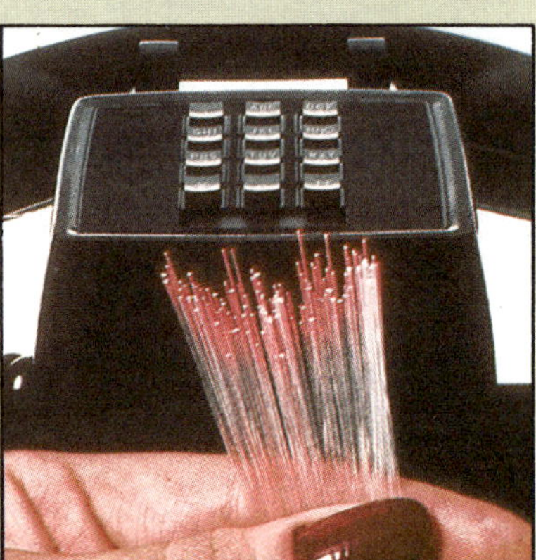

Each picture shows one of the new inventions described in this chapter.

1. Name each of these inventions.
2. Imagine that you were able to see these inventions when they first appeared. Choose any four of the inventions. Suppose that you are describing them to a friend who has not yet seen them. For each of the four inventions, write two or three sentences to explain what the communications equipment does and why it is exciting.

Using What You Have Learned

Think about how you use communications equipment in your life. List at least five ways your life would be different without telephones, radios, television sets and other communications tools you use.

3

How Is a Television Newscast Made?

In the last chapter you learned what communications in Canada was like in the past. In this chapter we're going to take a close-up look at one method of communication in Canada today—a television newscast.

You've probably watched a TV newscast at one time or another. Often it is a short program, maybe only 20 minutes long. During those 20 minutes you learn about 9 or 10 important things that happened in the world that day.

The person who reads the news is called a newscaster or announcer. The newscaster introduces each piece of news. For instance, he or she might tell you about a big fire. Then there may be pictures of the fire. Perhaps a reporter at the scene explains how it started or talks to people whose homes have burned down. The newscast gives you as much information about the fire as it can in just two or three minutes. Then the newscaster appears on the screen again to tell you about the next piece of news.

Many television stations produce newscasts. The newscast we will be learning about in this chapter is produced by the Canadian Broadcasting Corporation (CBC). The CBC National News is prepared in the newsroom in Toronto and is broadcast throughout Canada.

We'll spend one day in the newsroom and watch how the news is produced. Although this day never actually happened, it is a typical day. Let's go to Toronto now.

A newscaster reports the evening news to Canadians across the country. How might it feel to speak to so many people at once?

Choosing the News Stories

9:30 a.m.

Information pours into the Toronto newsroom from around the world. Telephones ring. **Video** pictures arrive by satellite and are stored on **videotape**. Morning newspapers pile up on the desks.

There is no shortage of information. There is, if anything, too much information. The difficulty is deciding which news stories are the most important. There will only be time for about 10 stories on the newscast. Which ones really count?

- What things would make a news story important?

The stories are chosen by the assignment **editors**. One assignment editor looks at the information coming in from eastern Canada. One looks at the news from western Canada. The foreign editor looks at what is happening in other parts of the world.

The assignment editors phone reporters across the country for further details. They pick the most important stories for the day. Then they ask reporters, camera operators and other members of the news team to prepare those stories for the newscast.

Not all the stories they work on will appear on today's newscast. Some will turn out to be unimportant and will be scrapped. Others will be dropped when new and more important stories come into the newsroom during the day. The final "line-up"—the list of stories that will appear on the newscast—will be decided early this evening.

Here are some of the stories the news team is working on today.

This map of the world shows the places mentioned in this chapter. The pictures show the location of six news events that the CBC may want to include in its evening television newscast. If you were a news reporter, which story would you like to cover?

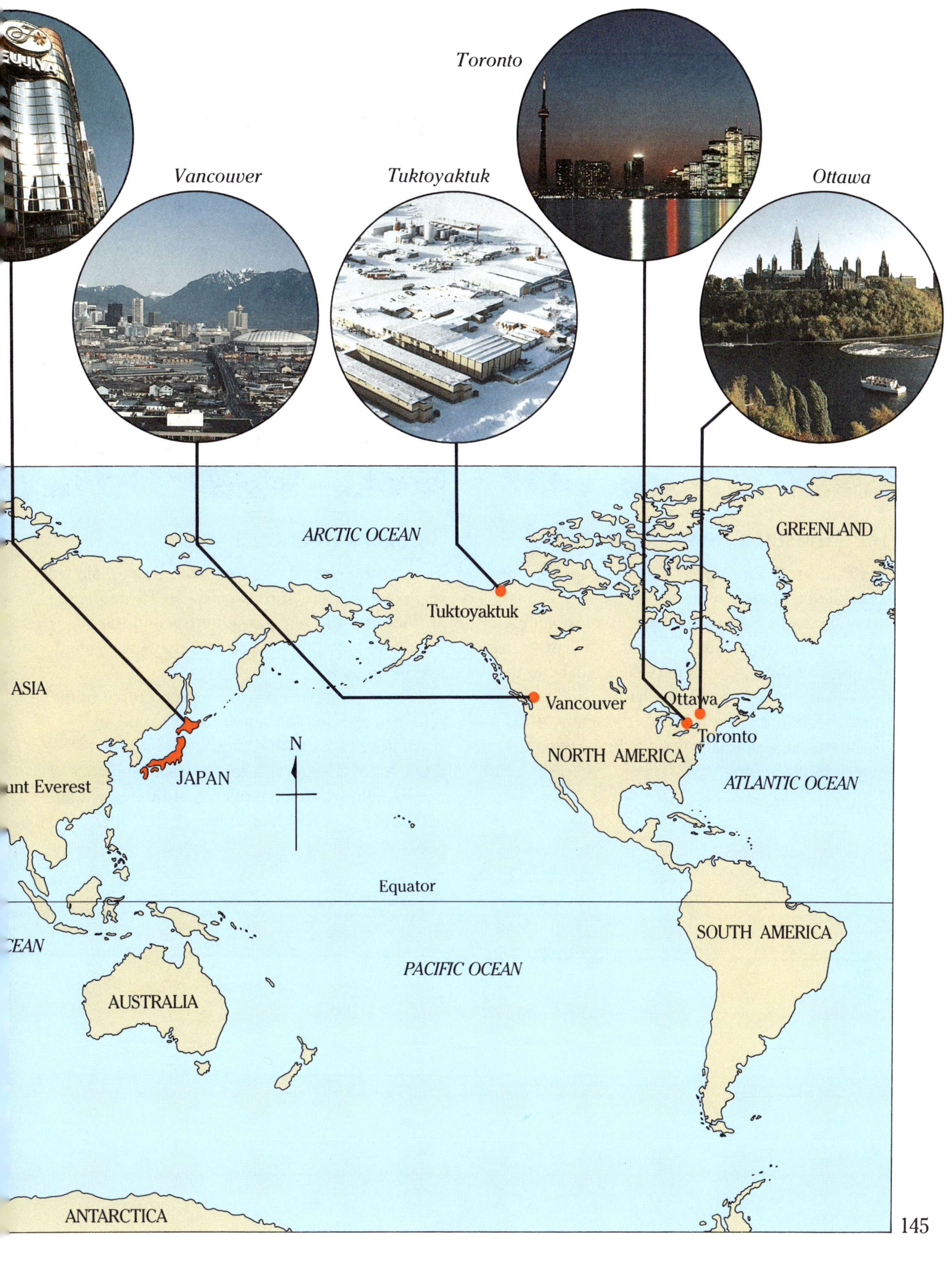
Toronto
Vancouver
Tuktoyaktuk
Ottawa
ARCTIC OCEAN
GREENLAND
Tuktoyaktuk
ASIA
Vancouver
Ottawa
Toronto
JAPAN
N
NORTH AMERICA
unt Everest
ATLANTIC OCEAN
Equator
SOUTH AMERICA
CEAN
PACIFIC OCEAN
AUSTRALIA
ANTARCTICA

The federal Minister of Employment and Immigration holds a news conference.

Canada has accepted many refugees, including these from Guatemala.

The Minister's News Conference

The Minister of Employment and Immigration has scheduled a news conference for 10:00 a.m. She has an important announcement to make about a new program to provide more jobs for Canadians. Members of the CBC staff in Ottawa will be at the news conference to find out what the minister has to say. That information should definitely be on the newscast. Canadians want to know what their government is doing.

Refugees from Guatemala

At any moment, 50 refugees from Guatemala will be arriving at the Toronto airport. These people are not safe in their own country, and the Canadian government has said they can come to live in Canada.

The assignment editor wants pictures of the refugees arriving in Canada, and maybe some short interviews with refugees who speak English. He asks a reporter to prepare a story. It will explain what is happening in Guatemala and why these refugees had to leave.

A drilling ship works in the Beaufort Sea.

In British Columbia a faller cuts down a tree.

Oil Discovery

A "stringer" has phoned in from the Arctic. Stringers are people who call the CBC with information from time to time, whenever something important happens where they live. These stringers are important because the CBC doesn't have enough regular staff to have reporters everywhere.

The stringer is calling from the village of Tuktoyaktuk, on the shores of the Beaufort Sea. Oil companies use Tuktoyaktuk as a base while drilling for oil under the Beaufort Sea.

The stringer has heard an interesting rumour. A mechanic who has just flown in from a drilling platform thinks that oil has been discovered. He believes that it is a huge discovery, the most oil anyone has ever found under the Beaufort Sea.

If the rumour is true, that could be an important story. The CBC would want to send a reporter to the scene. Oil companies have worked for years and spent hundreds of millions of dollars looking for oil in the Beaufort Sea.

The assignment editor asks the stringer to do more research to find out if the rumour is true. He also assigns a reporter in Calgary, where the oil company has its main office, to see if she can find out anything.

B.C. Forest Study

An important report will be released in Vancouver today. It is about forestry in British Columbia. Although this news is about one province, it is important to the rest of Canada, too. Ups and downs in British Columbia's forest industry affect all Canadians. In addition, people in one part of Canada should know what is happening in other parts of the country.

It is an important story, but the assignment editor is not sure how to make it interesting for the viewers. A forestry report does not sound as exciting as a plane crash, for example. The assignment editor asks the CBC staff in Vancouver to find some good video pictures to go with the story.

A volcano erupts unexpectedly.

Volcanic Eruption

Earlier this morning a volcano in Japan erupted. At this moment, lava is still pouring down the mountainside. This should make an exciting story for the newscast, with lots of good pictures.

More news about the eruption will be sent to the Toronto newsroom during the day. This news will be prepared by an American news team. The CBC does not have enough people to cover news all over the world. So when something important happens in another country, the CBC often uses news stories prepared for American television.

A Canadian climber nears the top of Mount Everest.

Mount Everest

There's one more story that just might arrive in time for today's newscast. At this moment, a Canadian women's team is in Nepal climbing Mount Everest, the highest mountain in the world. The climbers hope to reach the top today. At a camp at the base of the mountain, a video camera is mounted on a very powerful telescope. If the weather is good, it will be able to take pictures of the climbers at the top.

Also at the base camp, there is equipment for sending television signals up to a satellite. This equipment was flown to the mountain by helicopter. Video pictures can be sent to Canada in less than a second, even though Canada is halfway around the world.

Collecting the News

10:02 a.m.

In Toronto, across Canada and around the world, the news team gathers information for these and other stories.

Reporters spend hours on the phone, chasing down the latest, up-to-date information. They interview people connected with the news story and read background reports. They end up with pages of notes.

Camera crews go out to the scene of the story. They shoot interviews with people and try to get good shots of whatever happens.

Artists prepare maps and drawings that will help explain the stories. These drawings allow the news team to tell stories in an interesting way even if there are no video pictures to go with them. Librarians find videotapes in the CBC library that might be useful, such as pictures of British Columbia forests or oil drilling in the Beaufort Sea.

- Which job on the news team would you find most interesting?

1:23 p.m.

The stringer in Tuktoyaktuk calls about the Beaufort Sea oil story. He has had no luck. Nobody at the oil company will admit that there was an oil discovery. The stringer even got a ride to a nearby drilling rig, but he couldn't get any facts about the oil discovery.

He still thinks the rumour is true, but he cannot prove it. Oil companies like to keep their discoveries secret. If other companies found out where there was oil, they would start drilling in the same area.

The assignment editor checks with the Calgary reporter. She has not been able to find out anything from the company's headquarters there, either. The editor scraps the story. A rumour just isn't good enough. A news story needs facts.

2:00 p.m.

It will be a long day. As the "dayside" staff gradually leave for home, the "nightside" staff will take over.

At the 2:00 p.m. editorial meeting, the dayside and nightside editors get together to discuss the stories they are working on. The nightside staff will continue shaping the newscast through the afternoon and evening. Some news stories are still unfolding, and other information may arrive at any time.

An assignment editor checks with a reporter to see how a news story is developing. So far the reporter has not been able to get more details. Why might the editor decide to scrap the story?

Editing the News

When the information has been collected, the writing and editing can begin. Editing means making changes to the news stories until they sound just right and are exactly the right length. Somehow the news team must shrink pages of notes and hours of videotape into news stories that are only a few minutes long. The news team must choose just the right combination of words and pictures. It is not an easy task. Let's see how the team is doing with some of today's stories.

A reporter works on a story for the evening news. He reduces a long report to a short script. Why might this task be difficult?

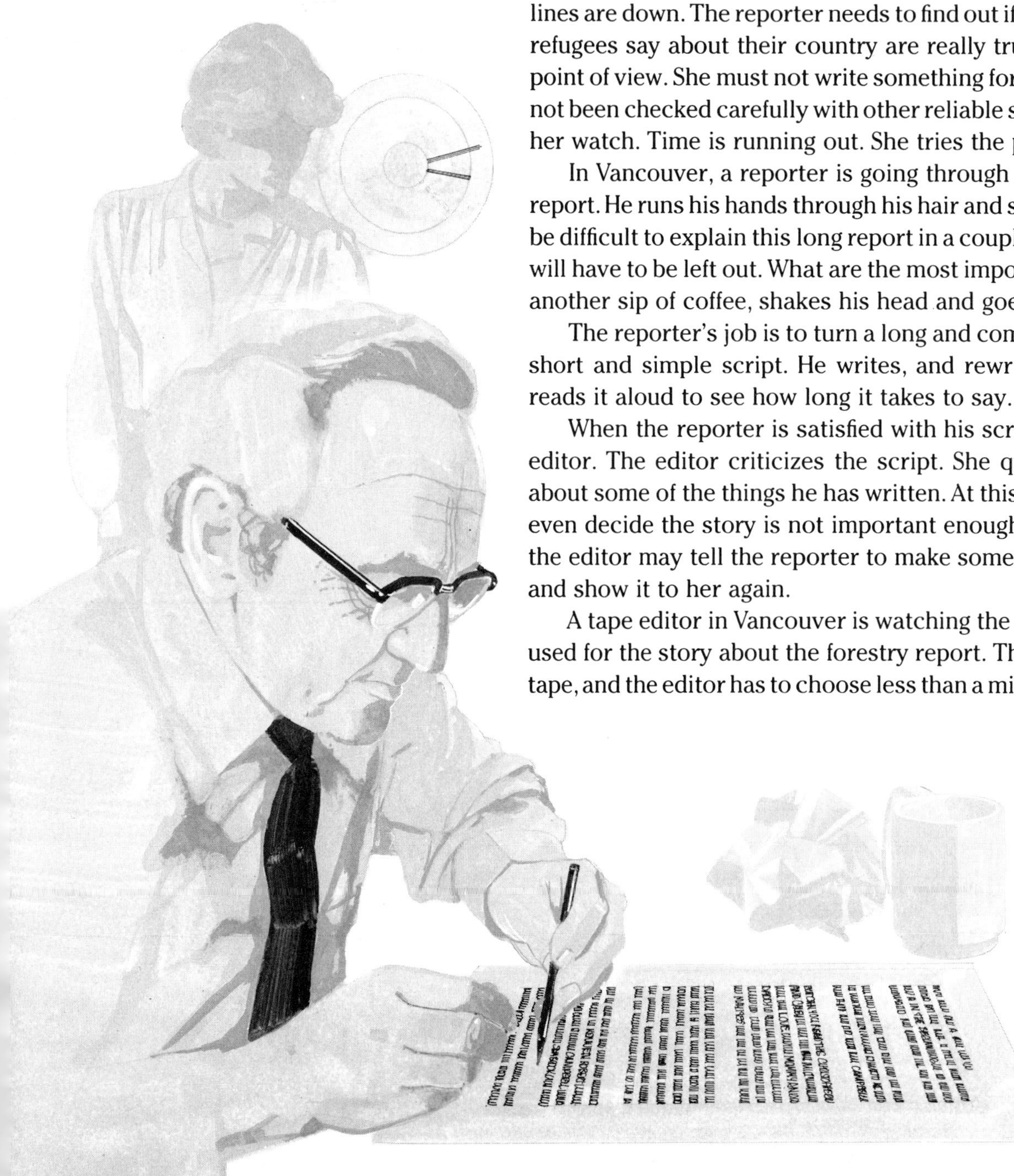

3:12 p.m.

In Toronto, a reporter is working on the story about the Guatemalan refugees. She is having a hard time getting information from their country. People are at war there, so communication is difficult. Phone lines are down. The reporter needs to find out if some of the things the refugees say about their country are really true. She wants another point of view. She must not write something for the newscast that has not been checked carefully with other reliable sources. She glances at her watch. Time is running out. She tries the phone again.

In Vancouver, a reporter is going through a copy of the forestry report. He runs his hands through his hair and sighs a lot. It is going to be difficult to explain this long report in a couple of minutes. So much will have to be left out. What are the most important points? He takes another sip of coffee, shakes his head and goes back to work.

The reporter's job is to turn a long and complicated report into a short and simple script. He writes, and rewrites, and rewrites. He reads it aloud to see how long it takes to say.

When the reporter is satisfied with his script, he shows it to his editor. The editor criticizes the script. She questions the reporter about some of the things he has written. At this stage, the editor may even decide the story is not important enough for the newscast. Or the editor may tell the reporter to make some changes in the script and show it to her again.

A tape editor in Vancouver is watching the videotape that will be used for the story about the forestry report. There are 20 minutes of tape, and the editor has to choose less than a minute for the newscast.

The director sits in front of a bank of television monitors in the control room of the television studio. The screens show several pictures of stories that have been edited for the evening news. Why is the editing of a news story so important?

The videotape includes two interviews. One is with the leader of the forest workers' union. He is very pleased with the forestry report. He shakes a copy of it in the air and says he's been waiting to see a report like this for years. The interview is exciting, so the tape editor uses 23 seconds of it. The other interview is with the president of a large forest company. He disagrees with the forest report. It is not such an exciting interview, but, to be fair, the tape editor chooses a little bit of that interview, too. That way the viewers will hear both points of view.

- Why is it important to hear different points of view? Do you and your friends have different points of view on some subjects?

Choosing the right pieces of videotape is as important as choosing the right words for the script. People watching the newscast will be influenced by what they see on the screen. If the tape editor is not careful, the news can be unfair. Here is an example of how that might happen.

During his interview, the union leader says, "This report is full of good suggestions. But it should have said more about retraining workers to use new technology." What if the tape editor decided to use just that last sentence on the newscast? People watching the news would hear the union leader criticize the report. They would not hear the whole interview, so they might think the union leader did not like the rest of the report, either. That would not be true.

Here is another example of bad tape editing. During the other interview, the president of the forest company says, "We are already doing many things the report suggests. We are already spending more money to plant new trees." What if the tape editor used those words for the newscast, and then followed them with a picture of a logged hillside with no new trees in sight? That would be unfair. It would make the president of the forest company look like a liar.

5:00 p.m.

The work goes on. Finally, the scripts are written; the videotape segments are chosen; the maps and other drawings are ready. The next job is to put all these pieces together in the right order to make a complete news story. For instance, here's how the news story about the B.C. forestry report looks when it is finished.

What You See	What You Hear	How Long It Takes
	Sound of logging machinery. Sound fades as the reporter explains that many workers in the forest industry are losing their jobs. The reporter says that the government has hired experts to help it decide what to do.	13 seconds
	The reporter explains that the experts' report has just been published. It contains many **recommendations.**	17 seconds
	The reporter explains the six most important recommendations in the report.	32 seconds

	A union leader explains what he thinks of the report.	23 seconds
	The president of a forest company explains what he thinks of the report.	17 seconds
	The reporter explains that the government wants time to think about the report before deciding if it will follow the recommendations. The reporter finishes by saying, "Harry Drew, CBC news, Vancouver."	16 seconds

TOTAL TIME = 1 minute, 58 seconds

This news story on forestry in British Columbia is prepared in Vancouver. Then it is sent by satellite to Toronto. In Toronto, all the stories are stored on videotape, ready for the newscast.

Then there is one more job to do. The editors prepare the short introductions that the newscaster will read.

7:00 p.m.

The line-up editor hands out the line-up, the list of stories for tonight's newscast. Now the news team knows which stories will probably be used. However, the line-up could still change at any moment. The editor must be ready to add the latest news.

This is rush hour in the newsroom. Last-minute news is still arriving. Writers and editors are making last-minute changes. The newscaster is in the newsroom, looking over her introductions. She makes some changes so that the scripts sound right to her as she reads them.

The newscast will be seen by most Canadians at 10:00 p.m. However, Atlantic Canada is in an earlier **time zone** than Toronto. It will be 10:00 p.m. in that part of eastern Canada an hour before it is 10:00 p.m. in Toronto. That means the Toronto news team must be ready to send the newscast to the Atlantic regions at 9:00 p.m. Toronto time.

This map shows the six time zones across Canada. How many hours' difference is there between Newfoundland and British Columbia?

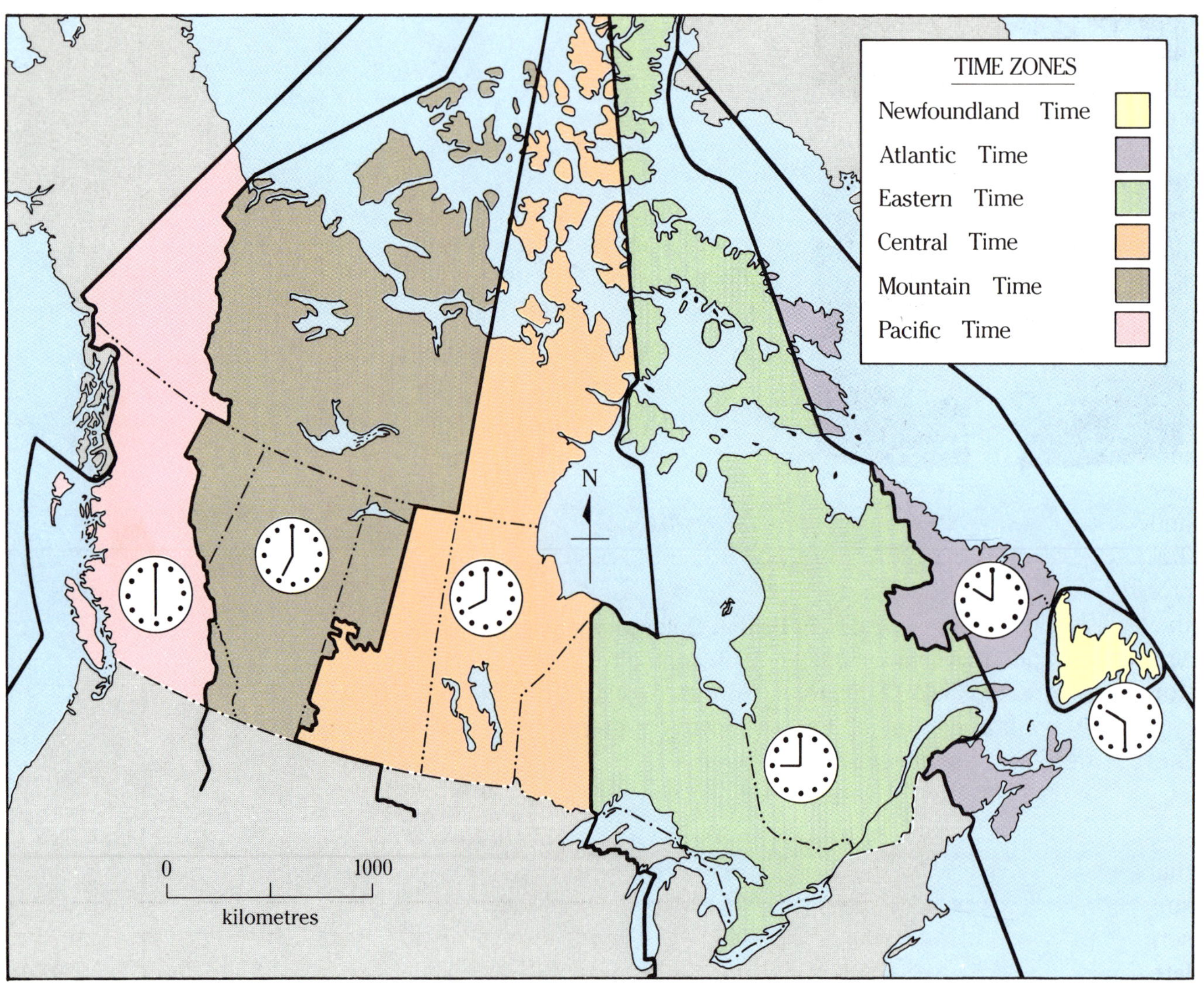

Broadcasting the News

8:45 p.m.

The newscaster is ready and waiting at her seat in front of the camera. The final script for her introductions is given to the teleprompt operator. He rolls the script through a machine that shines the words onto a screen on the camera. That way the newscaster can read them as she looks into the camera. She does not have to memorize everything.

Other people are getting ready, too. The camera operators are checking their cameras. Through their headphones, they listen to instructions from the director in the control room. The newscaster counts to 10 so that the person in charge of sound can check her microphone.

9:00 p.m.

The newscast starts with a short bit of music and flashing words that say "The National" and give the date. Then the newscaster turns to the camera and says, "Good evening." Travelling at the speed of light, her picture and her words fly up to the satellite and are sent back down to satellite antennas in the Atlantic region. The television signals speed out along the communications network. People in the Atlantic region find out about the most important news of the day. It is 10:00 p.m. in the Atlantic time zone and 10:30 in the Newfoundland time zone.

10:00 p.m.

At 10:00 p.m. Toronto time, a second newscast is broadcast. That newscast is seen by people living in the Eastern time zone. That includes parts of Ontario, Quebec and the Northwest Territories. The newscast is also sent to CBC regional centres in Winnipeg, Edmonton and Vancouver. Those western cities are in later time zones than Toronto. It is not 10:00 p.m. there yet. So CBC workers in those centres store the newscast on videotape. When it is 10:00 p.m. in their region, they will broadcast the news to people living in that time zone. By the time the news is broadcast from Vancouver, it will be 1:00 a.m. in Toronto.

- Do you think 10:00 p.m. is a good time for people to watch the news? Why or why not?

Usually, people living in western Canada see the same newscast that people in Ontario saw earlier. Sometimes, however, there is some last-minute news. Something new and important happens, something so important it should be on the newscast. It arrives too late for the 10:00 p.m. newscast in Ontario. But there is still time to add it to the newscast for western Canada. Let's see what happens then.

Canada's Communications Network

Canada is a huge country. Broadcasting the news throughout Canada is much more difficult than broadcasting in a smaller country.

To get the television signal out to all Canadians, the CBC uses a communications network. To understand how it works, think of the transportation network we have in Canada. Roads, railways and airports make it easier to send things from one part of the country to another. A communications network is much like a transportation network, except that it is used to send information from one place to another. The communications network uses wires, microwave towers and satellites to send messages.

10:32 p.m.

The pictures from Mount Everest arrive! They show two Canadian climbers at the top of the highest mountain in the world. One of the climbers waves at the camera and sticks a Canadian flag in the snow. Her face is brown and wind-burnt.

There is already a short story about the Mount Everest climb on the newscast. The editor decides to expand the story for the newscast that will be shown in western Canada. He wants to include at least two minutes of the new Mount Everest videotape. He takes a look at the line-up. What should he leave out to make room?

Some members of the news team have stayed late in the Toronto newsroom. A writer quickly prepares a new script for the Mount Everest story. A tape editor chooses the videotape clips. The newscaster returns to her seat in front of the camera to introduce the news item. The updated newscast is broadcast to people living in Manitoba, Saskatchewan and part of the Northwest Territories. Later, Canadians farther west see the same newscast.

In all, 2 million Canadians watch the CBC National News that evening. A further 800 000 watch the French news broadcast, Le Téléjournal, from the CBC's Montreal newsroom.

Canadians all across the country sit in their living rooms and watch the newscast. They find out what has been said by the Minister of Employment and Immigration; they learn what is happening in Guatemala; they watch a volcano erupting in Japan; and they see the top of Mount Everest. In a short time, they learn about the most important news of the day.

The evening news goes on the air. Why do you think the television studio has more than one camera in operation?

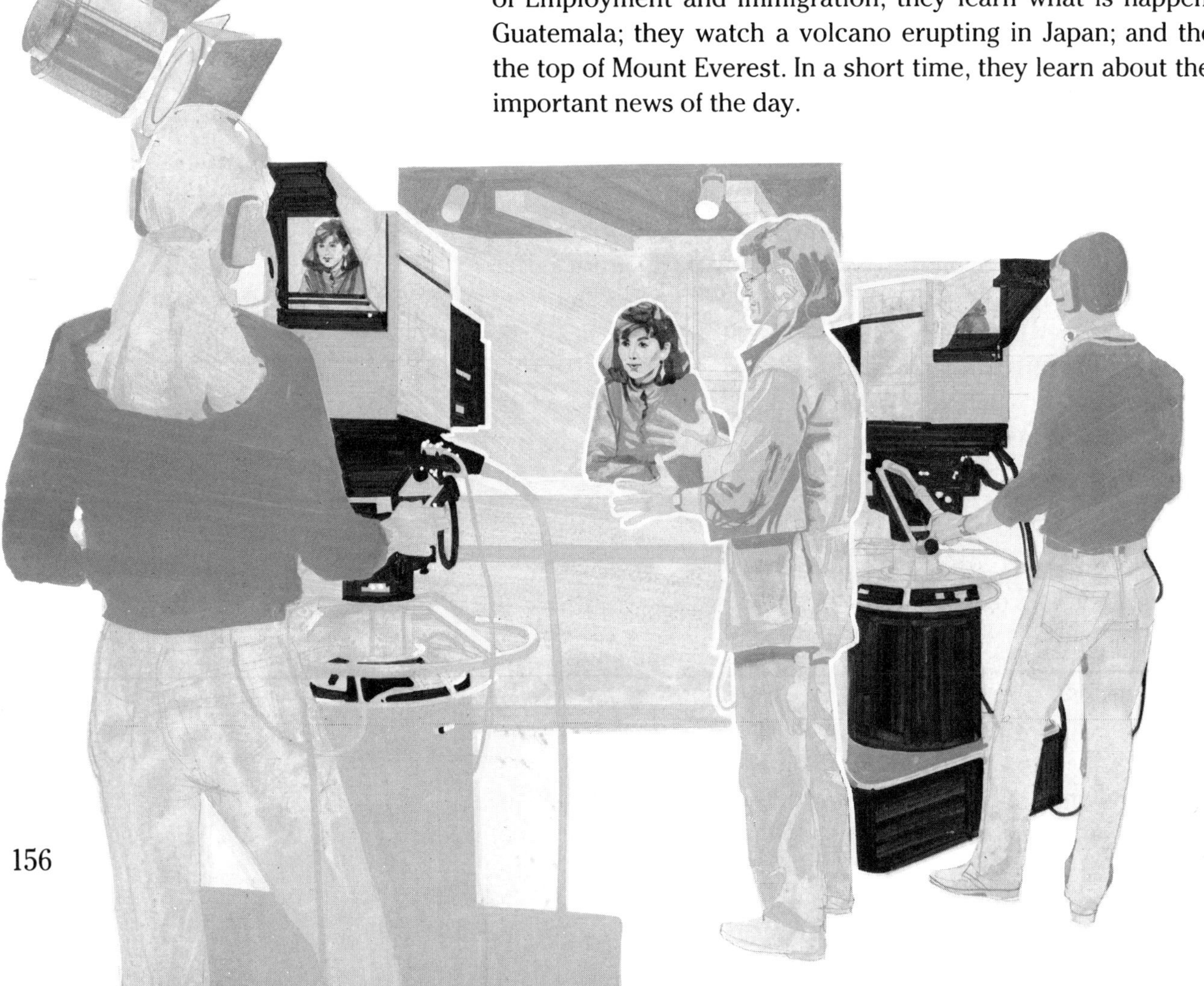

The CBC

Did you know that you own part of a radio and television network? Not just you, but all Canadians own this network. The Canadian Broadcasting Corporation is owned by the government of Canada. It is paid for with money collected from all Canadians.

Most Canadians receive many different radio and television stations. Almost all of these stations are privately owned. Owners of private stations make money from advertisers who want to broadcast commercials to the people who listen to the programs. The CBC is different. Although CBC television makes some money from commercials, there are no commercials on CBC radio. Most of the money needed to run the CBC comes from the government.

With so many privately owned stations to watch, why do we need one owned by the government? The CBC's programs help Canadians learn about their country. People can see Canadian films, plays, music and sports.

It is very expensive to bring radio and television to remote places. The government did not think private stations would be willing to spend this money. Yet the government wanted as many Canadians as possible to receive radio and television. The CBC network now reaches almost all Canadians, including some who do not receive any other radio or television stations. There are programs for people of all ages and from all parts of the country.

The CBC broadcasts in both English and French. About three quarters of the television programs on the English network are Canadian. On the French network, even more are Canadian. In the north, CBC broadcasts programs in Indian and Inuit languages as well. CBC radio is also broadcast overseas. Programs tell people in other countries about Canada.

The CBC costs Canadians about $800 million a year. When you are working, you will help to pay for CBC programs. You should think about whether or not the CBC is important to you.

This picture shows the CBC symbol.

The Power of Television

Forty years ago there was no television broadcasting in Canada. People got their news from newspapers or radio. Today almost all Canadian families own a television set, and they often have a choice of different stations to watch.

Since so many people watch television, it has become a very powerful method of communication. One program may be seen by millions of people at once. That program may change the way people think about things.

Advertisers know the power of television. They are willing to spend many thousands of dollars to show a one-minute commercial for a breakfast cereal.

Think about the television programs you watch. Do those programs affect the way you think about some things?

Watching the News

Because of modern communications technology, the CBC is able to gather information from around the world. It is able to broadcast this information to almost every Canadian home.

Some people live in communities with cable television. The newscast is picked up on the community antenna and sent to each home along a cable. Other people live far from any community. In northern British Columbia, the members of one family watch the news in their mobile home. They have a small antenna on their roof which catches the satellite signal. The antenna is powered by electricity they make themselves with a water wheel in a nearby creek.

Watching a television newscast can help us learn more about what is happening across Canada and around the world. It can also be interesting and exciting. Good action pictures and on-the-spot interviews make the news "come to life." We almost feel as if we were there ourselves.

Television is a very powerful kind of communication. Millions of people watch it, and they believe what they see and hear. They believe they are getting the facts. They believe that the newscast is showing them the most important news of the day. That means the people who prepare the newscast have a big responsibility. They must do a good job of communicating the news.

Now that you've learned how a newscast is made, you probably realize that there is really no such thing as "The News." The news can be very different, depending on who prepares the newscast. If you were an assignment editor, you might choose different stories than the CBC editors did. If you were a reporter, you might explain the story in a different way. If you were a tape editor, you might choose different bits of videotape. In fact, on the same day, two different television news teams may prepare very different newscasts, even though they both started with the same information. If you switch from one television channel to another, you can see these differences.

Most news teams do their best, but they are not perfect. They are often rushed, and they can make mistakes. While trying to make the news stories short, they may leave out important information. When you watch the news, you should remember that. Ask yourself if the news is presented fairly. Ask yourself if there is another point of view that the newscast does not show. If you don't like somebody you see on the news, ask yourself why. Maybe the tape editor chose a bit of videotape that makes that person look worse than he or she really is.

This is the community of Pangnirtung in the Northwest Territories. Why is communication so important to the people in this community?

If we use it wisely, television can be a very good thing. A television newscast is an easy, enjoyable way to get information. It can take us places we could never get to ourselves, such as the top of Mount Everest. It opens our eyes to what is happening in the rest of the world, such as in Guatemala or Japan. It helps us understand our country better and learn what our government is doing.

- Would it be better if all television stations showed exactly the same newscast? Why or why not?

CHAPTER CHECKUP

Recalling the Main Ideas

Preparing a newscast is a hectic job. During one day, the following activities may take place:

1. A reporter phones to find out more information about Guatemala.
2. An editor checks to see what news stories were printed out by the teletypewriter during the night.
3. In Japan, a camera operator rides in a helicopter, videotaping an erupting volcano.
4. More news arrives in the newsroom at the last minute. An editor decides whether it is important enough to go on the newscast.
5. A tape editor chooses 45 seconds of a 10-minute interview to use in the newscast.
6. A reporter shows a two-minute script to an editor, who suggests more changes.
7. The CBC regional centre in Winnipeg receives the newscast from Toronto by way of satellite.
8. At 10:00 p.m., the CBC regional centre in Winnipeg broadcasts the national news to homes in its region.

Although many of these different activities may happen at once, each can be placed in one of the following categories:

a. Choosing the News Stories

b. Collecting the News

c. Editing the News

d. Broadcasting the News

Make four columns, one for each of the above categories. Decide which activities belong in each category. Put each activity in the correct column.

Using What You Have Learned

Imagine you are part of a news team working on a news story about your school. The story is about a student who has won an important prize or about a school team that has won a championship.

1. Describe more exactly what the news story is about. (Make up an imaginary story that you think could be on the newscast.)
2. List at least three important pieces of information the reporter will want to find out.
3. Name at least two people who should be interviewed.
4. Describe what videotape should be shot.
5. Describe any additional photographs, maps or drawings that will be needed to explain the news story.

4

How Does Communications Help Canadians?

In the last chapter we took a close-up look at a television newscast. We saw how a news team gathers information from around the world. It uses this information to prepare a newscast that is broadcast throughout Canada.

Just as a carpenter needs tools to build a house, a news team needs tools to do its job. The tools it uses are video cameras, telephones, satellites and other communications equipment. These tools make the job of preparing the newscast much easier.

- What communications equipment do you use?

In this chapter, we'll look at three other areas where communications tools have become very important. First we'll see how they can be used to find boats or planes that have crashed. New communications equipment helps rescuers reach the scene of the accident much faster than before. Second, we'll look at students in schools far from the city. New communications equipment helps these students and their teachers get much more information than they could get before. Finally, you'll meet a deaf child. New communications equipment can help deaf people communicate with other people.

In each of these three areas, you'll see what life was like before today's communications equipment was available. Then you'll read about the situation today. You'll see the difference new technology has made. The people in the stories are not real people, but their stories show typical events in the past and present.

A rescue hovercraft arrives at the scene of a boat accident. How might rescue workers communicate with the rescue centre on shore?

How Communications Helps Search and Rescue

Many areas of Canada have very few people. Travelling in these areas can be difficult. The weather is often harsh. The high mountain ranges and the rugged coastline make travel dangerous, too. If you got lost or hurt somewhere in the wilderness of Canada, you could be in serious trouble. You could be far from help, far from food, and very, very cold.

If you are lost or hurt, communication is very important. You need to be able to send a message quickly so that you can be rescued. Doctors say that a badly injured person probably will not live more than six hours without medical help. Yet years ago, the chance of a quick rescue was slim. The following story will show you what a rescue might have been like in the past. Then you can compare it with a rescue that might take place today.

Search and Rescue in the Past

On the west coast of Vancouver Island there is a wild stretch of shore called the Graveyard of the Pacific. Many ships have been wrecked on the rocks there.

About 80 years ago, a sailing ship left Vancouver. It was carrying a load of timber from the forests of British Columbia. As it sailed around the southern tip of Vancouver Island and reached the open sea, it ran into a storm. Huge waves swept the ship northward. The wind ripped the sails away. The crew could do nothing to stop the ship from drifting towards the Graveyard of the Pacific. There was no way to call for help. The ship crashed onto the rocks and was thrown onto its side. The waves continued to pound it against the rocks.

One of the sailors managed to swim ashore with a rope, which he tied to a tree. One by one, the people on board were pulled to shore along the rope. Some had been injured in the wreck, and they cried with pain. That night, in the pouring rain, they huddled around a fire.

The next morning, two of the sailors set off on foot to find help. It took two days of hiking through the thick forest before the sailors reached a lighthouse. The lighthouse keeper telephoned the nearest village, 50 km away, for a rescue party.

At dawn the next morning, the rescue party arrived by boat at the scene of the accident. Unfortunately, two of the injured people had already died. If they had been rescued earlier, they might have lived. The survivors, weak and suffering from cold, were taken by boat to the nearest town. It was too late to save anything from the ship.

- What might have been different if the ship had been able to call for help?

Above: This map shows the location of the Graveyard of the Pacific. Approximately how many kilometres long is this area?

A sailing ship has been wrecked off the shores of Vancouver Island. How might the crew try to get help?

Now let's look at the situation today. Canada still has huge areas of wilderness. People still have accidents. Today, however, more people are found quickly. The difference is that Canadians now have equipment that helps them send messages much faster. They can call for help as soon as they are in trouble, no matter where they are. Let's look at an accident that could happen today. You can see how communications technology has made a difference.

Search and Rescue Today

The small plane roared across the water and lifted off. Mike Dolan took his eyes off the controls for a moment and grinned at his daughter. They were off on a fishing trip to a lake at the north end of the island. Now that Mr. Dolan had his pilot's licence, it was easy to go fishing for an afternoon. They could be back by suppertime.

But by suppertime, the Dolans were not back. They were in trouble. On their flight home, they ran into strong head winds. The plane used up a great deal of fuel fighting against the wind. Mr. Dolan was not an experienced pilot, and he had not realized he would need so much fuel. As the needle on the fuel gauge dropped lower, Mr. Dolan looked around desperately for a place to land. There was nothing but mountains. The engine sputtered and quit. The plane crashed into the trees.

Mike Dolan was badly injured and knocked unconscious. His young daughter was only bruised, but she was shaken and very frightened. She did not know that help would soon be on the way.

The jolt of the crash started up the emergency locator ***transmitter*** *in the plane. The transmitter automatically sends out radio signals after a crash. All planes today are required to carry these emergency transmitters. The radio signals can be picked up by a satellite when it passes overhead, about 1000 km above the earth. An earth station in Ottawa picks up the satellite signal. A message is sent to the Mission Control Centre in Trenton, Ontario. There, a computer calculates the approximate location of the radio transmitter sending the signals. This information is sent across the country to the Rescue Co-ordination Centre nearest the scene. Just 45 minutes after Mr. Dolan's plane crashed, the supervisor at the Rescue Co-ordination Centre was planning the rescue.*

The Air Traffic Control Centre at the airport had already informed the Rescue Co-ordination Centre that a small plane was overdue. After checking with the airport for new information, the supervisor called out the Search and Rescue team. In less than an hour, the team was flying over the area of the crashed plane. Using special equipment, the team tried to locate the radio signal.

This map shows the communications network that goes into action when there is a plane crash or an accident at sea. What are the five steps in the rescue process?

A small plane is forced down in an isolated area. Why might it be difficult for rescuers to reach this location?

Workers at the Mission Control Centre receive information about a plane crash. What might they do next with this information?

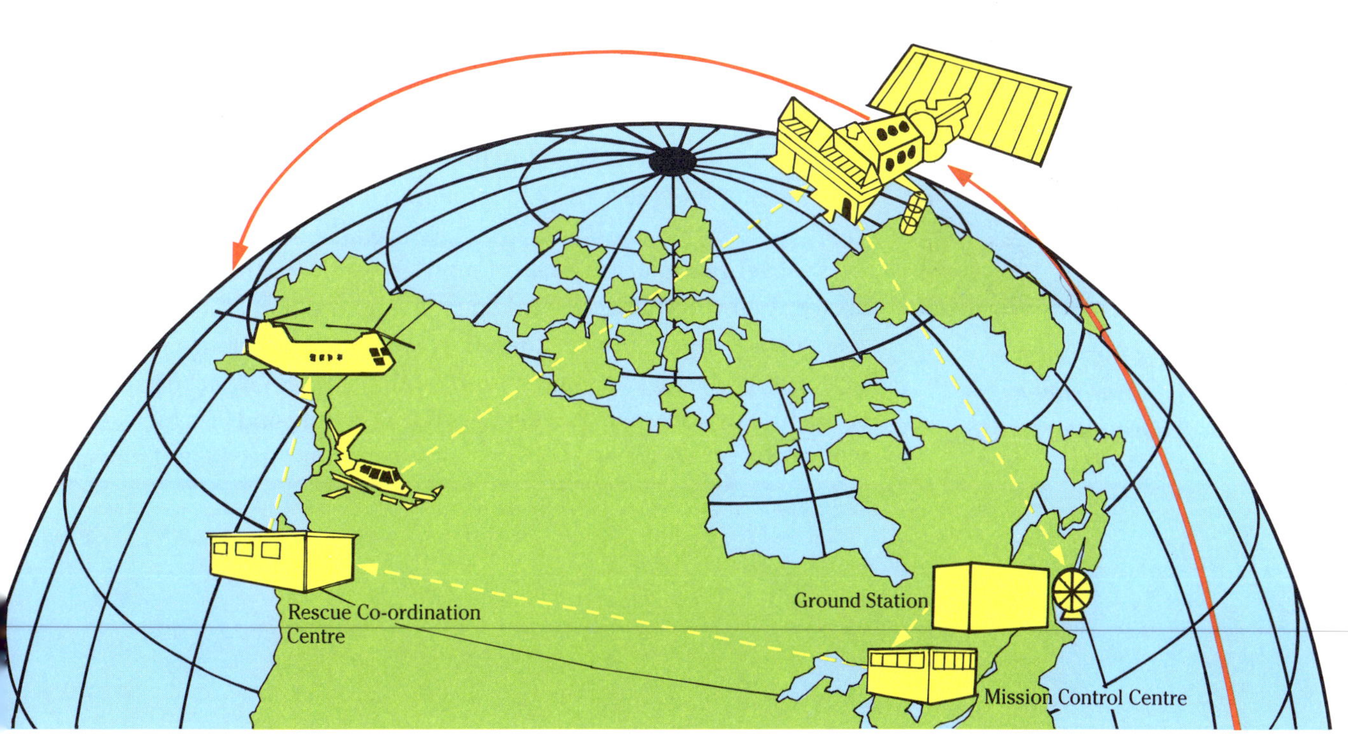

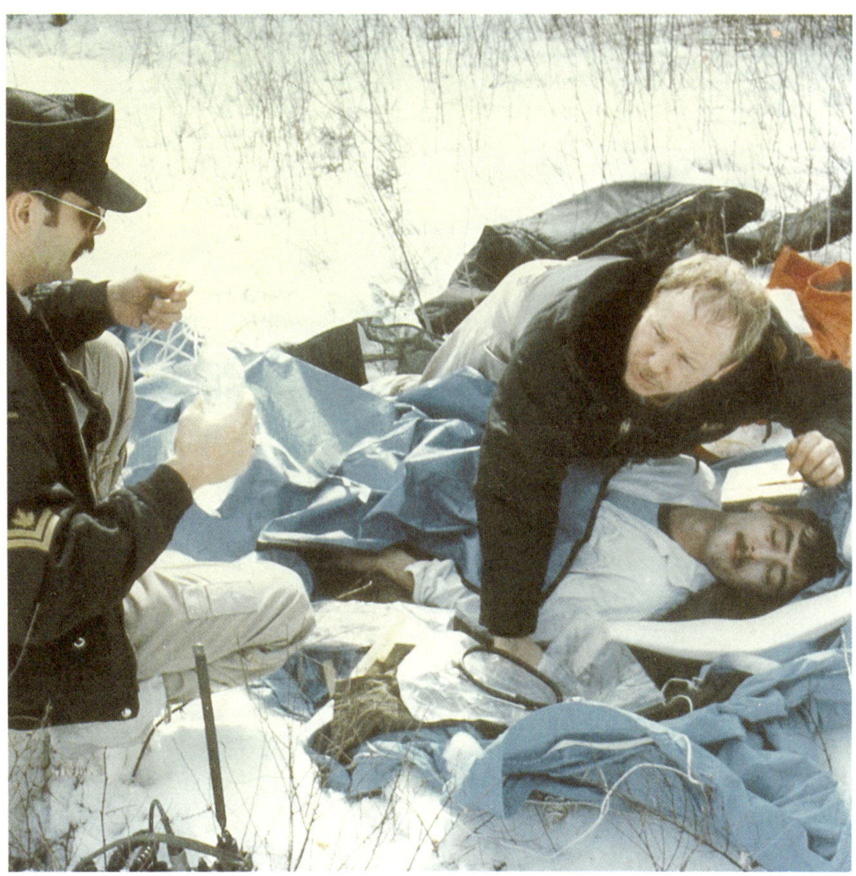

Rescue workers give medical aid to the victim of a plane crash. How might communications equipment help them?

A pilot searches for a plane crash. How is he staying in touch with the Rescue Co-ordination Centre?

When the team found the plane, there was no room to land. Two specially trained members of the Search and Rescue team parachuted down to the plane. They used their portable radio to report on the condition of the passengers. They gave Mr. Dolan medical treatment until the helicopter could arrive. Then the Dolans were hoisted by a sling into the helicopter. Less than three hours after the crash, they were safe in the hospital.

- How would this rescue be different if the plane had not been carrying an emergency locator transmitter?

Not all plane crashes are found as easily as the one described above. Bad weather and broken radios can delay rescue. Yet most rescues are much quicker than they were many years ago, thanks to new methods of communication and transportation. This speed saves money, because the rescuers use less time and less fuel searching for the crash. Most of all, speed is important because it can save lives.

How Communications Helps Students in a Country School

New methods of communication make it easier to receive information. Schools need lots of information. For instance, in your school you use information that explains how to add and subtract fractions. You use information that describes how people lived in the past. Information like this helps you learn new things.

Where do you get all this information you need? Some of it comes from your teacher. Some information is written in textbooks. You probably also receive information from books in the library, from maps, from films, from television, from newspapers, from field trips, from guest speakers and even from computer programs. Your information comes from many sources.

- What information have you used in the last hour? Where did you get that information?

Imagine how learning would be different if you did not have all these sources of information. Imagine, for instance, what learning would have been like in northern Ontario 100 years ago. Students in one-room country schools back then had fewer sources of information. In the following story you'll see what learning might have been like in a school in the past. Then you will compare that classroom in the past with a classroom in northern Ontario today. You'll see how much more information is available to students today. You'll see how changes in communications have helped students.

These students attended a one-room school in Ontario almost a century ago. What do you notice about the ages of the children?

A Country School in the Past

The pupils, ranging in age from four to twelve, sat in rows of desks screwed to the floor. On the front wall there were a blackboard and a map of the world. A wood stove was heating up one side of the room. The students sitting at the other side of the room kept their coats on.

The younger children were copying arithmetic sums from the blackboard. Their slate pencils squeaked across the slates. Older students were studying a lesson in their geography textbooks. The lesson was about fishing in the Atlantic Ocean. They had never seen the sea. They could not imagine what fishing in the ocean would be like, but they memorized everything in the textbook. The teacher would test them later.

These students relied on the teacher and the textbooks for most of their learning. However, the teacher had students from grades 1 to 8 in one class. He could not spend much time with any one group of students, so he usually assigned them work from their textbooks.

Besides the textbooks, there were not many other books to learn from. The library was very small. As for films, or television sets, or computers—they had not yet been invented.

At the back of the room, Jacob was struggling with his reading lesson. He had never learned to read properly. The teacher did not know much about teaching children like Jacob who had reading problems. There was no one he could turn to for advice. There were no other teachers nearby. The school inspector only made the long trip from the city once or twice a year. There were no special textbooks for students like Jacob. So Jacob just stared at the words in his textbook and looked confused. Soon he would quit school and work on the farm.

- How is your school different from this school in the past? How is it the same?

That is what a one-room country school in the last century might have been like. Now let's compare it with what a schoolroom in northern Ontario might be like in the 1980s. Let's see how new communications equipment has changed the amount of information that students can use.

This is a modern classroom. In what ways is it different from the classroom in the picture above?

This picture gives you a good idea of how students used to spend their school days. What teaching materials were used to help children learn?

A Country School Today

Sarah carried the stack of books to her desk and looked through them. With all these books, she would have no trouble finding enough information for her project on satellites. She picked up her pen and opened her notebook to a clean page.

When Sarah chose satellites for her topic, her teacher telephoned the resource centre in a nearby community to ask for information on the subject. The books arrived by truck just a few days later. The resource centre also sent filmstrips and videotapes about satellites.

Since new satellites are being built and put into space all the time, books do not usually have the latest, most up-to-date information. Newspapers have more recent information. To get the latest newspaper stories about satellites, Sarah's teacher helped her use a computer information bank. An information bank is like a library, but all the information is stored in a computer instead of on paper.

The information bank is not in Sarah's classroom; it is in a computer in Toronto. To get the information in the bank, Sarah used a telephone. With the phone, she was able to connect the small computer in her classroom to the big computer in Toronto. When Sarah typed the right message on her computer keyboard, her computer asked the Toronto computer for all the newspaper articles about satellites that were in the information bank. The articles appeared on Sarah's computer screen. She even received an article written just the day before!

Learning by Television

Learning by television is becoming more and more popular. Television courses can help you learn math or another language. They help doctors learn about new diseases and teach people how to repair their cars.

Think of the advantages of learning by television. It can bring courses to people who live far from schools or universities. It can show people, places and things that students could never see in an ordinary classroom. Television lessons can be stored on videotape and shown over and over again.

Television is also a source of information in Sarah's school. For instance, Sarah's class watches a French program after recess. The television programs are sent by satellite from Toronto. The school has an antenna on the roof to receive the television signal from the satellite. Sarah likes having her French lessons on television.

- What would be the differences between learning by television and learning from a teacher in your classroom?

Schools in northern Ontario can receive much more information today than in the past. Now, students living in the country can have almost the same information at their fingertips as students in the city. Students can get their information from many sources, not just from the teacher and textbooks. Through films and television, students can see places and things that students in the past could only read about. Students today can receive up-to-date information. Although schools may not yet use computer information banks such as the one Sarah used, they are available. Students will be using them in the future.

Modern equipment does not mean students no longer have to work. Students still have to work hard to learn new things. Still, today's communications equipment can make learning more interesting and exciting. It connects students with a whole world of information that is outside the classroom.

This dish-shaped antenna is located on top of a school. What communications equipment might students use in their classrooms?

A teacher uses an overhead projector to help a student practise speech. What kind of equipment is the student wearing?

How Communications Helps Deaf People

The most common way we communicate with others is through spoken words. We whisper secrets to our friends, share jokes with our family and take part in class discussions. We use a telephone to send our spoken words to people far away. Spoken words are the source of much of the information and entertainment we get from radio, television and movies.

People who are deaf cannot hear spoken words. In some cases, they also have difficulty speaking words to others. Because of this, deaf children often feel cut off from other children. They would like to be able to telephone their friends. They would like to get together with other children to watch a movie on television. When they cannot do these things, they may feel frustrated, angry and lonely.

In the last few chapters, you have been learning about new inventions in communications. Unfortunately, these new inventions have not usually helped deaf people at all. Radios, telephones and even television use the spoken word to communicate, and deaf people cannot hear the spoken word.

Deaf people can communicate well in other ways, though. For instance, they can use sign language—a way of talking using hand signals. They can also read and write messages. Finally, new equipment is being developed for deaf people. It uses printed words to communicate. Some of this new equipment was invented by scientists who are deaf themselves. They understand the difficulties deaf people have.

In the stories following you'll see how communications technology has helped people who cannot hear. First you'll see what life was like for a deaf child growing up 25 years ago. Then you'll see what life is like for a deaf child growing up today.

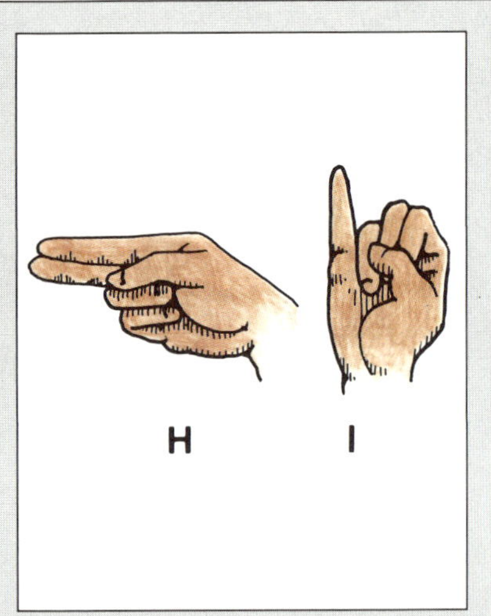

Talking with Your Hands

These two hand positions stand for the letters H and I. By quickly moving your fingers from one position to the other, you are saying "HI" using fingerspelling. Fingerspelling is a way of spelling out words so that deaf people can understand them.

Fingerspelling is too slow for ordinary conversations. Instead, deaf people use a method of communication called sign language. Certain movements of the hands, called signs, have different meanings. For instance, a wave of your right hand, starting at your forehead, means "hello" or "goodbye." These signs can be combined to make sentences.

A Deaf Child in the Past

Marion jumped off the school bus and waved at her friend through the window. "See you tomorrow," she said, using her hands. "Goodbye," said her friend, also with her hands, as the bus pulled away. Marion and her friend were using sign language.

At the School for the Deaf, Marion was surrounded by other deaf children. They talked to each other in sign language. Their teachers taught them lessons using sign language. Marion felt comfortable at her school.

Every afternoon, when she got off the school bus, Marion entered the world of hearing. The children living in her neighbourhood could all hear. None of them knew sign language. Marion could understand some things they said by lip reading, which means watching their mouths move. She still missed many of their words. Marion played with some of the smallest children, but she felt nervous with children her own age. She was afraid she would not understand them and might do something that would look silly. So Marion kept to herself most of the time.

Marion's family could use sign language, but even at home Marion sometimes felt left out. For instance, she did not watch television with her brother anymore. Lip reading was very tiring, and most of the time Marion could not figure out what was going on anyway. She did not like to keep asking her brother to explain what was happening.

Marion could not use the telephone, either. When her grandfather phoned at Christmas, someone else in the family had to interpret. Her father would listen to what her grandfather said and tell Marion in sign language. Then he would watch what Marion answered in sign language. He would tell this to her grandfather.

Marion relied on her family to be her link with other hearing people. They often had to communicate for her. Although Marion was as smart as other children her age, she did not always feel very smart, because she could not explain things for herself. It was frustrating.

That is what life might have been like for a deaf child 25 years ago. What has changed today? Today communication can still be difficult for children who cannot hear. They can still feel cut off from the hearing world around them. Yet, as you'll see, new equipment can make communication for deaf children easier in some ways.

A Deaf Child Today

Don gave a hoot of laughter. He was watching his favourite television program. He liked the comments the robot was always making.

Don is deaf. He knew what the robot was saying, though. Every time the robot talked, its words were printed in a line at the bottom of the screen. That line of print is called a caption. By reading this caption, Don could understand the robot.

On most television sets, this caption would not appear. People who can hear would not need it. Don was watching a special television set that is made to show the captions for some programs. Don's mother, who is also deaf, watches the news every night with captions. But not all TV programs have captions. Don and his mother do not have as much choice as people who can hear.

Captioning on television is one example of how new technology has helped Don do things that hearing people take for granted. Captions turn spoken words into printed words that deaf people can understand.

These deaf students in the past and present are using equipment that allows them to communicate with others. How might such equipment make life easier for these students?

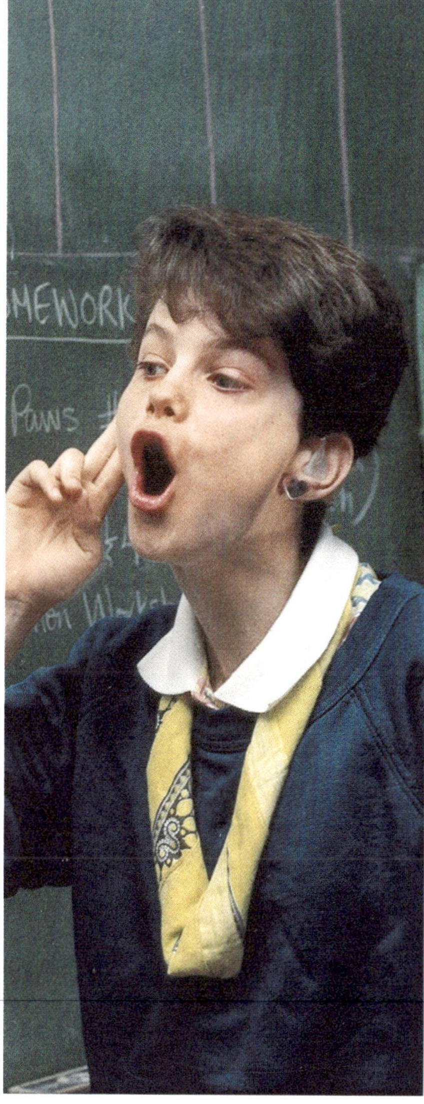

This person is using a Visual Ear to receive a telephone message. This equipment allows deaf people to send typed messages by telephone. Why is this a slower form of communication than an ordinary telephone?

Don can even use a telephone. His phone is attached to a machine called a Visual Ear. It has a keyboard like a typewriter and a small screen. When Don wants to say something on the telephone, he types out his message on the keyboard. When his friend answers, the printed words appear in a line that moves across the screen. Typing on the Visual Ear is slower than speaking, but it allows Don to use the telephone.

- Imagine having a telephone conversation with a friend using a Visual Ear. How would it be different from a spoken conversation?

The Visual Ear has made a big difference to Don's life. He can call other people who also have a Visual Ear. He likes to call his friends or his grandmother. If his mother is going to be home late from work, she can phone and tell him. If he is alone at home and needs help, he can call the operator.

Inventions like television captions and the Visual Ear have given Don and his mother more confidence. Instead of guessing what people are saying, they can read the actual words. They can communicate for themselves, instead of asking hearing people to help. They can learn more about what is going on in the world, and they can understand what people are saying.

Communication is important to all people, whether they can hear or not. Communication is what makes human beings special. No other animals use language for speaking and writing like we do. Only people can share so many thoughts, feelings and ideas. Communication links us together in this world.

Deaf people do not want to be shut out of this world. They, too, want to receive information, learn new things and share ideas. New inventions in communications can sometimes help them do this.

Communications and Computers

Computers were almost unknown when your parents were your age. Today they are found in stores, offices, banks, factories, schools and homes. Computers are changing our lives.

A computer can do many tasks. It can store huge quantities of information. With the correct instructions, a computer can do almost anything with this information. It can add long lists of numbers or keep track of the items for sale in a department store. It can use hundreds of pieces of information about the weather to prepare a weather forecast. A computer can guide you through a spelling exercise. People are able to do these things, too. But computers do them many, many times faster.

Computers are important in new communications technology. In some cases, computers are used to design and develop new equipment. In other cases, computers are needed to operate this equipment. The pictures show some examples of how computers help communications.

Satellites are placed in orbit by a space shuttle. Computers control every aspect of the launch, the flight direction and the speed of the space shuttle.

Telephone exchanges use computers. Computers make the phone connections and keep track of long-distance calls. If we had to pay people to do all the jobs of computers, it would be very expensive to make a telephone call.

Videotex systems allow people to order information from a computer information bank. There may be millions of pages in that information bank.

Communications Technology: A Tool We Can Use

Canada has often been a leader in new communications technology. The first radio broadcast of a human voice was made by a Canadian. Alexander Bell tested his new invention, the telephone, in Canada. Canadians still design some of the best telephone equipment in the world. Canada was also one of the first countries to use communications satellites.

It is not hard to understand why Canadians have tried so hard to find better methods of communication. People often live far apart in a country as large as Canada. New methods of communication have been necessary to develop the country.

Although it is easy to be excited about new communications technology, we should remember that these new inventions are just tools. They are tools that people find very useful, but they cannot replace people.

For instance, we can use communications equipment to call for help in an emergency, but we still need someone to receive the call and organize a rescue. Students in remote schools can use new communications equipment to bring television programs to their classroom. But people are still needed to make useful and interesting programs. New equipment can make communication easier for deaf people. Yet deaf people still want to talk to other people, not to machines. Today's technology does not make people any less important.

- What are some of the things people can do that equipment will never be able to do?

A Canadian satellite rockets into space from its American launching pad. How might this satellite help Canadians communicate?

Even if we could get all the information we need from machines, we would not want to. Imagine what it would be like if you lived all alone on an island. You might have a computer bank that could give you any information you want and all the best books and movies that were ever made. Just the same, you would have nobody to talk to when you were feeling sad. There would be nobody to tell if you discovered something interesting. Nobody would come if you called for help. Nobody would be there to share your thoughts and feelings.

We need to be able to talk to other people. The best way to talk is face-to-face, without using any special equipment at all. Since that is not always possible, we use tools that make other kinds of communication possible. They help us communicate with people far away or with people unable to understand our spoken words. We can share our thoughts and information with other people, even if we live all alone on an island.

In this chapter, you've seen three examples that show how new inventions in communications have helped Canadians keep in touch. Probably you can think of more examples. What new communications tools do you think Canadians will invent in the future? How will we use them? What differences will they make in our lives? In the next chapter, we'll explore these questions.

Above: These microwave towers are an important part of the communications network that links all Canadians. Why might Canada have a greater need for communications equipment than some other countries?

How Could You Communicate with a Blind Person?

“In two weeks, a blind student will be joining the class,” the teacher announced. “His name is Stephen.” The teacher explained that Stephen was used to working in a regular classroom. “But in the beginning,” she said, “some of you may have difficulty communicating with a blind person. Let’s discuss some ways we could prepare for Stephen’s arrival.”

Carlo suggested that the students could spend some time with blindfolds over their eyes. This would give them an idea of what it might be like to be blind.

Another student wanted to know how Stephen would read and write. The teacher explained that Stephen would use an alphabet called **braille**. Braille is a pattern of raised dots like little bumps on the paper. A blind person can read what was written on the paper by running a finger over this pattern of dots.

“Would it help Stephen if we learned braille?” Marie asked. The students discussed her suggestion. One student felt that it would not help Stephen, since he was the only one working in braille. Another student thought that learning about braille would help the students understand how Stephen did his work.

Carlo said, “We could have a guest speaker who knows about being blind. That would help us learn about communicating with Stephen.”

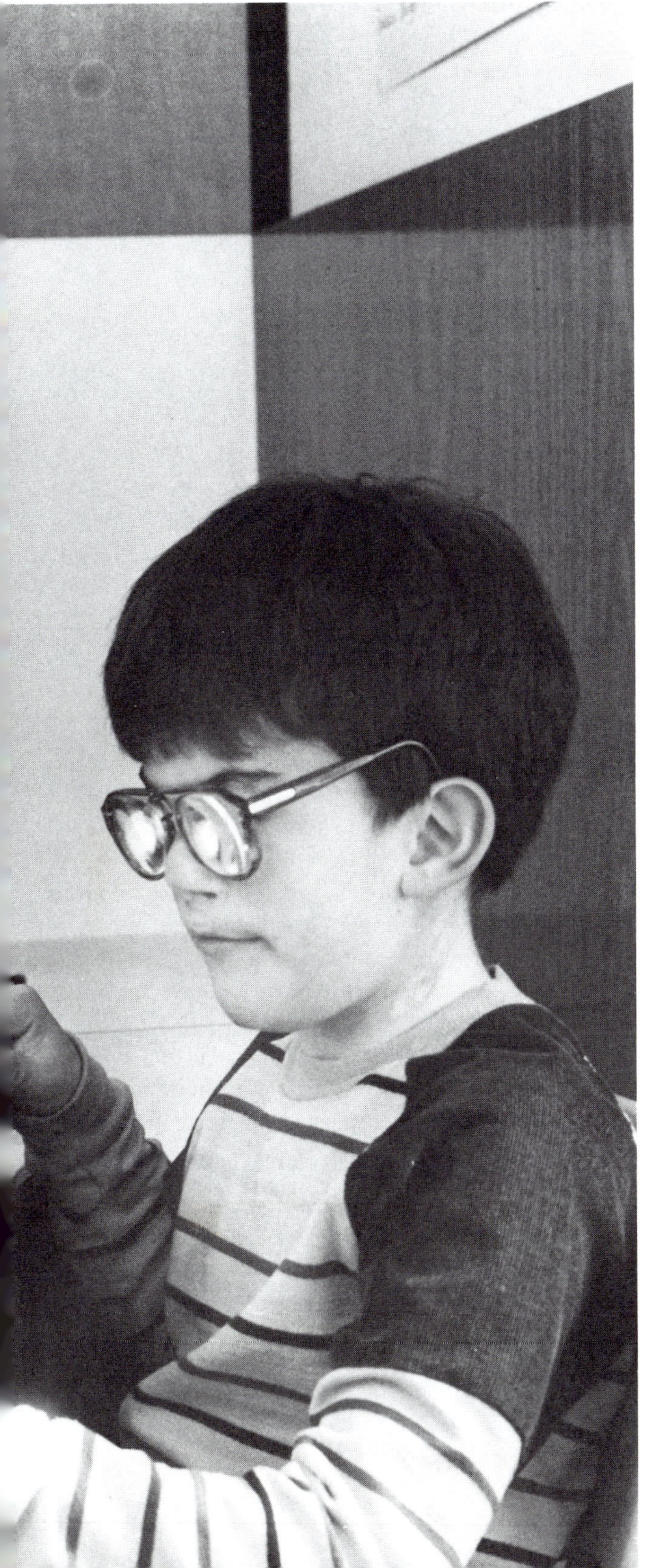

The teacher pointed out that at first Stephen might have trouble knowing who was talking to him. Jan suggested that students could practise identifying themselves before speaking. That would help them remember to give Stephen their names.

After further discussion, the students decided to invite a guest speaker to talk to the class about communicating with a blind person.

- What could you do to make communication with a blind person easier?
- What problems might you have and how would you solve them?

This student has limited vision. He is using a machine that increases the size of the type he is reading. The machine also reverses the colour of the type so that the black type appears white on a black background. What might you learn from this boy if he were a student in your classroom?

CHAPTER CHECKUP

Recalling the Main Ideas

Some of the communications tools mentioned in this chapter are listed below. For each one, write one or two sentences to explain what the tool does and why it is important.

Search and Rescue Team Uses — emergency locator transmitter
— satellites

Students in a Country School Use — computer information bank
— television programs sent by satellite

Deaf People Use — television captions
— Visual Ear

Using What You Have Learned

New communications equipment helps Canadians in many other ways. Below, you can read about the jobs of a police officer and a weather forecaster. Choose one of the two jobs. List at least three ways communications equipment is used in that job. Could the job be done just as well without this equipment? Why or why not?

Police Officer

A phone call comes into the police station. The caller reports a robbery at a store. The dispatcher radios the information to the patrol car in the area. The car rushes to the scene. The officers find a man in the alley behind the store. He says that he hasn't done anything. The officers take the man to the patrol car and tell him to get into the back seat. One officer radios the man's name to the police station. At the station an officer uses the computer information bank. In a few seconds he discovers that the man is wanted for another robbery. The officer radios the information back to the patrol car. One of the officers in the car turns to the man in the back seat. "You're under arrest," she says.

Weather Forecaster

Every three hours there is a new weather forecast. The latest information is gathered in different ways. A satellite sends pictures of the earth's surface. These pictures might show clouds, rainfall or storms. Ships and planes radio information about the weather where they are. Weather stations collect information about temperature, rainfall and moisture in the air. Hundreds of these stations do not have people there; machines do the collecting. Information gathered by weather stations might be sent to a satellite. Or it might be sent over a network of microwave towers.

The information is used to make forecasts and weather maps. These are then sent to weather centres across the country. A map can be placed in a machine in one centre and a copy printed out in another centre. People at the weather centres make up local weather forecasts. They record them on tape, ready for people who telephone to hear them. Forecasts are also sent by radio to ships at sea.

5

How Might Communications Change in the Future?

Saturday, November 9, 2002

VOICE OF RADIO HOST: Good evening, everyone. Welcome to another edition of the cross-Canada radio show.

Thirty years ago today, Canada launched its first communications satellite. That satellite, called *Anik A-1,* was a major step forward in communications. Since then, Canada has taken many more steps. Tonight, we are going to look at what is happening in communications today. Our guest is Dr. David Cheng of Lunar Communications Corporation. Lunar Communications is a Canadian company specializing in communications in space.

We've reached Dr. Cheng in his office at Copernicus International Research Centre on the moon. Hello, Dr. Cheng.

DR. CHENG: Hello there!

RADIO HOST: Dr. Cheng, could you briefly describe what Lunar Communications is doing on the moon?

DR. CHENG: My company has been hired to plan the communications network that will be needed by people living and working in space. You know there is a large international research station here on the moon. Hundreds of scientists from many countries are doing research. There are also four large mines operating on the moon. There are already several solar power stations orbiting in space. They use sunlight to make electricity that is then sent to earth. Many people work at the research centre, in the mines and on the power stations. My job is to make sure all these people are able to communicate with each other and with people on earth, too.

In the year 2002, people at a communication centre on earth prepare to talk with people on the moon. Do you think you will ever talk with someone on the moon?

RADIO HOST: It sounds like a big task.

DR. CHENG: There's no doubt about that. For people working in space, a reliable communications network is very important. For one thing, it's easy to feel isolated and far away from family and friends at home. We need to be able to keep in touch with life on earth.

A good communications network is also important because we need to know right away if something goes wrong with our equipment here in space. People cannot survive outside our space colonies without special pressurized suits and oxygen supplies. So if something goes wrong with someone's equipment, we must be able to send messages right away.

Finally, communications helps people understand one another. With people from so many different countries here, it is very important that we understand each other. One of our challenges is to set up instant **translation** equipment so that people using different languages can communicate. Translation reduces misunderstanding that can lead to arguments. We want a peaceful community here in space.

RADIO HOST: Canada's first satellite was launched 30 years ago. Are the challenges today different from the challenges in the 1970s?

DR. CHENG: Today we are working with newer and more complex equipment. It allows us to communicate more efficiently. But our purpose has not really changed. We are still looking for ways to send information from one place to another. In the old days in Canada, we wanted to reach people living in small communities on the prairies or in the north. When I was a teenager, I wanted to send my music to children around the world. Thanks to satellites, which were still quite new in those days, my dream came true. That seemed very exciting to me back then. Today I'm just as excited about communications in space. Today's communications technology is different, but our reasons for communicating are the same.

RADIO HOST: Do you mean that people still want to talk to each other?

DR. CHENG: That's right. We're human beings, and human beings communicate. Since human beings don't always live or work within speaking distance of each other, they have had to find ways of communicating over longer distances. That's why Canadians strung up telegraph wires on poles across the prairies. That's why we developed our satellites. And that's why I've been hired to develop a communications network here in space.

That was an imaginary radio broadcast that might take place in the future. Dr. Cheng is David, the musician you met in Chapter 1. He was talking to a radio host about communications. The radio broadcast is imaginary, of course, because nobody knows for sure what will be happening in the year 2002. What new communications technology can you imagine people might use in the future? How might it change your life?

The next few pages will give you some ideas about the future. You may be able to think of other ideas. Think about how communications has changed in the past. You can be sure that there will be more changes in the years ahead.

A radio host on earth interviews Dr. Cheng at a research station on the moon. Do you think that an audience will find this interview interesting?

What New Communications Technology Might We Use in the Future?

In the past, people discovered how to send messages over long distances, first using wires and then without using wires. Human voices and then television pictures were broadcast to people living far away. People are always inventing new tools to improve communications. While today we use telephones to send our voices, in the future we will probably use something like a telephone to send and receive pictures and drawings, too.

Some of the technology described on these pages already exists. It may be just a matter of time until you are using it. Whether this new technology will actually improve our lives depends on how we use it. The messages we communicate are as important as how far, how fast or how easily we can send them.

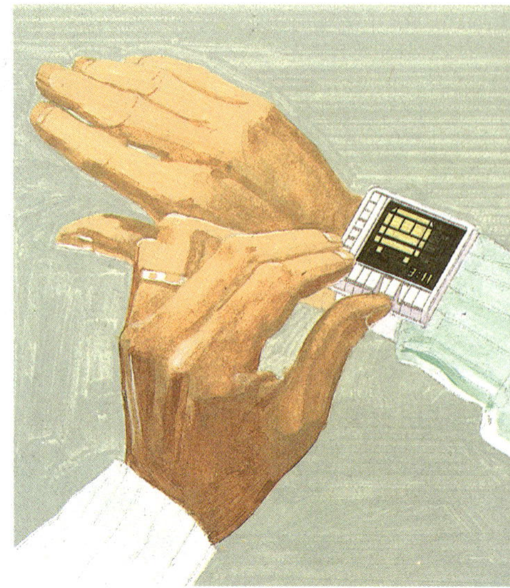

Above: Will we wear tiny wrist computers that we can use to telephone home, to find out when the next bus is coming, or to check which movies are playing?

*Below: Will all telephones be equipped with scribble pads for sending drawings or doodles over the phone lines? Will these **videophones** send your picture as well as your voice?*

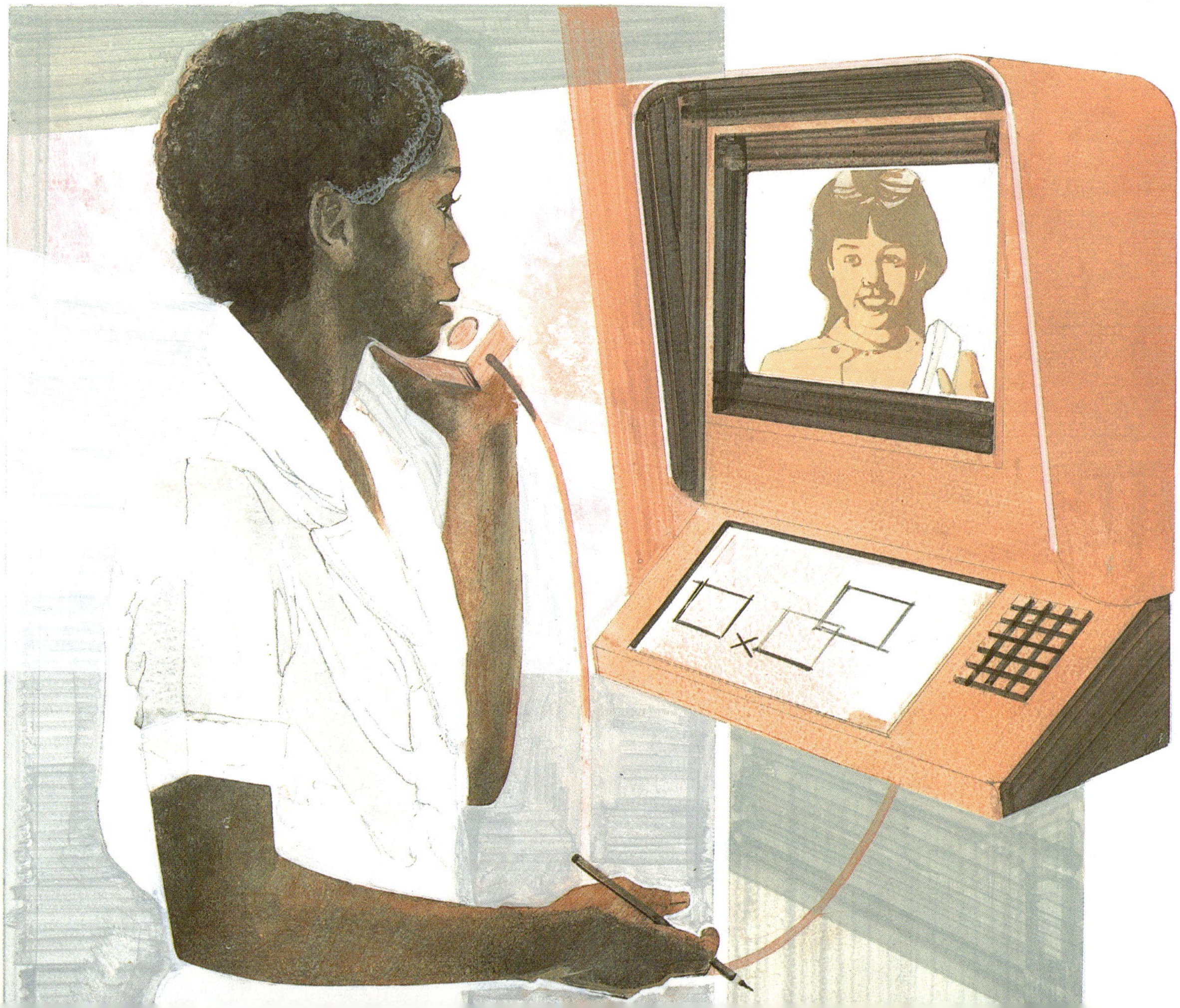

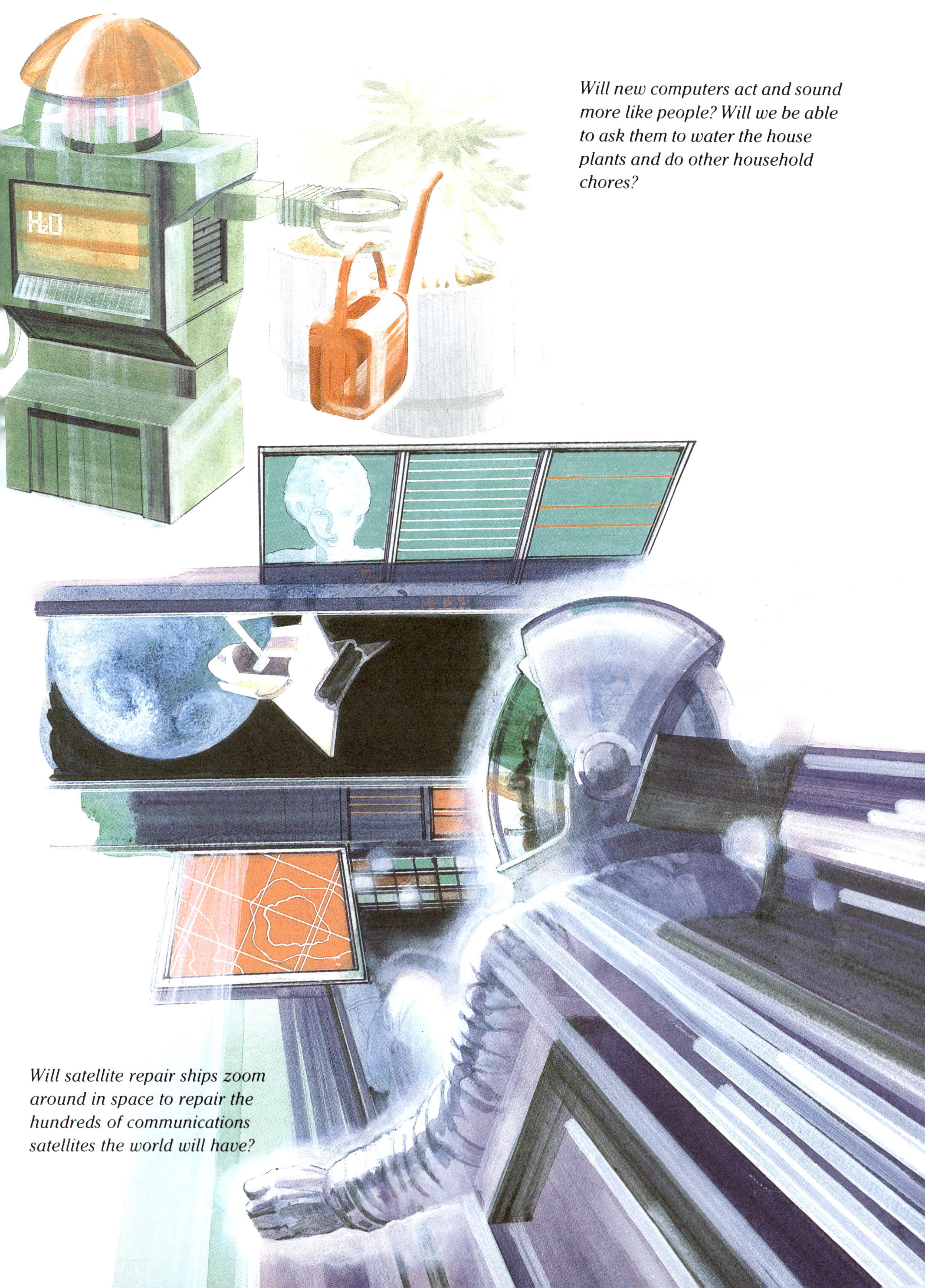

Will new computers act and sound more like people? Will we be able to ask them to water the house plants and do other household chores?

Will satellite repair ships zoom around in space to repair the hundreds of communications satellites the world will have?

How Might Changes in Communications Affect Our Lives at Home?

When people in the past started using telephones, they no longer had to leave home to talk to their friends. When they bought television sets that showed movies, people no longer had to travel across town to movie theatres. The technology of the future will make more and more information available to us in our homes. We may be able to do our shopping and banking, take courses and mail letters without stepping out the door.

Although we could stay at home the whole time, we probably won't. We will still want to meet with other people. For instance, it would be impossible to have a soccer game or a birthday party without getting everyone together in the same place.

Above: Will our mail appear on our home viewscreen? We would check our computer, just as we now check the mailbox, to see if anyone had sent us letters. Then we could read them on the screen or print them out on our home computer.

Will we be able to go shopping without leaving the house? We might see pictures of 10 different egg beaters on our home viewscreen. Then we could order the one we want. It would be delivered to our home.

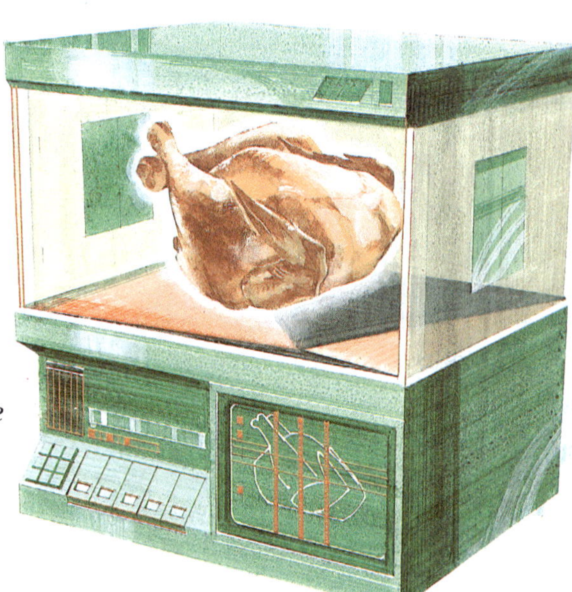

Right: Will our household appliances be computerized? If we are away from home, will we be able to use a telephone to instruct our computer to turn on the oven for dinner or turn on the porch light?

Left: Will we be able to learn any hobby we want by ordering a course to appear on our home viewscreen? For instance, we could order courses that teach us how to play the ukelele, how to keep pet spiders or how to make fudge.

How Might Changes in Communications Affect Our Lives at School and at Work?

Students need information to learn. Working people need information to do their jobs. Most of this information can be found in schools, offices and other buildings that are often located in the city. That means that people living in the country are at a disadvantage.

As communications equipment improves in the future, more of this information will be available to people no matter where they live. More and more information will be stored in computer banks. Students and workers everywhere, but especially those living in the country, will find it easier to do their work.

Will schools have equipment that can produce three-dimensional images of dinosaurs and other things the students are studying? These holograms would look real until you tried to touch them. They would be better than ordinary pictures of dinosaurs because students would be able to walk around and look at them from all angles.

Left: Will business people be able to dictate letters to a machine that can turn spoken words into printed words? The letters could be checked on a viewscreen before they are sent electronically. They would arrive in seconds.

Below: Will nurses at health clinics in the country be able to talk to doctors at city hospitals by videophone? The doctors would be able to see the patients on the videophone and look at them closely with a camera. The doctors could then decide whether patients needed to make the long trip to the hospital.

Above: Instead of driving to work, will people work at home? Home computers would be connected to the main office computer and would be able to receive all the information usually kept in the main office. Will children living in the country learn from computer programs at home instead of taking a long bus ride to school every day? Will people become lonely working and studying on their own at home?

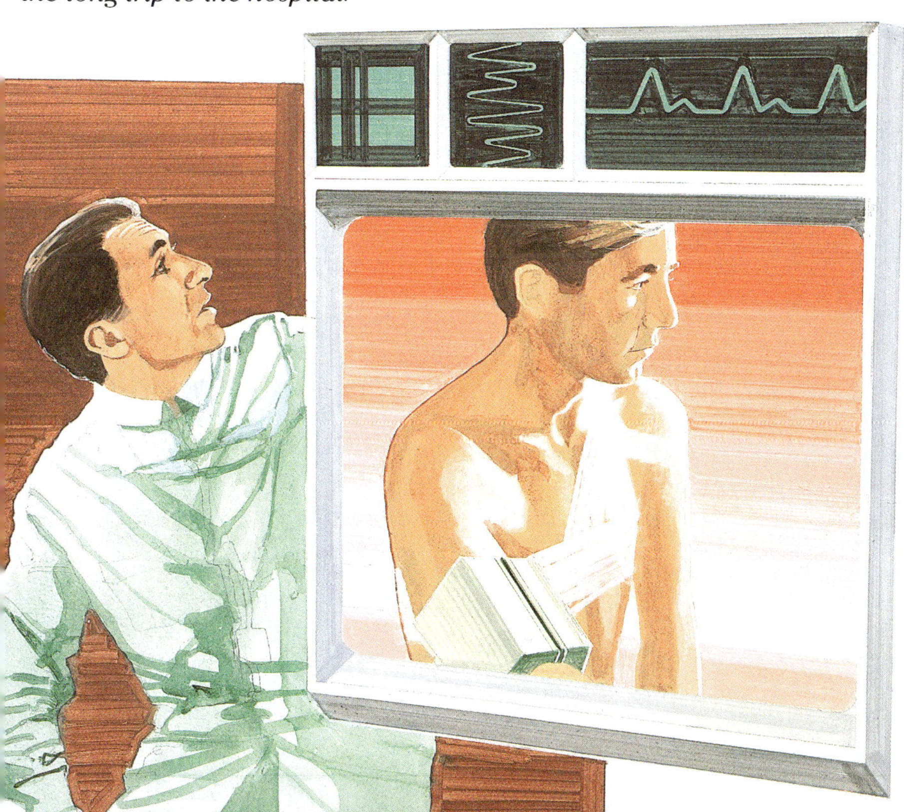

How Might Changes in Communications Affect Our Relations with Other People?

Some people see good changes ahead as we develop new communications technology. They see that better ways to communicate can help people learn more and understand each other better. New inventions can help bring people together. They can improve relations between people.

Other people worry that new communications technology may have its bad side. Already they see some bad effects on children who watch too much television. They wonder whether we will use future communications equipment wisely. They wonder if people will care as much about other people when they communicate with them more and more through machines.

Will there be translating machines that allow English-speaking people to communicate with people speaking French or Japanese? Will you make friends with a child in another country?

Left: Will satellite television make life more difficult for people in poorer countries? Will they feel worse when they see programs and commercials about things they cannot afford? Or will only rich people and wealthy countries be able to get communications equipment and the information it brings?

Above: Will business and government people spend less time travelling and more time at home? Will people across the country hold meetings by teleconferencing—seeing one another on a television screen?

Will satellite television help people in other countries learn more about Canadians? Will it help Canadians learn more about other people in the world? Will there be more peace in the world when people understand each other better?

Looking to Your Future

What about you? What does your future hold? How will changes in communications affect your life?

When the first telegraph wire reached the town of Napanee, Ontario, in 1847, all the school children were given a holiday to watch how it worked. A man walked 30 km to see if messages really *did* fly over wires! In those days, the telegraph was a tremendously exciting invention.

Your future could be just as exciting. There will be new inventions, and you may help develop them. These new inventions will make communication even easier than it is today.

Yet communication is much more than the equipment that sends our message from one place to another. The new technology is exciting, but it is not everything. The message we send is also important. Just because we know how to send words to the moon doesn't mean we should do so if we have nothing useful to say.

When used wisely, communications equipment can make this world a better place. By sharing information, ideas and friendship, we can help each other. However, communications equipment can also be used to spread lies, hate and messages that will hurt people. Television and radio have a great power to change people's ideas. In the future, as in the past, it will be important to think about *what* we communicate, not just how far or how fast we can send the message.

You will be one of the Canadians of tomorrow. You can help decide how we will use communications technology. You can help shape the future. It could be an exciting time.

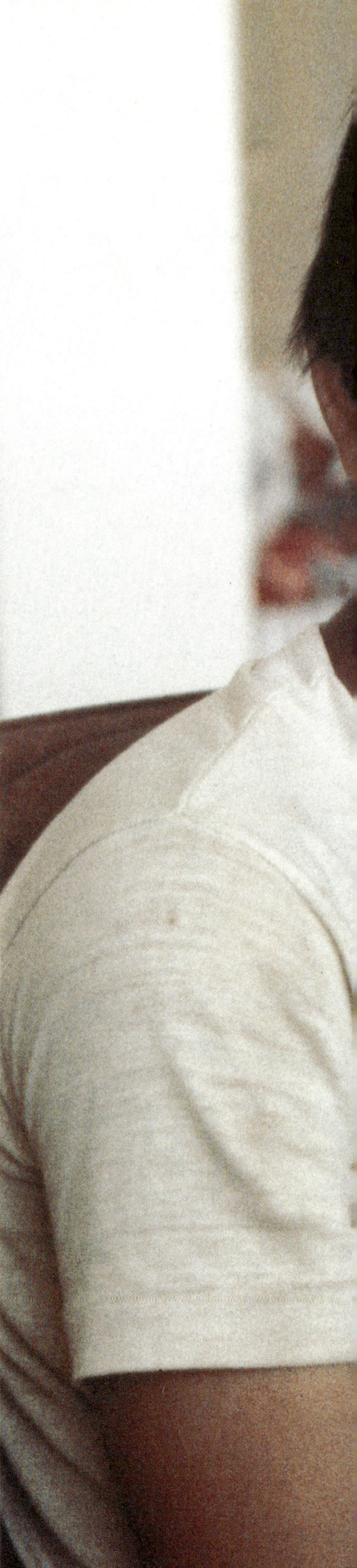

The telephone is an important form of communication for many people today. What forms of communication do you use most often?

UNIT CHECKUP

Learning from the Past

The picture on the left below shows people travelling to the prairies in the 1800s. The picture on the right shows people travelling today.

Imagine that you and your family are moving from Montreal to the prairies

—in 1850

—today

You are sad to leave your friends and promise to keep in touch with them.

1. How could you communicate with your friends across the country in 1850? How long might it take?
2. How could you communicate with your friends today. How long might it take?

Looking to the Future

Communications equipment reduces the amount of travelling that people must do. For example, if you want to talk to a friend who lives two kilometres away, you can use the telephone.

Write down three places that you visit regularly (for example, the corner store). For each place, explain how communications technology might make it unnecessary to go there 50 years from now.

Example:

Today I travel to ____.
In the future, I may not need to travel to ____ because ____.

Getting Involved

Imagine that your school is holding a fair to raise money. You want as many people as possible to come. Make a list of at least six ways you could let the community know about the fair. Put check marks beside the three methods of communication you think would reach the most people.

Summing Up

In this unit, you have read how communications equipment is important in a vast country like Canada. List three ways that communications equipment is important in your life.

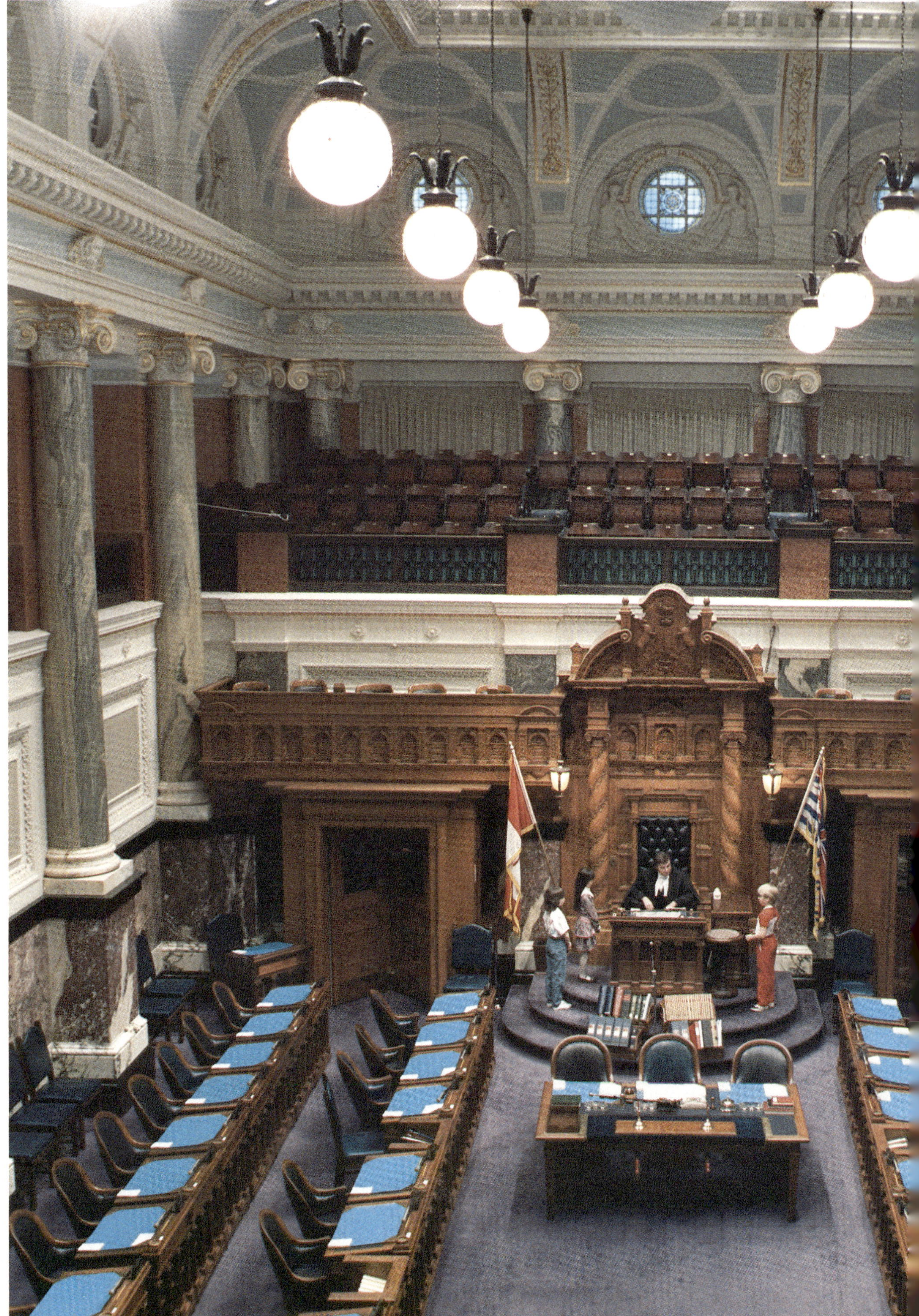

UNIT III

Exploring Government

1

What Is Government?

In some provinces, people are required to wear seat belts when riding in a car. Are people required to wear seat belts in your province?

Catherine Hears about Laws

Catherine's long, dark hair clung to her neck every time she leaned back in her seat. Bosley, her old English sheepdog, was panting on the floor of the car. Normally, Catherine liked to take Bosley everywhere. But in this Saskatchewan heat, they both would have been cooler and happier at home.

Catherine tugged angrily at her seat belt. "Do I have to keep this thing on, Mom? I'm hot."

"We're almost home," said Mrs. Adams.

"But Mom . . ."

"It's dangerous not to wear a seat belt, Catherine. Anyway, I couldn't tell you to undo your seat belt even if I wanted to. You know we all have to buckle up. It's the **law**," said Mrs. Adams. She sounded hot and a bit cranky herself. Catherine thought it might be best not to argue.

In another five minutes they were home. Bosley bounded out of the car and ran to the sprinkler. Mr. Adams appeared at the front door.

"I'm glad you're back," he said to Catherine. "Would you please go to **city hall** and get a dog **licence** for Bosley?" Mr. Adams handed her some money.

"But Dad, I'm hot," said Catherine.

"Please don't fuss. We don't want any trouble for Bosley—or for us—just because he has no licence."

Then he pulled an extra bill from his pocket and added, "Stop by Mr. Larson's on your way. Have a cold milkshake or something."

Bosley was torn between staying under the sprinkler and following Catherine. But before she had reached the corner, Catherine found that Bosley was by her side. She pulled his leash out of her pocket and snapped it on.

"We have to get you a licence, pal," she said to Bosley. "I don't know why. You can't read it anyway."

Three blocks later Catherine could see the bright awnings on Mr. Larson's ice cream parlour. The thought of a creamy, cold milkshake made her walk a little faster. She always liked talking with Mr. Larson, too.

Catherine tied Bosley's leash to the bicycle rack under the awnings and then opened the door to the ice cream parlour. A little bell jingled above her head.

"Well, Catherine," said Mr. Larson, looking up as he polished the already shiny countertop. "Come in, come in. Sit down and cool off. It's such a hot day."

"Thanks," said Catherine as she plopped down on a stool. "It's really cool in here. I wish I could bring Bosley in, too."

"Poor Bosley," said Mr. Larson, looking out the window at the panting dog. "If I let him in, both he and I would be in trouble. It's against the law to have a dog in a place that serves food."

Then he had an idea. "Here, Catherine," he said, handing her an ice cream carton that was nearly empty. "Take this to Bosley and let him lick it out. I'll bring a pail of water. He'll have his very own ice cream parlour outside."

Bosley pulled excitedly against his leash when he saw them coming. As soon as Catherine set down the ice cream carton, his big woolly head disappeared inside it.

"He loves it," laughed Catherine. "Look at him go. I think I'll have something cold, too, Mr. Larson. Could you make me a chocolate milkshake, please?"

"Sure thing, Catherine," said Mr. Larson, heading back in.

- Have you ever had to obey a law you didn't agree with? If so, how did you feel?

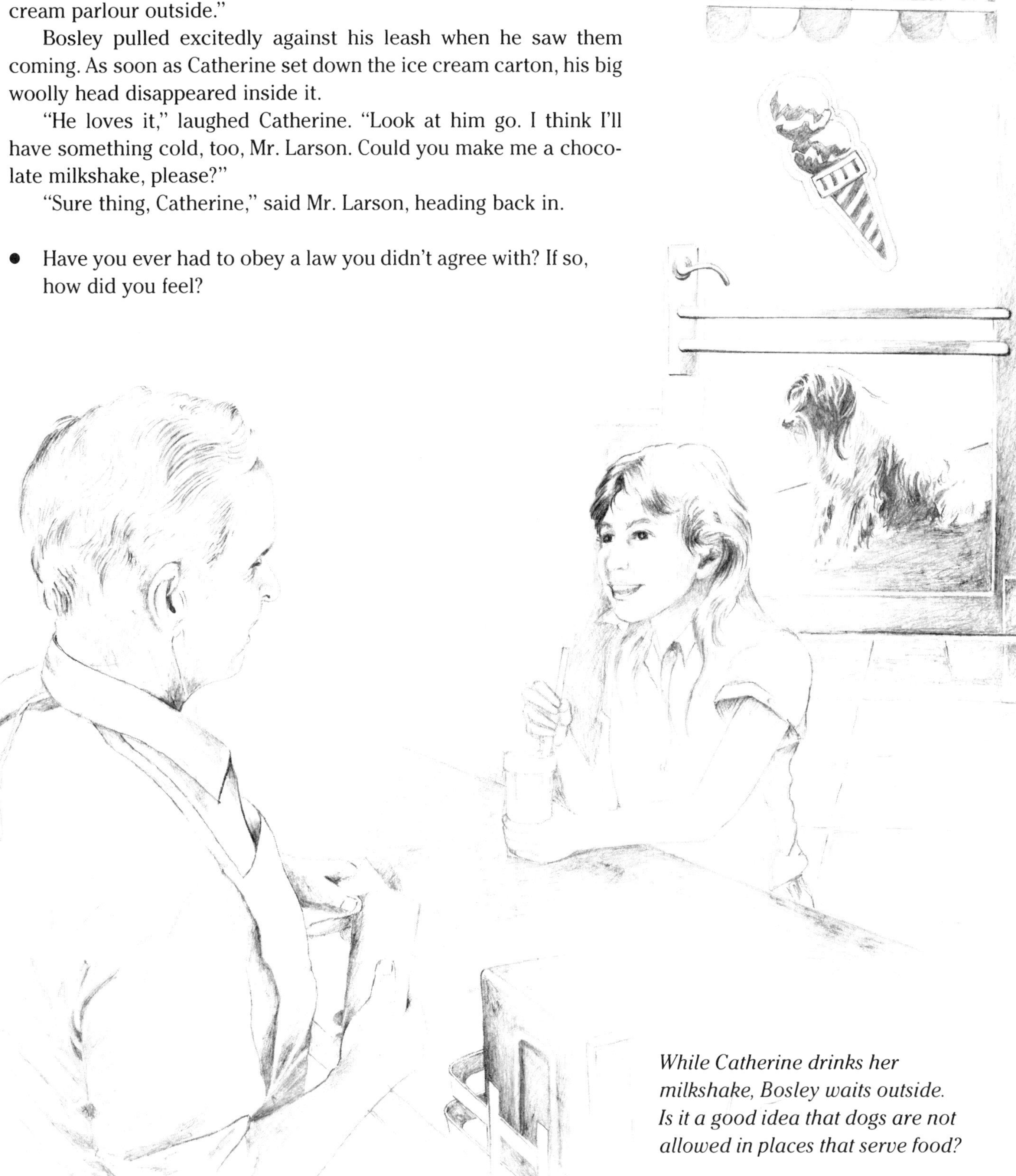

While Catherine drinks her milkshake, Bosley waits outside. Is it a good idea that dogs are not allowed in places that serve food?

What Are Laws?

Laws are rules made by **governments**. In a family, rules about mealtimes and chores help people live together. Governments make laws for the same reason. Laws help you get along with other Canadians.

Laws both limit and protect your freedom. For example, traffic laws limit your freedom by stating that you must ride your bicycle on the right side of the road. You are not allowed to wander all over the road. But traffic laws protect your freedom by making it safer for you to ride your bicycle.

Laws are for everybody. Even the most important or powerful people in Canada must obey the laws.

Thinking about Government

Inside, Catherine sat down on her stool, plunked her elbows on the counter and rested her chin in her hands. "Gee, Mr. Larson, there sure seem to be a lot of rules. Do this, do that. Don't do this, don't do that. And they are not even our own rules."

"What do you mean, Catherine?" asked Mr. Larson, turning on the milkshake machine.

"Well, it's your ice cream shop, but it's not your rule about dogs having to stay outside. And Bosley's my own dog, but somebody else says I have to get a licence for him. Even in our own car, we have to wear seat belts, whether we like it or not."

"So, Catherine, you are angry with our government," said Mr. Larson. He handed her a milkshake.

"Government?" said Catherine. "Well, if that's government, I wish we didn't have any."

"I can't imagine what it would be like having no government at all," said Mr. Larson.

"Poor Bosley wouldn't be stuck outside in the heat, and he wouldn't have to wear some dumb licence. I wouldn't have to ride strapped into a seat belt either. That's what it would be like," said Catherine. "What other laws could we get rid of if we didn't have a government?"

"Well," Mr. Larson said, "I suppose you wouldn't have to go to school if you didn't want to."

"No school? Terrific."

"If there were no government, I guess there wouldn't have to be any **taxes**. I'd sure like that," said Mr. Larson, laughing.

Catherine looked at him blankly.

Mr. Larson explained, "All of us have to pay taxes to the government. That money helps to pay for some of the work the government does. For instance, people who work pay **income tax** every year. We give part of what we earn to the government."

- Pretend that you and your classmates were shipwrecked on an island. Would you need to make a simple set of rules to live together? Would you likely form a simple government?

Above: Canada's police services are paid for by taxes. What are some of the things a police officer does for you?

These are some of the signs the government puts up. What does each sign mean?

Finding Out about Government Services

Mr. Larson went outside to pick up Bosley's empty ice cream carton. He came back into the shop and put it with the other empty cartons.

"There's another side to government," he told Catherine. "I'd soon have enough empty ice cream cartons to fill my whole shop if the garbage collectors didn't haul them away. This **service** is provided by our city government. If we got rid of the government, we'd get rid of some laws and taxes. But we'd also get rid of a lot of special kinds of help. We'd have to look for other ways to get the help we need."

"I can look after myself and Bosley really well. Anyway, we have my mom and dad to look after us, too."

Mr. Larson started to polish the shiny countertop again. He moved slowly and thoughtfully. "There are some things that are very hard for you to do yourself, Catherine, or even for your parents to do for you. But we can do many of those things, quite easily, if we all work together. That's really all government is."

Catherine looked doubtful.

"What if there were no government at all, and you discovered a big fire in your house?" asked Mr. Larson.

"I'd call the fire department. I know the number," said Catherine quickly.

"There'd be no one to answer," said Mr. Larson. "In our community, the government looks after fire protection. It has made sure there are roads for the fire truck to reach you, and water pipes and hydrants for the fire hoses. It pays for firefighters to put out fires."

Catherine sucked hard on her straw. "I sure wouldn't want to try putting out a fire myself. I didn't know that fighting fires had anything to do with our government."

Just then Bosley let out a short, impatient bark. Catherine stood up. "Bosley must be tired of being tied up. I'd better get going and buy his licence. I sure hate walking in this heat, though."

Then she paused. "I know. I'll cut through the park and keep cool."

Above: Fire protection is usually provided by the government and paid for by taxes. What do you think would happen if there were no fire protection?

Above: Catherine and Mr. Larson talk about different kinds of government. Why is it important for Canadians to discuss their government?

Garbage collection services are usually provided through the government. Why is garbage collection important to a community?

Above: This is a petroglyph, a picture carved by the Indians in rock. Why is it important to preserve such carvings?

"The park" repeated Mr. Larson. "That's something else that the government in our community looks after."

"Bosley would miss all the walks he gets in the park, if it weren't there" said Catherine.

"Everybody in the community enjoys that shady park, especially on a hot day like this. We have city parks because we share the costs of buying the land and of looking after it."

"There are lots of parks I like," said Catherine. "Last summer, my cousin in Assiniboia took us to his favourite park. We saw drawings of faces and animals that the Indians had carved in rock a long time ago. It was neat."

"That park is called St. Victor Petroglyphs Historic Park," said Mr. Larson. "Those rock carvings you saw are called petroglyphs. That park is special to everybody in Saskatchewan. The government of the whole **province** owns it."

Mr. Larson explained that people work together through their local government to do many things for everybody in the community. They also work together through the Saskatchewan government to do things for everybody in the province.

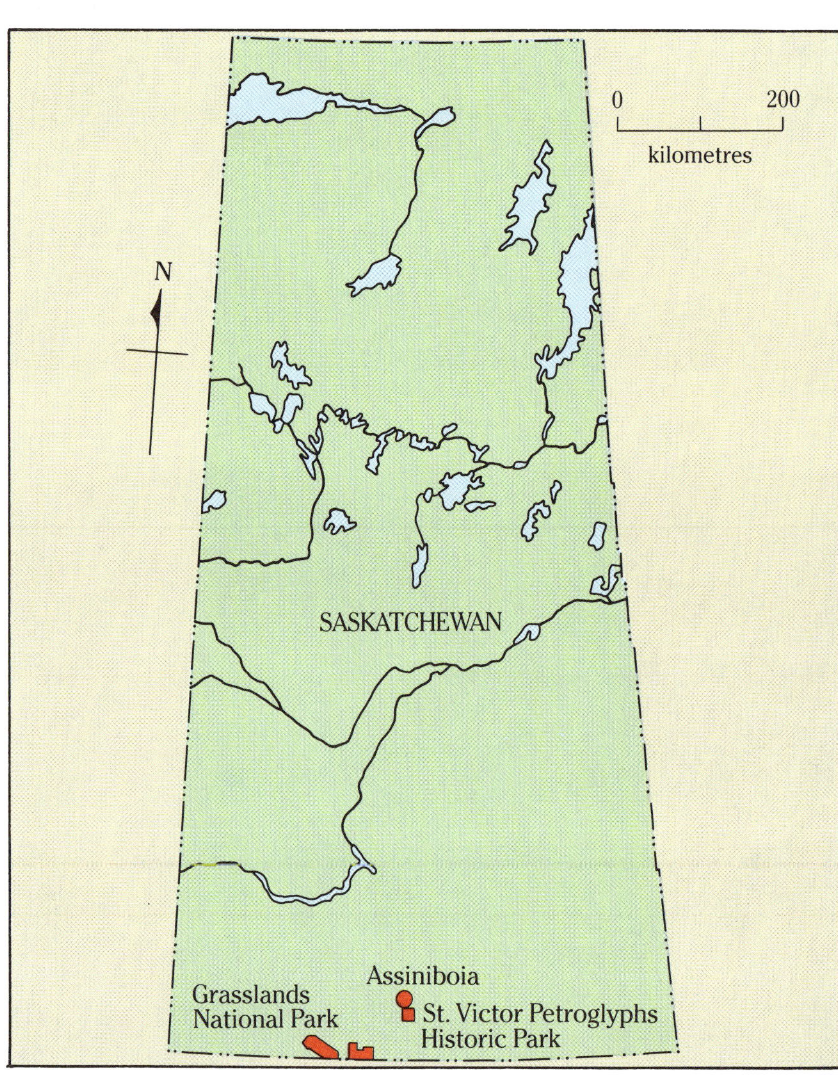

This map of Saskatchewan shows the locations of Grasslands National Park and St. Victor Petroglyphs Historic Park.

Mr. Larson told Catherine about another park in Saskatchewan. "It's called Grasslands National Park. It has plants, birds and other kinds of animals. It shows us what the prairies looked like long ago, before all the farms were built. It's called a **national** park because it belongs to everybody in Canada."

"Then does the government of Canada look after it?" Catherine asked Mr. Larson.

"That's right," said Mr. Larson. "Now you're moving ahead of me. Our government comes in different sizes and kinds—just like my milkshakes. We have local government for the community. Each province or **territory** also has a government. And Canada has a **federal** government for the whole country. Each government protects us and gives us services."

- What is your favourite park? Does your community own it? If not, who does?

What Is Government?

Government is the way people organize themselves so that they can do together what they cannot easily do alone.

The government is the small group of people chosen to make decisions for a large group. Canadians have three kinds of government—local, provincial or territorial, and federal. These governments make decisions for their community, for their province or territory, and for the country. Each government makes laws for its people.

Governments also provide many of the services people need, such as roads, education and libraries. Canadians pay for these government services through taxes.

As its name suggests, much of Grasslands National Park is flat grasslands. This picture shows the rocky land that you can also find in that area. Who owns this park?

Government Services in Canada

A service is work that helps other people. Stores offer a service by selling things you need. Governments also offer services. Governments provide services that are available to everyone who needs them. Everyone helps to pay for government services through taxes.

This chart lists a few of the services Canadians receive through their governments. Some services are provided or paid for by two or three governments. Not all local or provincial governments provide the same services. People in different places have different needs.

Governments in the territories provide many of the same services provincial governments provide. But a province and a territory are not exactly the same. Provincial governments manage their own natural resources. The federal government manages most natural resources in the territories.

LOCAL	PROVINCIAL	FEDERAL
parks	parks	parks
roads and sidewalks	highways	airports
museums	museums	museums
schools	education	post offices
water supply	universities	universities
health care	health care	health care
police	police	police
buses	workers' safety	defence
fire protection	pensions	pensions
garbage collection	forest management	forest research
public libraries	agricultural research	agricultural research

Understanding Laws and Taxes

"I still don't like all the laws made by governments," said Catherine.

"No one likes all the laws," agreed Mr. Larson. "But when we are living and working together, we have to do what's best for most of the people. That's only fair. You wanted to bring Bosley into my ice cream parlour. The government has a law against that. The law requires places that sell food to be kept clean so that people won't get sick."

"That makes sense, but why does Bosley need a licence?" asked Catherine.

"Two reasons, I guess. It's one way the community keeps track of all the dogs and their owners, just in case the dogs run around alone, bothering people. I know Bosley doesn't do that, but the law must apply to all dogs."

Mr. Larson continued, "Licences are also a way to make money. When you buy a dog licence you are helping the local government pay for animal shelters. The city gets money in other ways, too. It collects **property taxes** from everybody who owns land."

This animal shelter is maintained by local government. What service does it provide to the people who live in the community?

In some provinces, people pay sales tax when they buy something in the store. How much sales tax do you pay in your province?

"I pay tax, too," said Catherine, "every time I buy a game or something."

"That's **sales tax**," said Mr. Larson. "It goes to the government of the province."

"And don't forget income tax," Catherine added.

"Oh no, I could never forget that," laughed Mr. Larson. "That's how both the federal government and the provincial government get a lot of their money."

"Okay, I see why I have to buy a licence for Bosley. I still don't see why the law says I have to wear a seat belt," said Catherine, thinking of the hot car ride home. "That doesn't make money for the government and it doesn't help anybody else if I'm buckled up."

"That's harder to understand," Mr. Larson admitted. "Think of it this way, Catherine. If you are in a car accident, your seat belt keeps you from flying out of the car and getting badly hurt."

"I know that, Mr. Larson, but it's just *me* that gets hurt," said Catherine.

"Remember, we all put our money together to pay for things like doctors and hospitals. People who are badly hurt in car accidents need lots of care. That costs everybody lots of money. So we're all worse off if you get hurt."

"My dad didn't wear a seat belt when he was a kid. He told me that," said Catherine.

"You're right. He didn't use computers like you do either," answered Mr. Larson.

Catherine wondered what computers had to do with laws. Mr. Larson continued to explain how things have changed. "Government works for the people. So if we change, government changes. When we learned that seat belts save us from getting badly hurt, the provincial government made a law requiring everybody to wear one. When we realized that those Indian rock carvings are part of our **heritage**, the government made the land around them a park. We gain a lot through our governments, Catherine, but we have to obey the laws, too. It all goes together."

"Well, I'd better get to city hall," said Catherine as she opened the door. "It was fun talking to you, Mr. Larson."

"Drop into the shop again soon, Catherine. You, too, Bosley," Mr. Larson called out. "There's always a nearly empty ice cream carton to lick out."

- Can you think of any laws you would like to change?

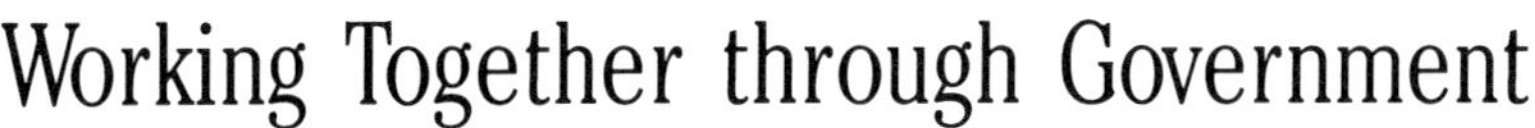

Working Together through Government

The story of Catherine and Bosley has introduced you to government in Canada. You have learned that government is a way for people to work together. It is a way to provide many of the services Canadians need. There are different kinds of government in Canada: local, provincial or territorial, and federal. Each government provides services.

Canadians share the costs of services. Buying licences, such as dog licences and car licences, is one way. Most money for services comes from taxes. Canadians share the services and their costs, so the government must do what's best for most of the people. Sometimes that means making laws, such as seat belt laws, that not everybody likes to obey.

As you read the rest of the chapters in this unit, you will learn much more about your government. You will learn about how Canada became one country with a federal government. You will find out how Canada's government works today. And you can use your imagination to see what government might be like in the future.

Catherine runs through the park with Bosley. Why do some communities require dogs to be on leashes?

CHAPTER CHECKUP

Recalling the Main Ideas

In this chapter Catherine talked to Mr. Larson about laws. These pictures illustrate some laws that Catherine did not like. For each picture, write

1. what the law is,
2. why Catherine did not like the law,
3. why the law is important to the people in Catherine's community.

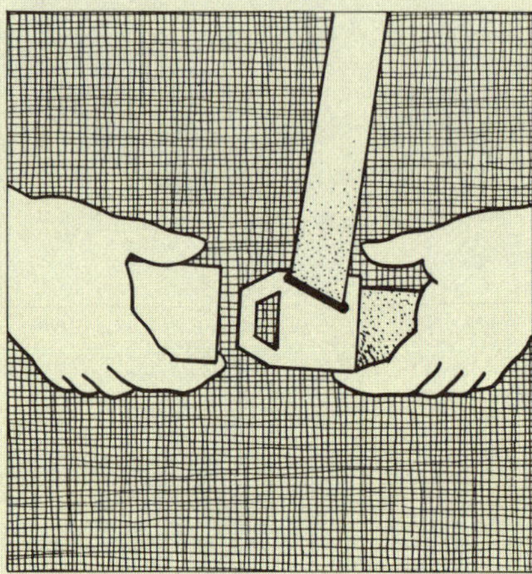

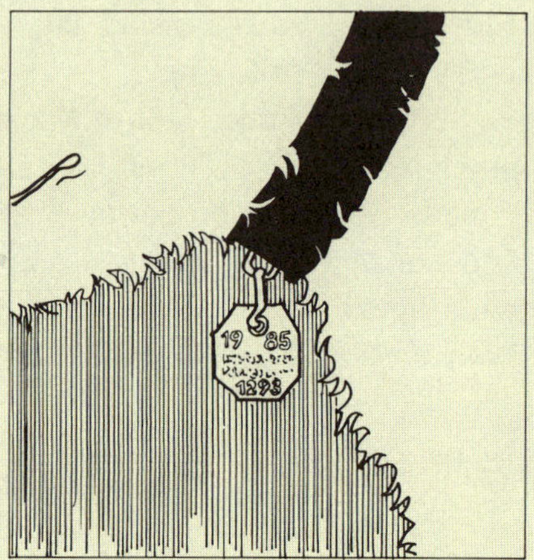

These pictures illustrate some of the services that are provided by local governments. Name each of these services and write a sentence or two explaining how the government gets money to pay for them.

Using What You Have Learned

Think of two government services and two laws not shown in the pictures. For each,

1. name the law or service,
2. write why it is important to you.

2

How Did Canada Become a Country?

When we look at a map of Canada, we see one country divided into ten provinces and two territories. But did you know that the map has not always looked like that? It has changed many times over many years. In fact, the map that we have today didn't exist until 1949.

When settlers first came from Europe about 400 years ago, Canada was not a country. The federal, provincial or territorial, and local governments that we have today did not exist. Canada's native people had their own ways of **governing** themselves. Later, settlers came to Canada and started **colonies**. They gradually introduced ideas about government from their homelands. They did not try to use the native people's ways of governing. Over many years, the government we have today grew from the government of the early **colonists**. This chapter tells the story of how Canada changed over the years and became a country with ten provinces and two territories.

This picture was drawn by a Canadian artist to celebrate Canada Day in 1983.

Government for Colonists

People from Europe started colonies in Canada in the early 1600s. These colonists hunted, farmed and fished for their own food. They built their own homes, made their own clothes and sold their goods in small shops. Although they lived very independently, they did not have a **democracy**. A democracy is a type of government that allows the people to make their own laws and decisions. The early colonists did not have any say in their government. Even if they did not like the laws and taxes, they could not change them.

For example, the colony of New France was governed by a **council**. Although the members lived in New France, they were appointed by the government in France. The council made the laws for the French colonists. It decided what taxes the people should pay. The council also told merchants what prices they could charge in their shops and how much money they could make.

In Nova Scotia, a **governor** and council members lived in the colony. But these people were appointed by Great Britain. They decided on laws and taxes for the colony. As Nova Scotia grew, the colonists wanted to have a say in their government. They wanted a democracy. The colonists demanded the **right** to **elect representatives** to speak for them in the government. So in 1758, Britain allowed Nova Scotians to elect representatives and have a democratic government.

At this time Britain and France were fighting a war. At the end of the war the French colonies in Canada were given to Britain. Britain later gave people in all its colonies—English and French—the right to elect representatives.

- Why did the colonists want a democratic government?

Above: Colonist Louis Hébert sows seeds on the land he has just cleared. Where might he have obtained these seeds?

The English begin to build Halifax in 1749. What kinds of problems do you think the builders faced?

Above: Jean Talon was a member of the council of New France. Here he is pictured in 1672, studying plans for a ship at a shipyard in Quebec. Why was the shipbuilding industry important to New France?

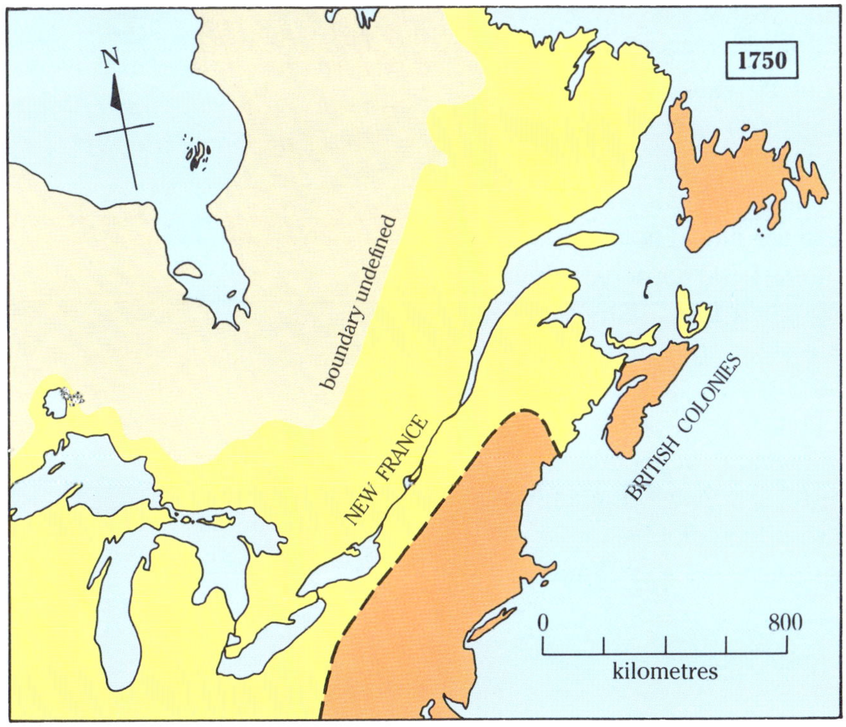

This map shows New France and the British colonies in 1750.

Government for Canadians

By 1860, there were eight British colonies. In the east there were five colonies: Newfoundland, Nova Scotia, New Brunswick, Prince Edward Island and the Province of Canada. Farther west, separated from the five eastern colonies, there were three more colonies: Red River, British Columbia and Vancouver Island.

As you can see on the map, the five eastern colonies were close together. Many people in those colonies were talking about forming one country. They wanted to **unite**. But they did not consider uniting with the western colonies. At that time there was no railway across the country and there was very little communication between east and west.

The 1850s had been good years for many people in the eastern colonies. They had grown crops on rich soil. They had cut lumber from forests and hauled fish from the ocean. Many people had moved to the colonies. Cities, such as Montreal and Toronto, were growing very quickly. Factories were being built. Messages and news were travelling from town to town through the electric telegraph. Railway companies were laying hundreds and hundreds of kilometres of track across the colonies.

By 1860, the colonists were interested in uniting. The people wanted to link the railways in the Province of Canada with railways in New Brunswick and Nova Scotia. Then each colony could send its products to the other colonies.

The colonists also wanted to be part of a country that could grow westward. Most of the good farmland in the Province of Canada had already been claimed. Farmers hoped that their children would be able to find new land in the west.

The colonists were also afraid they might be attacked by the United States. They thought they would be safer if they united. Britain agreed and encouraged the colonists to unite.

However, it was a lot easier to talk about forming one country than to do it. The people in the colonies had different ways of life.

Nova Scotia and New Brunswick were the oldest colonies. Many people lived in older towns with large homes and gardens, schools, theatres and many stores. Both colonies had busy seaports. The people sold lumber and wooden sailing ships to other countries. Nova Scotia also had good farms and fishing.

In contrast, the people in Newfoundland were poor. The thin soil was not good for farming. Newfoundland depended almost completely on fishing. Newfoundlanders traded their fish mainly for goods from Britain. They did not trade with the colonies in Canada. Sometimes the people did not catch many fish, and sometimes they could not sell the fish they did catch.

Above: Halifax, Nova Scotia, was a busy seaport by the 1850s. How do you think the shipping industry helped the people of Halifax?

Below: *By the 1860s Montreal was a large city with many shops and services. What might you see if you walked down a Montreal street at that time?*

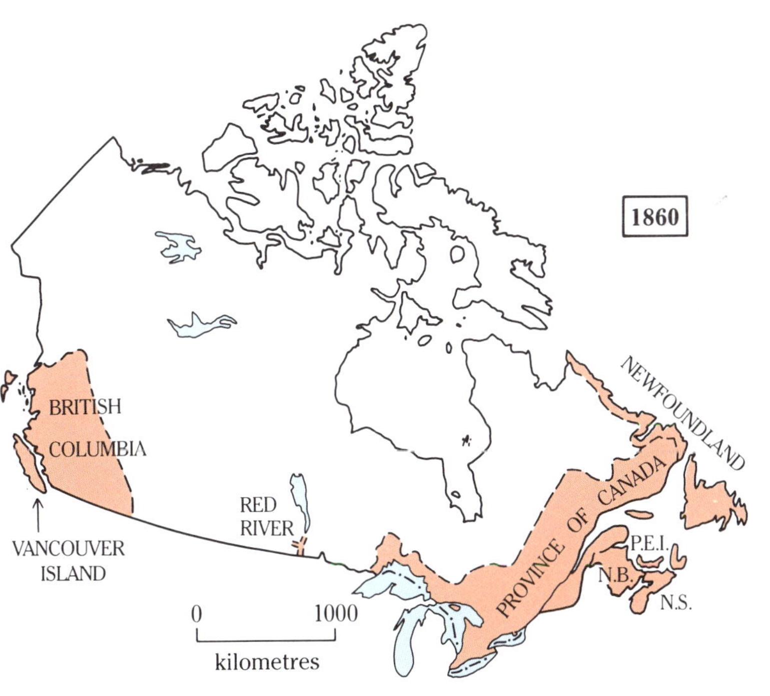

Left: This map shows the British colonies in 1860. The five eastern colonies wanted to unite.

Fathers of Confederation

In 1864, representatives from all five eastern colonies met first in Charlottetown, Prince Edward Island, and later in Quebec. We call these men the Fathers of Confederation. They wrote the *BNA Act*, which made Canada one country with four provinces. The picture above shows some of the Fathers of Confederation arriving in Charlottetown.

After 1867, the Fathers of Confederation continued to work hard for their country. One of them, John A. Macdonald, became Canada's first **prime minister**. Another, Charles Tupper, became Canada's sixth prime minister. Several Fathers of Confederation became **premiers**, or heads of provinces.

In Prince Edward Island, most of the people were farmers. They grew enough food for their own needs and were quite independent. They did not need to trade with the other colonies. The people of Prince Edward Island, like most of the people of Newfoundland, lived on an island and seldom visited other colonies.

The largest colony was the Province of Canada. The people farmed, fished, logged the forests and worked in factories. The Province of Canada had two parts—Canada West and Canada East. Like the people in the other colonies, the colonists in Canada West were mainly English Canadians. But the people in Canada East were mainly French Canadians. The two groups spoke different languages and attended different kinds of schools and churches.

The leaders from the five eastern colonies (Newfoundland, Nova Scotia, New Brunswick, Prince Edward Island and the Province of Canada) knew that it would not be easy to form one country. They knew that the people in each colony would still want the freedom to keep their own ways of life.

After many meetings, the leaders decided it would be best for

the colonies to join together in one country. This country would be made up of separate provinces. The leaders called this union of the colonies **Confederation.**

This picture shows the Fathers of Confederation and several other people who helped Canada become a nation. Why might it be difficult for this group to agree on how Confederation would work?

The leaders discussed how Confederation would work. There would be a federal government for everyone in the country. The federal government would make some laws and provide some services for everyone. For example, the federal government would be responsible for defending Canada against enemies and for trading with other countries. As well, each province would have its own government, laws and services. For example, provinces would be responsible for education and hospitals.

- What disadvantages might there be if each province looked after certain needs and services?

Canada's First Prime Minister

As a child, John A. Macdonald moved from Scotland to Canada with his parents. The family was poor. John Macdonald worked hard and became a lawyer when he grew up. When he was 29, he was elected to the government of the Province of Canada.

Macdonald was not a great speaker, but he loved to meet and talk with people. Many people thought that the colonies would never have formed a single country without him.

Macdonald was one of the Fathers of Confederation. He wrote much of the *BNA Act.* On July 1, 1867, he became Canada's first prime minister, the leader of the federal government. Macdonald said that no one had ever loved a country better than he loved Canada.

Confederation seemed to be the best way the people could unite and still be independent. The French settlers in Canada East, for example, could be part of the country. But they could still have their own language, religion, schools and laws. Even so, two of the colonies—Prince Edward Island and Newfoundland—decided not to join Confederation. The colonists on these islands felt isolated from the other colonies. They did not want to help pay for railways in the other colonies.

To create the new country of Canada, the leaders wrote a **constitution**. A constitution contains a set of rules for running or governing the country. That constitution was called the *British North America Act,* or the *BNA Act* for short.

- Many clubs and groups have constitutions. Why is a constitution important?

When Britain passed the *BNA Act,* a country was born. On July 1, 1867, cheering Canadians gathered to hear the announcement: they had a new country called Canada. Ottawa became the **capital** of the country. John A. Macdonald became Canada's first prime minister.

The new country of Canada had four provinces: New Brunswick, Nova Scotia, Ontario and Quebec. On the map you can see that the Province of Canada had been divided. Canada West became Ontario, and Canada East became Quebec. The *BNA Act* also allowed the provinces to create local governments to provide services and make laws for communities. So right from the start, Canada became a country with local, provincial and federal governments.

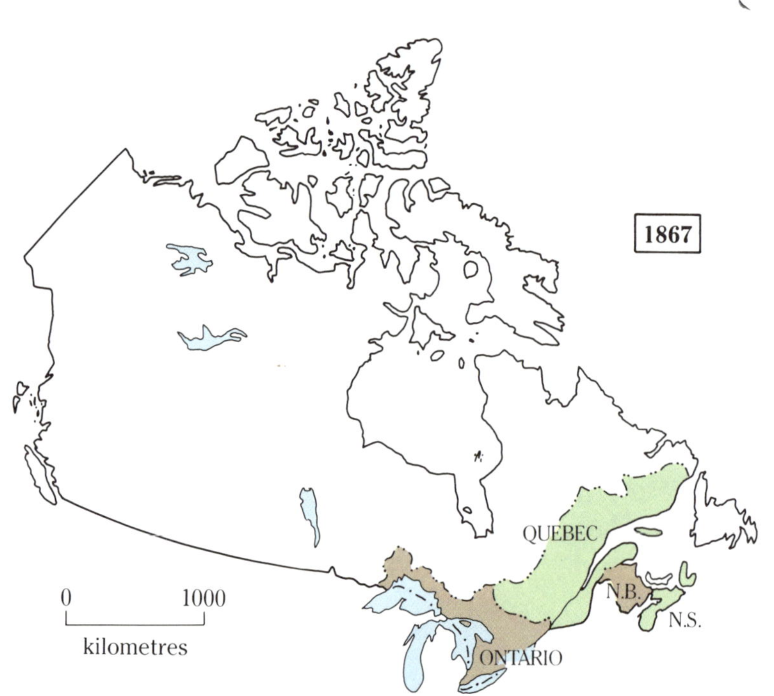

Right: This map shows the four provinces in the new country of Canada in 1867. The provinces included Ontario, Quebec, New Brunswick and Nova Scotia.

Canada Grows and Changes

The *BNA Act* created the country of Canada. But it was not the country we have today. After 1867, many more people came to this land. Times changed. Needs changed. So the country changed, too. Let's look at a few of the important years in the growth of Canada. The maps and photographs on the following pages show how the country changed as new provinces and territories became part of Canada.

Below: This map shows how Canada looked when Manitoba and the North-West Territories joined the country. The new province of Manitoba included the Red River Colony. Before 1870, that land was governed by the Hudson's Bay Company.

1870: Manitoba and the North-West Territories Join Canada

Above: Native Indians formed a large part of the population of the North-West Territories in 1870.

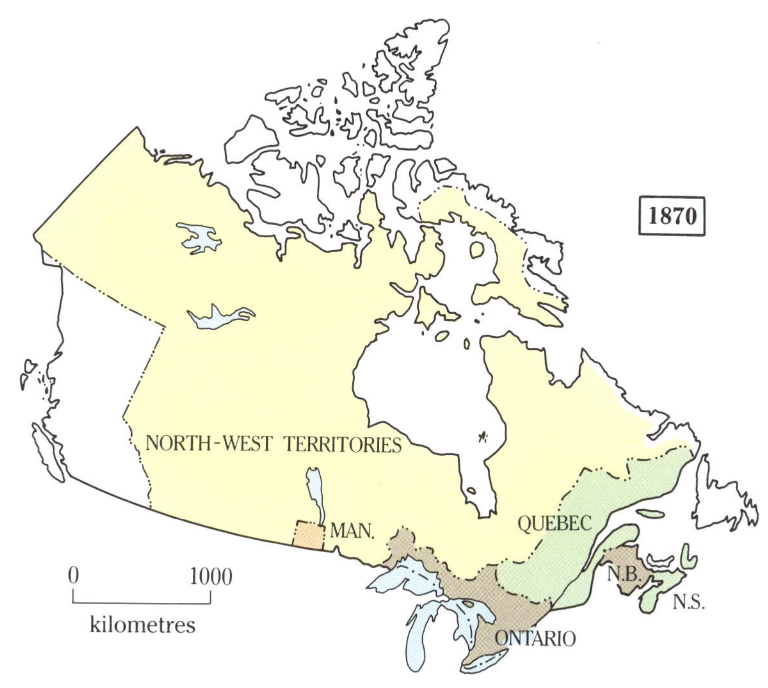

In the 1800s, many farms like this one were located along the Red River in Manitoba.

1871: British Columbia Joins Canada

Right: The colonies of Vancouver Island and British Columbia had united in 1866 to form one colony called British Columbia. When British Columbia joined Canada in 1871, the country finally extended from the Atlantic Ocean to the Pacific Ocean.

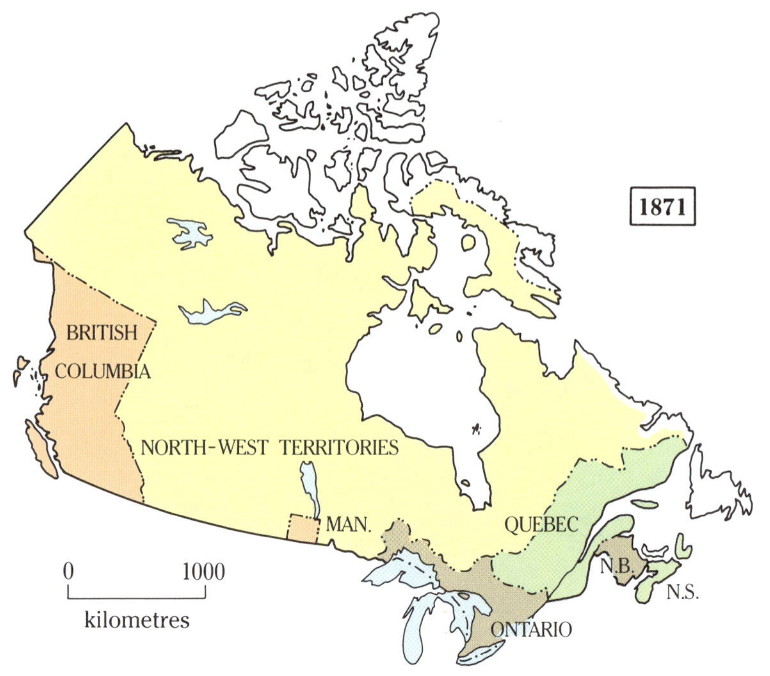

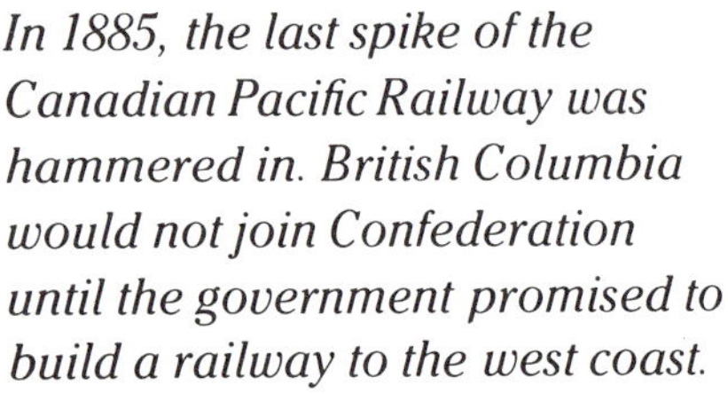

In 1885, the last spike of the Canadian Pacific Railway was hammered in. British Columbia would not join Confederation until the government promised to build a railway to the west coast.

Above: A gold digger works at a mine in British Columbia. The discovery of gold in the 1850s brought many people to British Columbia and Vancouver Island.

1873:
Prince Edward Island Joins Canada

Right: This map shows Canada when Prince Edward Island joined the country.

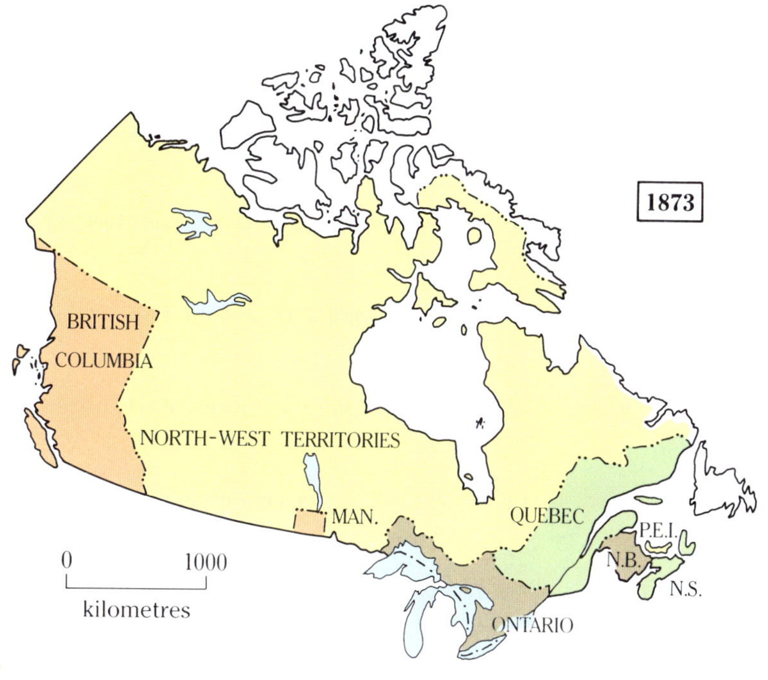

Left: Most of the people on Prince Edward Island were farmers when the colony joined Canada in 1873.

Above: Canada offered Prince Edward Island a year-round ferry service to and from the mainland if the colony joined Confederation.

1880:
The Arctic Islands Join Canada

Right: This map shows how Canada looked when the Arctic Islands became part of the North-West Territories. By this time the District of Keewatin had been formed and was governed by Manitoba.

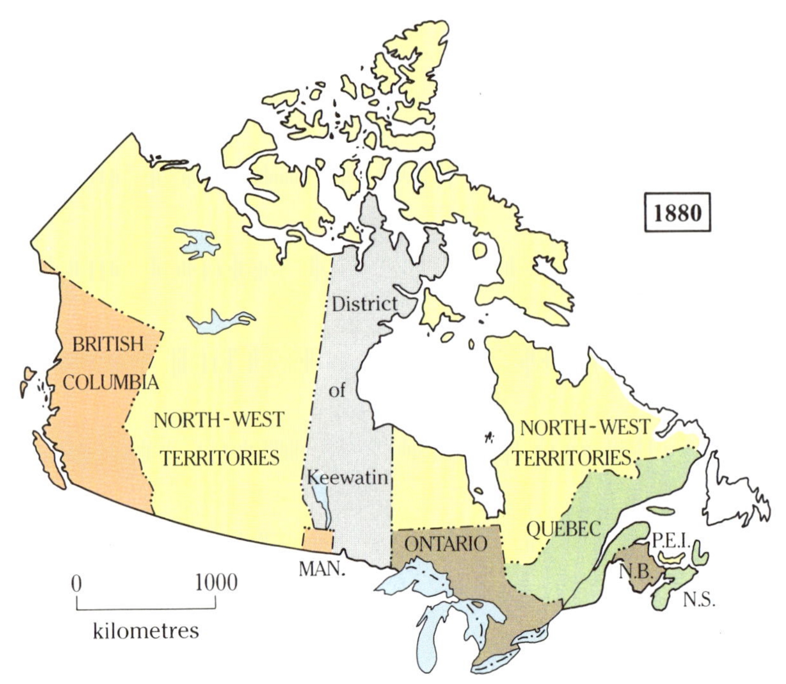

Most people living on the Arctic Islands were Inuit. This picture shows an Inuit family sitting on an ice platform inside their igloo.

1898: The Yukon Joins Canada

Right: In 1898 the Yukon became a separate territory. Before then it had been part of the North-West Territories.

Native Indians formed a large part of the population of the Yukon.

People hoping to find gold travelled in single file over the Chilkoot Pass on their way to the Yukon. So many people moved to the Yukon during the 1890s gold rush that it became a separate territory.

1905: Alberta and Saskatchewan Join Canada

Right: This map shows how Canada looked when Alberta and Saskatchewan joined the country. Notice that "Northwest Territories" was no longer spelled with a hyphen.

Left: Many settlers arrived on the Canadian Pacific Railway to farm the prairies. Here a settler milks the family cow.

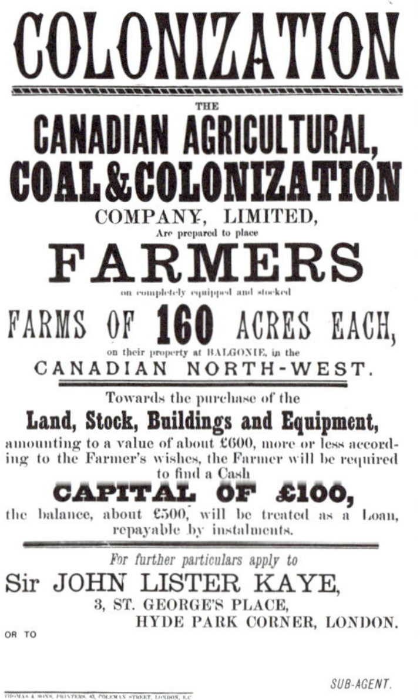

COLONIZATION

THE

CANADIAN AGRICULTURAL, COAL & COLONIZATION COMPANY, LIMITED,

Are prepared to place

FARMERS

on completely equipped and stocked

FARMS OF 160 ACRES EACH,

on their property at BALGONIE, in the

CANADIAN NORTH-WEST.

Towards the purchase of the

Land, Stock, Buildings and Equipment,

amounting to a value of about £600, more or less according to the Farmer's wishes, the Farmer will be required to find a Cash

CAPITAL OF £100,

the balance, about £500, will be treated as a Loan, repayable by instalments.

For further particulars apply to

Sir JOHN LISTER KAYE,
3, ST. GEORGE'S PLACE,
HYDE PARK CORNER, LONDON.

OR TO

SUB-AGENT.

THOMAS & SONS, PRINTERS, 83, COLEMAN STREET, LONDON, E.C.

Right: The federal government and some private companies offered free or cheap land to anyone interested in settling on the prairies.

1949: Newfoundland Joins Canada

Right: When Newfoundland joined Canada the country looked exactly as it does today. There are now ten provinces and two territories.

Fishing has always been an important industry in Newfoundland. Here some workers are loading salt codfish for export to Portugal in 1949.

Above: For hundreds of years many Newfoundlanders have lived in small fishing villages like this one along the coast.

Indian Government

Past and Present

Indian people have lived in Canada for thousands of years. The way they have governed themselves has varied from **tribe** to tribe. In the past, some Indians were governed by a chief, while others were governed by a council. Sometimes the chief or **councillors** inherited their positions, and sometimes they were chosen for their abilities.

As more and more settlers moved into Canada, the British made agreements, called **treaties**, with some of the Indians. Under these treaties, the Indians gave up their claim to large areas of land. In return, the British paid the Indians some money and set aside land, called **reserves**, for their use. After Confederation, Canada made several similar treaties with some other Indian groups and also provided schools or teachers for the reserves.

In 1874 the Plains Indians signed a treaty with the Canadian government. Indians from several tribes attended this important event. They included the Blackfoot, the Bloods, the Sarcees and the Stonies.

Not all reserves were created under treaties, and not all Indians live on reserves. But most Indians on reserves today are organized as **bands**. These bands usually elect chiefs and councillors to look after the affairs of the bands. For example, the council may make some laws for the reserve and manage the band's property and most of its money. But the government of Canada still guarantees Indian education and health care.

Some Indian bands today are becoming more independent. They are beginning to control things like Indian education. They also want the right to collect taxes and to control their land and resources.

Because Canada did not sign treaties with all the Indians, there are still many **land claims** to be worked out. Agreement on these land claims will help the Indians work towards greater **self-government.**

Like other governments in Canada, Indian government has been changing. It will likely change still more in the future.

This picture shows the opening moments of the first Premiers' Conference on Native Rights, held in 1984. Indian leaders and government officials from across Canada attended the conference.

A New Constitution for Canada

You have read that Britain passed the *BNA Act* in 1867. Canada then had its own constitution, or rules for running the country. For the next 115 years, Canada was still tied to Britain in another way. Canadians had never agreed on how they could *change* their constitution. So any changes they wanted to make had to be approved by Britain.

For about 55 years our government leaders tried to agree on a way to change Canada's constitution. Finally, they decided that in general changes must be approved by the federal government and seven provincial governments that **represent** at least half the population in all provinces.

Then, in 1982, the new *Constitution Act* created an all-Canadian constitution. It still included the old *BNA Act,* but renamed it the *Constitution Act, 1867.* It included a plan of the way Canadians would make changes to the constitution in the future. It also included another section called the Charter of Rights and Freedoms. This section is very important to Canadians.

The Charter of Rights and Freedoms guarantees everyone fair treatment. No one can say that you are too young, too old, too light-skinned or too dark-skinned to be treated fairly by the government and its laws. The charter also says that you are:

- free to choose your religion
- free to say what you think
- free to go to meetings of any kind
- free to join clubs or groups
- free to move anywhere in Canada
- free to work in any province

The Queen signs the Canadian Constitution as the prime minister looks on. Why do you think this was an important moment for Canadians?

Although you have these freedoms, you cannot do whatever you want. For example, you can practise your own religion, but you cannot stop other people from practising theirs. You can say what you think, but you cannot spread lies or urge people to kill others. You can join a club and hold meetings, but your group cannot riot or break the law. As you see, your freedom is limited. You are not free to hurt others or break the law.

The Charter of Rights and Freedoms also guarantees that Canadian **citizens** have the right to **vote** in **elections** and the right to try to become elected representatives in government.

Although Canadians had many of these rights all along, they had never been written down. Now the Charter of Rights and Freedoms makes sure that you and your family will continue to have these important rights.

- Which of these rights is most important to you and your family?

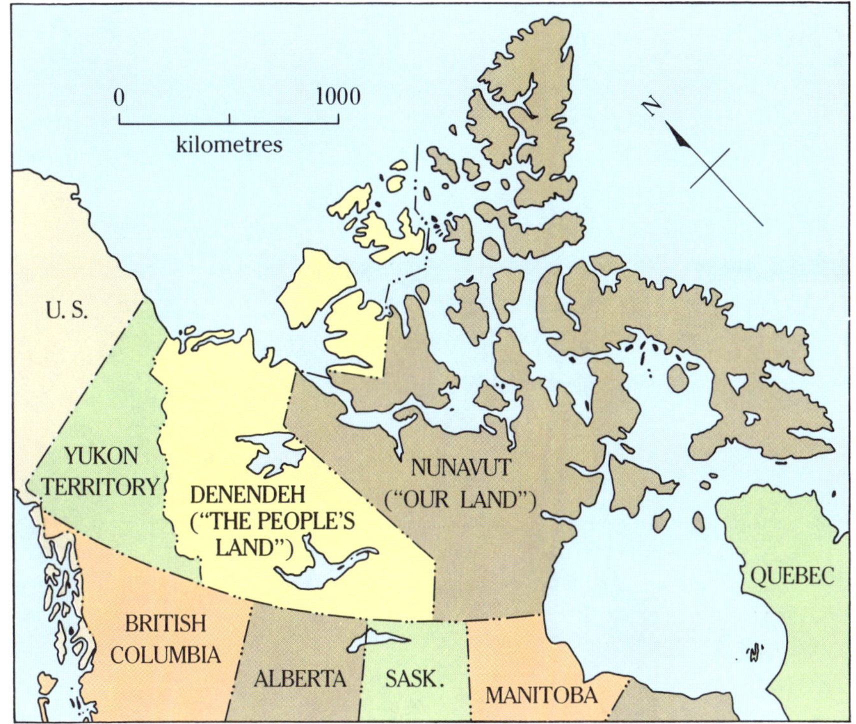

This map shows the division of the Northwest Territories proposed in 1987. Nunavut *means "Our Land" in the Inuit language.* Denendeh *means "The People's Land" in the Dene language. Why might these be good names for the new territories?*

Canada: A Changing Country

Settlers from Europe first lived here in colonies. Soon they wanted to elect representatives so that they could have a say in their own democratic government. Eventually all the colonists joined together in one country so that they could help each other. Together, they could do things they couldn't easily do alone. Confederation gave the people one government for the whole country. It also gave Canada provinces with their own governments so that each province could look after its own special needs. The provinces allowed local governments to look after some of the local needs and services.

Canada and its government are always changing. Since 1867, Canada has gained the territories and several provinces. Some provinces have become larger, and the territories have become smaller. In 1985, the government of Canada announced another possible change. The Northwest Territories may be divided into two new territories in the future.

You can see that the story of government in Canada is a long one. It hasn't always been a peaceful or a happy story. People had different needs and different ideas. They often argued about what kind of government they should have and what work it should do. Over the years, Canadians have made many changes in their government. But out of it all has come the country we have today.

You will never come to the end of the story of Canada's government. Even when you are grown up, the story will still be going on because government will still be changing.

MAKING A DECISION

Should You Always Say What You Think?

The teacher turned to the class. "I have a question for you. This morning we read about Canada's Charter of Rights and Freedoms. It says that people in Canada are free to say what they think. Does that mean that people can *always* say what they think? Let's discuss the things we say here in class."

Maria said, "We have to say what we think, or we'd never have class discussions." Another student said that hearing other people's opinions was a good way to learn things. The teacher asked the other students what they thought.

Shawna said, "We probably shouldn't say things that are untrue. Telling lies can cause trouble for other people." Another student pointed out that people sometimes said untrue things without meaning to.

"Then we shouldn't say something that we *know* is untrue," Shawna replied.

Ilsa suggested that the students should not say hurtful things.

"But sometimes you can't help it," said Noel. "If I tell you that your face is dirty, your feelings might be hurt. But if it's true, I should be free to say it."

Then the class talked about saying things that others disagreed with. Most of the students thought that they should be free to give their opinions, even if other people disagreed.

"What if I disagreed?" the teacher asked.

"We'd get into trouble," said Marc. The students laughed.

Two students are having a discussion. Why might you decide not to say what you think in some discussions?

Jon said, "Even if you disagree, we should say what we think. After all, you might be wrong and we might be right. Or we might have different opinions on things."

The teacher asked, "What should we decide? Do you think you should be free to say whatever you want in class? Or are there some limits on your freedom?"

"I think we should say what we think, unless we know it's untrue," said Amy. After further discussion, the students decided to follow her suggestion.

- Should students in your class always say what they think?

CHAPTER CHECKUP

Recalling the Main Ideas

Imagine that time machines really exist. With the flick of a switch, you could go backwards in time. The following years are some of the ones you might like to visit:

1. 1758
2. 1864
3. 1867
4. 1870
5. 1871
6. 1873
7. 1880
8. 1898
9. 1905
10. 1949
11. 1982

Write down each year. Then write what events you might see in that year. Choose the events from the list below. More than one event happened during some of the years.

— Canada has a new, all-Canadian constitution.
— Canada becomes a country with four provinces.
— British Columbia joins Canada.
— The colony of Nova Scotia gains the right to have a democratic government with elected representatives.
— Saskatchewan and Alberta join Canada.
— The Yukon becomes part of Canada.
— John A. Macdonald becomes Canada's first prime minister.
— The Charter of Rights and Freedoms becomes part of Canada's constitution.
— Representatives from five eastern colonies meet in Quebec to write a constitution to create Canada.
— Newfoundland joins Canada.
— Britain passes the *BNA Act.*
— Manitoba and the North-West Territories join Canada.
— The Arctic Islands become part of Canada.
— Prince Edward Island joins Canada.

Using What You Have Learned

After 1867, Canada gained more provinces. Choose any one of these provinces. Write the name of the province and answer each of the following questions:

1. How might the people in the province have benefited from joining Canada?
2. How might the rest of the country have benefited when this province became part of Canada?

3

What Does an M.P. Do?

In the mid-1980s, there were about 25 million people in Canada. Imagine everybody standing together, shoulder to shoulder. There would be enough people to form *two* lines along the railway track from Vancouver, British Columbia, to Halifax, Nova Scotia!

That's a lot of people. All these people work at different jobs, attend different churches and enjoy different things in their free time. Some are young and some are old. But they all need help and services from the government. That means their representatives—the people Canadians elect to speak for them in government—have a very big job to do. In this chapter, we'll look at the work federal representatives do for Canadians.

In 1985 there were 282 federal representatives. A representative represents the people who live in a voting area called a **constituency**. A constituency may be a small area, like part of a city. It may also be a huge area, like the Yukon Territory. The people who live in each constituency are called **constituents**. Canada has not always had 282 representatives. The number changes as the population changes.

Representatives from all the constituencies gather in Ottawa, the capital of Canada. They meet in a set of buildings called the **Parliament Buildings**. The word "parliament" means "a talk," and our representatives talk over the country's business when they meet. The representatives themselves are called **Members of Parliament,** or **M.P.s** for short. The M.P.s from all the constituencies in Canada form a group called the **House of Commons**.

Members of Parliament enter the Parliament Buildings to discuss the country's business. Why might the news media be taking pictures of the members?

An M.P. Helps Her Constituents

If you could spend a day watching an M.P. in the Parliament Buildings, you would learn a lot about how the federal government works. Imagine you are watching Jane Penney, an M.P. from a city in Newfoundland. Although she's not a real M.P., the work you will read about is what many M.P.s do.

It's 8:15 a.m. Jane Penney enters her office in the Confederation Building, one of the Parliament Buildings in Ottawa.

Timothy Warren, her member's assistant, is already there. A member's assistant is someone who is hired to help an M.P. For example, Timothy helps Jane answer the mail; he arranges meetings and gets the information she needs to do her job.

At her desk, the first set of papers Jane picks up is marked "URGENT." It arrived late yesterday from her other office—the constituency office in Newfoundland. There she has another assistant, Sylvia Tucker. Sylvia meets with the constituents and passes messages on to Jane in Ottawa. Sylvia has attached a note to this urgent set of papers. It reads:

> Mr. Schmidt's 70-year-old mother became very ill during her holiday in Germany. She is now in hospital there. Yesterday she phoned Mr. Schmidt to say she must have an operation this week. Mr. Schmidt wants to fly to Germany at once, but he does not have a **passport**. It will take about three weeks to get one. He has asked for your help in getting a passport much sooner.

Jane knows it is important for Mr. Schmidt to have a passport, which will allow him to travel in other countries. She checks through the set of papers Sylvia has sent. It includes a photograph of Mr. Schmidt and the information she'll need to help him get a passport.

Jane Penney discusses a problem with her assistant, Timothy Warren. What are some of the ways an assistant might help an M.P.?

"I'm going to handle this job personally," Jane tells Timothy, as she leaves her office. "I want to talk to the passport people myself."

Like all M.P.s, Jane hears from many constituents who want her help. An elderly man may ask her to find out why he has not received his pension cheque—the money the government pays to people over 65. A family that has just moved to Canada may not understand our laws and may ask her for advice. A Girl Guide company may want pictures of the Parliament Buildings to take on a visit to the United States.

Jane does as much as she can, especially for people with urgent problems, like Mr. Schmidt. But she doesn't have enough time to help all her constituents personally. Often she asks her member's assistants, Sylvia and Timothy, to help her constituents.

Just before 10:30 a.m., Jane returns to her office. "Mr. Schmidt will have his passport in 24 hours," she tells Timothy. "He can fly to Germany the next day if he wants to."

- How might your M.P. help you or your family?

An M.P. Works with Her Party

Jane picks up another set of papers from her desk and hurries off. She is going to meet with other M.P.s in her **political party**. A political party is a group of people who share many of the same ideas about what the government should be doing.

There are three main parties in the House of Commons. They are called the Progressive Conservative Party, the Liberal Party and the New Democratic Party. After an election, the party with the most M.P.s usually becomes the **Government party**. Its leader becomes the prime minister of Canada. The other parties become the **Opposition.** The leader of the largest of these parties is called the leader of the Opposition.

Jane is a member of the Opposition. Two or three mornings a week, she meets with other M.P.s in her party. This group is called the **caucus**. Today the caucus is discussing a new **bill** the Government party has introduced. A bill is a suggested law. It will become a law if more than half of the M.P.s agree to it.

The bill is supposed to make fishing safer. It says that only large fishing boats can be used on the ocean. Opposition members do not agree with the bill. They are not against making fishing safer, but they know that many people cannot afford bigger boats. If the bill becomes a law, then many people may be out of work.

Jane and her party agree to question the Government party about the bill later in the day.

- Who is the M.P. in your constituency? What party does your M.P. belong to? Does your M.P. belong to the Government party or the Opposition?

"Firsts" in the House of Commons

When Canada was a new country, no women or native people were elected to the House of Commons.

In 1921 the first woman was elected to the House of Commons. Agnes Macphail was a school teacher. She was elected as M.P. for a constituency in Ontario.

In 1968, the first native Indian to become an M.P. was Len Marchand. He represented a constituency in British Columbia. Marchand had been an agricultural researcher.

The first Inuit in the House of Commons was Peter Ittinuar. In 1979, he was elected as M.P. for a constituency in the Northwest Territories. He had worked as a professor, broadcaster and film maker.

Today Canadian citizens of any race or sex may be elected M.P.s in the House of Commons.

How a Citizen Becomes a Member of Parliament

The Nomination

Members of a party in a constituency ask a citizen to try to become the party's **candidate**. A candidate is someone who wants to become the M.P. Usually other people in the same party also want to be candidates. There is a **nomination** meeting. The person who gets the most votes is **nominated** to be the candidate. Other parties nominate other candidates.

Below: Candidates who have been nominated speak to their supporters.

The Campaign

The candidate **campaigns** by meeting people in the constituency and telling them what he or she would do as their M.P. People in the party put up signs, talk to constituents and place ads in the newspapers so that lots of voters know who the candidate is.

A campaign worker gives out leaflets to the voters in the constituency.

A member of the candidate's party talks to a voter by phone.

A party member puts up a sign for the candidate.

The Election

Canadian citizens who are 18 years or older may vote in federal elections. People vote by secretly marking an X beside the name of the candidate they want. The candidate who receives the most votes is the M.P. until the next election.

An electoral officer puts a ballot into the ballot box on election day.

An M.P. Listens to the People

Just before noon, Jane Penney returns to her office. Timothy is opening a big pile of mail.

"Here are several more letters from your constituency, Jane," he says. "Many people want you to speak against the new bill on the size of fishing boats."

Jane just has time to read over the letters before lunch. She is pleased so many people have written to tell her what they think. Whenever she can find out what some of her constituents think, she can discuss their ideas with her party. Then the party members decide what they might do about these suggestions.

- If you mail a letter to your M.P. in Ottawa, you don't need a stamp. Why do you think no postage is needed?

At 1:00 p.m., Jane welcomes three members of a Newfoundland fishing association to her office. They have come to Ottawa to see about selling more fish. They have also come to talk with Jane about the new bill. They do not want any law that would make them buy bigger boats.

Members of a Newfoundland fishing association discuss a new bill with Jane Penney. They do not agree with the bill and explain their reasons to Jane. Why is it important for Jane to listen to their views?

One of the members explains, "We realize that a few small fishing boats have had some bad accidents. That's why the Government party wants us to use bigger boats on the ocean. But our association has just finished a study of the accidents. We now think many accidents happened because the boats were overfilled, not because they were too small."

"We think that we are safe on the ocean in our small boats if they are not overfilled with fish," says another member, handing Jane a copy of the study. "Besides, not many of our members can afford to buy bigger boats."

"I will be asking about the new bill this afternoon," says Jane. "Thank you for coming to see me and for bringing in this new information." She suggests they go over to the Centre Block, another of the Parliament Buildings. There they can hear her raise the question.

The Cabinet

The **Cabinet** is a group of people, mainly M.P.s, chosen by the prime minister. The members are called cabinet ministers. There is usually at least one cabinet minister chosen from each province in Canada. The prime minister is the head of the Cabinet.

Most cabinet ministers are in charge of departments. For example, there is a department of agriculture and a department of defence. Each has a cabinet minister. Some cabinet ministers are in charge of a special area, like tourism, within a department.

The cabinet ministers work together to decide on the programs and policies for each department. They also decide which bills to introduce to the House of Commons. The Cabinet is the most powerful group in the House of Commons.

An M.P. Speaks in the House of Commons

Soon Jane hurries off to the Centre Block herself. She joins other M.P.s. They meet regularly in the House of Commons **chamber** to discuss subjects that are important to Canadians. They also make decisions about things like new laws and new taxes.

Daily meetings of the House of Commons are called **sittings**. Everybody in Canada is represented by an M.P., so a sitting of the House of Commons really involves all Canadians.

At one end of the House of Commons chamber sits the **Speaker**. The Speaker is like a referee in a soccer game or a chairperson at a school meeting. The Speaker keeps order and makes sure the M.P.s follow the rules during sittings.

The prime minister and other members of the Government party sit on the Speaker's right. **Cabinet ministers** sit close to the prime minister. They are M.P.s chosen by the prime minister to be in charge of important resources or services, such as agriculture, fishing, health and transportation.

The leader and members of the Opposition sit on the Speaker's left. The Opposition has a very important job. Its members watch and question Government party members to make sure they are doing the best job they can for Canadians.

In a balcony high above the M.P.s, the three members of the Newfoundland fishing association watch the M.P.s during the question period. This is the time when M.P.s question the cabinet ministers on what the Government party is doing.

The members of the fishing association notice that some of the M.P.s and cabinet ministers speak in English and others speak in French. There are translators for both languages.

- Why are both French and English spoken in sittings of the House of Commons?

When Jane stands up to speak, the members of the fishing association lean forward with special interest. They notice she does not talk the way she did in her office. Instead she follows the rules of the House of Commons and talks in a formal way.

"Mr. Speaker," Jane says, "my question is for the Minister of Fisheries and Oceans. A Newfoundland fishing association and many of my constituents think that the new bill on the size of ocean fishing boats is unfair. Few of them can afford to buy bigger boats. Most of them think that bigger boats are not necessary anyway. Must the minister support a bill that is unfair and unnecessary? Must the minister force people out of work?"

On the other side of the room, a cabinet minister, the Minister of Fisheries and Oceans, stands up.

"Mr. Speaker, I wish to inform the honourable member that we do not mean to force anyone out of work. Our concern is for the safety of the people who are fishing. Is the honourable member not aware of the rising number of bad accidents with small ocean fishing boats?"

Jane stands up once more.

"Mr. Speaker, I am sadly aware of the rising number of accidents. Both my constituents and I want fishing to be safer. However, a fishing association has just finished a study of the accidents. It claims that many accidents are caused by overfilling the smaller boats. Has the minister considered this cause of the accidents? Perhaps we need a bill about how much should be put into boats, not about how big they should be."

"Mr. Speaker," says the Minister of Fisheries and Oceans, "my staff and I have studied the accidents carefully, but we have not seen the results of this new study. We will need time to review the new information."

After the question period, Jane hurries away. She wants to make a call to Newfoundland. From her office in the Confederation Building, she phones Sylvia at the constituency office.

"I've taken care of Mr. Schmidt's passport," Jane says. "Please let him know he'll have it tomorrow. And you can tell people that I questioned the cabinet minister about the fishing boat bill. I will be telling all my constituents about it in my next newsletter. Oh, and Sylvia, I'll be making a short trip home to Newfoundland on the 27th. If anyone wants to see me, please set up appointments. See you then."

The Speaker sits at the far end of the House of Commons chamber. Where might you sit if you were visiting the House?

An M.P. Looks for New Ways to Solve Problems

Timothy reminds Jane of a committee meeting at 4:30 p.m. Jane works on several committees that study ways to help Canadians. M.P.s from all parties belong to these committees. One committee is looking for ways the government can help disabled people. Another is looking for ways the government can improve **trade** with other countries. One of the committees that Jane works on is looking for ways to help young Canadians find jobs. That committee is meeting this afternoon.

Jane picks up a report she hopes to read that evening. Then she hurries off to her committee meeting—Jane's last job of the day.

How a Bill Becomes Law

M.P. introduces bill

Any M.P. may introduce a bill—a suggestion for a new law. Most bills are introduced by cabinet ministers.

House of Commons discusses bill and votes three times

M.P.s from all parties discuss the bill. They ask questions and suggest changes. Some bills are changed. Some are dropped. If a bill is passed on the third vote, it goes to the **Senate**.

Senate approves bill

The Senate has members, called **senators**, from every province and territory. The prime minister appoints them. The Senate studies bills from the House of Commons. Sometimes it suggests changes. The Senate can introduce some bills of its own. It also studies important public problems like poverty.

Governor General signs bill

The **Queen of Canada** lives in Britain. She has a representative in Canada, called the **Governor General**, to do her work here. The Governor General is a Canadian. A bill does not become law until it has been signed by the Governor General. Besides signing bills, the Governor General has other work to do. For instance, the Governor General opens each **session** of the House of Commons with a speech about the work the Government party plans to do. The Governor General usually closes each session with a speech reviewing the work that has been done. The Governor General also greets important visitors from other countries and attends special events.

Bill is proclaimed law

A new law must be registered and published in the *Canada Gazette*. This publication goes to libraries across Canada. Then the law can be enforced.

An M.P. introduces a bill in the House of Commons.

The Governor General signs a bill. With her signature, the bill becomes law.

Your Representative and You

You can see what a big job M.P.s have. Each one works for a large number of people in a constituency. Many people need special help with problems like getting a passport quickly. An M.P. spends a lot of time helping and advising people personally.

When the House of Commons sits in Ottawa, M.P.s must be there to represent their constituencies. M.P.s read letters and reports from their constituents. They talk with people who phone or come to the office. M.P.s want to know how constituents feel about suggested laws, services and taxes.

M.P.s report to their constituents through meetings, phone calls, letters and newsletters. They travel from Ottawa to their constituencies several times a year. M.P.s let their constituents know how new laws might affect them.

Looking for new ways to help Canadians is another important part of an M.P.'s job. M.P.s spend much of their time working together in committees. They try to learn about Canada's problems and how to solve them.

In this chapter, you have seen that M.P.s represent Canadians in the House of Commons. Canadians elect representatives to provincial, territorial and local governments, too. Elected representatives are the people who speak and vote for you.

Selecting representatives is one of the most important jobs citizens have. It is important to nominate candidates who want to work hard. It is important to know what parties the candidates belong to and understand what they want to do. It is important to get out and vote for candidates at every election.

Once representatives are elected, Canadians have another very important job. They must tell their representatives what laws, taxes and services they want. They must tell their representatives what they think about government decisions. After all, Canada will have good government only if Canadians choose good representatives and say what they think about laws, services and taxes.

- Some Canadians choose not to vote in elections. Do you think that there should be a law that people must vote?

Pretend you are a newspaper reporter interviewing Jane Penney. What questions would you ask her about her work?

Your Elected Representatives

Canadians vote at elections to choose representatives for local, provincial or territorial, and federal governments. These elected representatives have different titles and different jobs.

At the local level, councillors or aldermen make decisions about matters that affect the community. The head of the local government is called either a mayor or a reeve. School trustees make sure that schools in the community are well run. The leader of the trustees is the Chairperson of the School Board. Local representatives are usually elected every two or three years.

Provincial or territorial representatives discuss and debate matters such as educational services, health care services and the development of businesses and industries in the province or territory. The head of the provincial government is called a premier. The head of the territorial government is called the government leader. Provincial or territorial representatives are elected whenever the government decides an election is needed. However, a provincial or territorial election must be held within at least five years of the previous election.

At the federal level, M.P.s discuss matters that are important to all Canadians. They make decisions about new laws, taxes and services. The head of the federal government is called the prime minister. Like provincial or territorial representatives, M.P.s are elected whenever the government decides to call an election. However, an election must be held within at least five years of the previous election.

GOVERNMENT	REPRESENTATIVE	LEADER
Federal	Member of Parliament	Prime Minister
Provincial	Member of the Legislative Assembly Member of the Provincial Parliament (Ontario) Member of the National Assembly (Quebec) Member of the House of Assembly (Newfoundland)	Premier
Territorial	Member of the Legislative Assembly	Government Leader
Local	Councillor or Alderman School Trustee	Mayor or Reeve Chairperson of the School Board

CHAPTER CHECKUP

Recalling the Main Ideas

Pretend that you are a member's assistant working in the Ottawa office of Jane Penney, M.P. Help Jane organize her busy day. Use the events you have read about in this chapter. Write out a schedule that shows at what times she will do her office work and attend her meetings. You will need to make up some of the times. For example, the first entry in your schedule should be:

8:30 a.m.: Constituency work—Mr. Schmidt's passport

Using What You Have Learned

These pictures illustrate some of the work that M.P.s do. For each picture,

1. describe what the M.P. is doing,
2. write a sentence or two to explain why that activity is important to Canadians.

4

What Does Government Mean to Canadians?

Imagine that you are the "Roving Reporter" on a local radio show. Your job is to question people on the street. Today you ask them, "What does government mean to you?"

Some people say, "Government means getting my mail and having police to protect me." Other people yell angrily into your microphone. They say, "Government means paying lots of taxes." Still other people say, "Government means elections. It means crowds of people with signs at city hall."

Which answer is correct? All of them are. Local, provincial or territorial, and federal governments provide services such as mail delivery and police protection. People pay taxes to these governments to pay for the services. Canadians tell the governments what they need. One way they do this is by electing representatives to speak for them. People can also tell the government about their needs through committees and **protest groups**.

In the first part of this chapter, you will look at a few of the services Canadians get for their taxes. You will see that some services have changed over time. In the second part of the chapter, you will see how the people tell the government what they need. You have already read how your M.P. represents you in the House of Commons. In this chapter, you will see how citizens speak for themselves.

Every time you mail a letter, you are using a government service. How might this service be paid for?

Government Services

When Canada was a new country, there were fewer services than there are today. People paid less tax, too. At that time, most Canadians lived in large families on farms or in small towns. They looked after themselves and their neighbours. They didn't get as much help from the government as people do today. For example, if someone became ill, the family might ask the doctor to come. In those days, most medical equipment could be packed in the doctor's bag. The doctor might be paid with a chicken and a jar of homemade jam. Compare that to today's hospital with all its costly equipment. Canadians pay taxes so that all people can have medical care.

Today Canadians receive many services from the government, and they pay a lot of taxes. But people do not all pay the same taxes. People who earn a lot of money or own a lot of property pay high taxes. People who earn less money pay lower taxes.

Canadians pay taxes to local, provincial or territorial, and federal governments. Each government uses the taxes to help the people it serves. Some of the tax money is used to pay for things like hospitals and parks. Some is used to hire people like teachers and police officers.

- Can you think of other things that tax money is used for?

Let's look at some of the people who provide government services to Canadians. First we'll look at services that have existed for many years. You will see that the workers today provide the same service, but often in quite a different way.

The picture on the far left shows a forest ranger in British Columbia in the 1930s. Rangers checked for fires during the summer, often travelling by horseback into the interior of the province. Gradually their work increased. For example, they made sure that the forest industry paid for the trees it cut. Today the job of forest ranger no longer exists. Instead, district forest managers and their staff do the work that rangers once did. Like the man pictured on the left, staff members still watch for fires. From their offices, they work with maps and computers to plan where the forest industry can cut trees.

Since 1882, communities in Canada have built public libraries that everyone can use without charge. The picture on the far left shows a library in 1920. The picture next to it shows a library in the 1980s. Early librarians chose books for the library and kept track of what was borrowed and returned. They helped people find information. Today librarians do much the same kind of work, but many libraries use computers to keep track of books.

The top picture shows judges in the early 1900s. The bottom picture shows a judge in the 1980s. Governments in Canada appoint judges to decide whether or not laws have been broken and to settle arguments. Although many laws have been changed since Canada first became a country, judges have always done the same job.

One hundred years ago, many teachers taught in one-room schools like the one shown in the top picture. Teachers often did not have any special training. Textbooks were usually the only books that students had to learn from. Today the teacher's job has not really changed, but teaching conditions have. Teachers, like the one shown in the bottom picture, are well trained. Classrooms have many different kinds of learning materials.

Some services are new ones that no one even dreamed of when Canada was young. Let's look at some of the workers who do these new jobs.

Above: When airline services came into being about 60 years ago, new government jobs were created. One of these jobs was that of air traffic controller. An air traffic controller tells pilots when and where to land their planes.

When automobiles were invented over 80 years ago, nobody thought they would ever become as common as they are today. Their widespread use has created many government jobs. Here a meter inspector checks a parking meter.

A radio host broadcasts a program in northern Canada. Why is a communications system an important government service?

You have learned about a few of the services that Canadians receive for their taxes. There are many, many more. Federal, provincial, territorial and local governments all employ people to provide services.

Government services reflect the needs of the public. Some services have existed for many years. But they have often changed because people's needs have changed or because equipment and machines have changed. Still other services are new because there are new needs.

When you grow up, the government will likely provide you with some of the same services it does now. Just as it has in the past, the government will also change some services and provide new ones. The government provides services to meet your changing needs.

- What services do you use now? How might your needs change as you get older?

Taxes

Canadians pay many different kinds of taxes to their local, provincial or territorial, and federal governments. You have already read about three of these taxes:

— income tax on all money earned
— sales tax on purchases
— property tax on land and houses

There are other taxes, too. These taxes are more "hidden" because you do not directly pay the government. For example, when someone pays for a tank of gas, some of the money goes to the government. There are taxes on tobacco, alcohol and movie tickets, too.

All together, taxes take about one half of the average Canadian family's total income. You can think of it this way: for about six months of every year, a family pays all the money it makes to the government.

Taxes—especially income tax—are the main source of money for governments. Without taxes, they couldn't provide services for Canadians.

The chart shows how one provincial government spent its tax money in 1983/84.

How British Columbia Spent Its Tax Dollars in 1983/84

Department	Millions of dollars
Health and Social Services	$3890
Education	$1730
Transportation and Communication	$ 800
Natural Resources and Primary Industries	$ 440
Protection of Persons and Property	$ 370
General Government Expenses	$ 350
Aid to Local Governments	$ 310
Other	$ 460

Communicating with Government

Canadians must let the government know what they need. In Chapter 3, you learned how your M.P. represents you in the House of Commons. Writing to your M.P. is one way to tell the government what you need. Individuals can always get in touch with their elected representatives.

Sometimes people work together as a group to let the government know their needs. They share common concerns and goals. In this part of the chapter you will learn about two ways groups of citizens communicate with government: **public committees** and protest groups.

Public Committees

Groups of citizens have always helped the government. Their help became more important as the number of Canadians grew. People may join committees set up by the government. These public committees help the government learn what the people want. For instance, one public committee might help to decide where to build a new hospital or school. Another committee might help plan a new park.

Let's look at an example of how a committee worked with its local government. Together, they were able to provide what the people needed.

The oldest Chinatown in Canada is in downtown Victoria, British Columbia. For many years, all Chinese people moving to Canada came through Victoria. By 1900, Victoria's Chinatown was the largest in the country.

Hundreds of people lived in Chinatown. They had their own stores, temples, theatres and schools. After the 1940s, many people moved from Chinatown into other parts of Victoria. By the 1960s, Chinatown looked shabby and neglected. There were few customers in its stores.

Victoria City Council wanted to improve Chinatown. For 15 years, the council studied the problems. The council tried several plans for improving the community. Nothing seemed to work because the council had not involved the people of Chinatown.

In 1979, the Victoria City Council asked a university professor, David Chuenyan Lai, to get ideas from Chinese Canadians and other people in the community. He met people who lived in Chinatown or who owned property or businesses there. He asked them what they did not like about Chinatown and what changes they wanted. Lai found people to work on committees to improve Chinatown.

Lai made up a questionnaire—a list of questions about Chinatown. He wrote about his project in the Chinese-language newspapers. He spoke at meetings of Chinatown groups. Then Lai gave the questionnaires to hundreds of people who lived or worked in Chinatown. He also gave questionnaires to tourists.

- Do you think a questionnaire is a good way to find out what people want? Why or why not?

Above: A Chinese man sells vegetables in 1898. Why do you think he is carrying the vegetables in this way?

Young children walk along a sidewalk in Victoria's Chinatown. How can you tell this picture was taken in the early 1900s?

Most of the people wanted Chinatown to be improved. But they did not want to change the old, Chinese-style streets and buildings. Most people thought it would be very hard to fix up Chinatown. Gradually, people found ways to solve the problems.

One committee made plans to paint the buildings and decorate the streets. Another committee planned a new nursing home. Another raised money to build a big Chinese arch across Chinatown's main street. This group sold thousands of two-dollar **shares** in the arch. Each **shareholder** owned a tiny bit of the arch.

One committee told city council about the work of all the other public committees. Then the council approved the projects or suggested changes. The council also helped organize and pay for some of the projects.

For over three years, everyone worked very hard. People shared their ideas, their time and their efforts. They also shared many of the costs. Landlords paid half the cost of painting their buildings. The city council asked the provincial government to pay the other half. By 1981, many of the projects were finished.

If you visited Victoria's Chinatown today you would see the results brought about by people working together. The old buildings have been repaired and redecorated. The sidewalks are decorated with large Chinese letters. There are rows of pines and flowering cherry trees. The street lights are Chinese lanterns on red posts. Even the phone booths are bright red and gold, with curved, green roofs. There's a new Chinese nursing home.

You would notice the big Chinese arch in Chinatown. It is decorated with golden dragons, and its metal chimes blow in the wind. Chinese writing on the arch says, "Working together with one heart," and "Helping each other to achieve harmony."

Today Chinatown looks much better than it did before the project. It is also a busier place. There are new shops and more people. Many of them are tourists who like to take pictures of the arch.

- If you could visit Victoria's Chinatown, what things would you like to see and do?

The city of Victoria is proud of the Chinatown project. No one forgets to mention that the people made it possible. Lai said, "Chinatown is a place for everyone in the community. Chinese Canadians and non-Chinese Canadians worked together. And they worked with the government to improve Chinatown. That was the reason for its success."

The story of Victoria's Chinatown shows that the government on its own does not always understand what people want. Elected representatives can do a better job if they get help from the people. Public committees are one way to do this. Both the government and the people can gain by working together.

A Public Committee Today

There are many public committees all across Canada. One committee in Vancouver, British Columbia, runs a recreation centre.

The Britannia Community Centre has a swimming pool, an ice rink, a gymnasium, a library, meeting rooms and offices. It is used by the people who live in the eastern part of Vancouver. Although the Vancouver City Council provides money for the centre, it does not run it. Instead, some people in the Britannia neighbourhood sit on a public committee to run the centre.

The committee chooses all the programs for the centre. It decides what equipment the centre needs. Through the public committee, the people who use the Britannia Community Centre have a say in what the centre offers.

Today a Chinese arch extends across Chinatown's main street. How might the arch help the Chinese business community?

Protest Groups

Citizens are not always able to work successfully with the government on public committees. They do not always agree with the government. Sometimes the government makes laws that citizens don't like. Sometimes it does not provide what citizens want. The public is free to speak against—or protest—the work of the government. Protests are another way of letting the government know what the public needs.

If you joined a protest you might do several things. You might march along the street carrying a sign. You might block the entrance to a building. You might camp in a park so that the bulldozers could not dig it up. You might write letters or send out newsletters. These are a few ways that people protest the work of the government.

Citizens join together to protest an important public issue. How might this group help to change a government decision?

There have always been protest groups in Canada. Even before Confederation, colonists marched on the streets to protest their form of government. They wanted elected representatives. Over the years, Canadians have protested many government decisions. For example, Canadians have protested decisions to raise sales taxes. They have spoken against the government when it wanted to close a school or build a new airport.

- Why do some people join protest groups instead of just communicating with their elected representatives?

Public protests try to change government decisions. Some public protests are successful. Some are not. Let's look at an example of a very long, but successful, public protest in Manitoba.

When Canada was a new country, the federal government did not allow women to vote. The *Election Act of Canada* read, "No woman, idiot, lunatic or child shall vote." The provincial governments did not allow women to vote either.

Although women couldn't vote, they still had to pay taxes and obey laws. Women wanted the right to vote for the representatives who spent those taxes and made those laws. They wanted to vote for representatives who would change laws. In the early 1900s, women wanted labour laws for fair treatment of women. At that time many women worked long days in factories for very low pay. To make changes in the law, women needed the right to vote.

In the 1890s, several Manitoba women formed a group to work for voting rights. Many men supported the women's group, too. For years, the group wrote newspaper articles about why women should be allowed to vote. The group also sent **petitions** to the government. These petitions were lists of the names of people who wanted women to vote. At that time, women working for the right to vote were called **suffragettes**. "Suffrage" means "the right to vote."

In the early 1900s, many Canadian women worked long days in factories like this one. Usually their pay was very low. What might these women have done to help change their working conditions?

Other women's rights groups started up, too. They tried to discuss women's rights with the government. However, Manitoba's premier would not consider new laws to help women.

In 1912, Manitoba suffragettes formed another group, the Political Equality League. This group printed pamphlets explaining why women wanted to vote. Members went to meetings and spoke to groups of all kinds. They hung banners on streetcars in Winnipeg. Hundreds of people signed petitions supporting the women.

Two years later, many of the women's rights groups met with the Political Equality League. They chose five people, led by Nellie McClung, to meet the premier of Manitoba, Sir Rodmond Roblin.

Nellie McClung was an author, a talented public speaker and a hard worker for women's rights. After she and the others had spoken to Premier Roblin, he became angry. He said he was totally against votes for women.

As Nellie McClung left, she said to the premier, "I believe we'll get you yet!"

And the next night, they did. Nellie McClung and her friends put on a play that packed the theatre. McClung played the part of the premier. Other women played the parts of all the representatives in the government. The men in the play wanted to be able to vote. They asked the "premier" to consider it. McClung gave a very funny speech. She talked to them just as Premier Roblin had spoken to the women the day before.

Everyone laughed. The show was a hit! The women made enough money to pay for all the rest of their projects. What was more important, many people in the audience decided to support women's rights.

The next year, there was a provincial election. Premier Roblin and his party campaigned against women's rights. So the Political Equality League campaigned hard for the Opposition party. Nellie McClung was one of their most popular speakers. The suffragettes were disappointed when Premier Roblin and his party were elected once again.

The women's rights groups kept on working. And it's a good thing they did. The following year, Premier Roblin resigned. Suddenly there was another election. Nellie McClung joined the campaign for the Opposition party. This time, the Opposition won.

The new premier and his party agreed to introduce a law to allow women to vote. First the government wanted to have at least 17 000 names on a petition. It wanted to prove that many women wanted the right to vote. Once more, the women's rights groups went to work. After four months, they handed the premier a petition with over 43 000 names. One 94-year-old woman, Amelia Burritt, had collected 4250 of them herself!

- Have you or your parents ever signed a petition? Do you think petitions are a good way to protest a law?

On January 28, 1916, a new law was made: the women of Manitoba had the right to vote in their province.

The story of how Manitoba women won the right to vote shows that public protests can change government decisions. For years, elected representatives supported a law that kept women from voting. Many women protested that law. Eventually the law was changed.

You can see that a public protest is not an easy way to make changes. The women of Manitoba worked hard for over 20 years. They organized women's rights groups. They held many meetings. They wrote to newspapers, printed pamphlets and hung banners. They talked to many people to convince them that women should be able to vote. They gathered petitions. They campaigned in elections for the party that supported votes for women.

The victory for women in Manitoba was just the beginning. Suffragettes continued to work for the right to vote throughout the country. Because of these protest groups, women today have the same voting rights as men.

Public protests are usually more successful if they involve lots of people. The government cannot please everybody. If it is going to make changes, it must feel that many people want them.

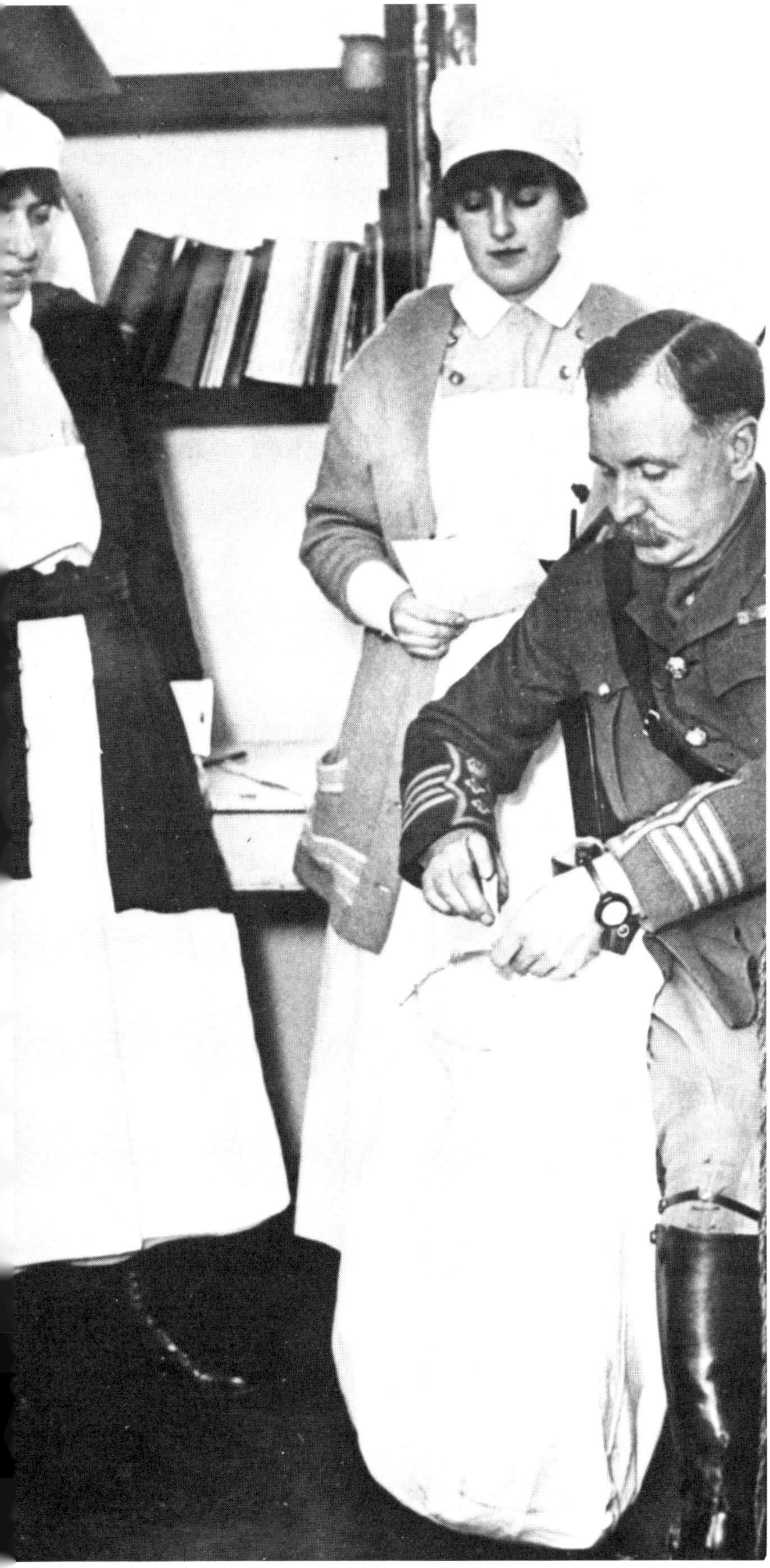

Women Get the Vote

Nellie McClung, shown in the picture above, helped women in Manitoba gain the right to vote. The list below shows the dates when women won the vote in each province for provincial elections and across Canada for federal elections.

Manitoba	1916
Alberta	1916
Saskatchewan	1916
British Columbia	1917
Ontario	1917
Canada	1918
Nova Scotia	1918
New Brunswick	1919
Prince Edward Island	1922
Colony of Newfoundland	1925
Quebec	1940

These Canadian nurses worked in Europe during World War I. They were among the first women to vote in a federal election. How do you think they felt as they voted for the first time?

The Right to Vote

The Charter of Rights and Freedoms guarantees that all adult Canadians can vote. In the past, many people were denied the right to vote because of their age, sex, race, ethnic group or lack of property.

The dates given below are important because they show how voting laws changed over the years in Canada. More and more Canadians were given the right to vote in federal elections.

Canadians vote by secret ballot. Voters put an X beside the name of the candidate they are voting for. Then the electoral officer puts the ballot into a locked box.

1918	Women could vote in federal elections.
1920	Men could vote in federal elections whether or not they owned property.
1948	Asian Canadians could vote in federal elections.
1950	Inuit could vote in federal elections.
1960	Indians on reserves could vote in federal elections.
1970	The voting age was lowered from 21 to 18 years for federal elections.

Government and Your Needs

Throughout this chapter, you saw that government means an exchange of services and taxes. That exchange works best when the government understands what Canadians need. Citizens can tell the government what they need through:
- their elected representatives
- public committees that work with the government
- protest groups that speak against some government decisions

- Is the freedom to protest government decisions an important freedom? Why or why not?

The government provides you with many services that you cannot easily provide yourself. But good services cannot happen without good citizens. Canadians must be prepared to pay taxes and tell the government what they need.

As people's needs change, government services and taxes change. In the future, your taxes may pay for services you cannot imagine today. You may pay more taxes for more services. Or you might pay fewer taxes for fewer services. Still, you should always try to let the government know what services you need. If you communicate with the government, you are more likely to receive the government services you need most.

Students climb onto a school bus. If you needed bus service to your school, what could you do about it?

A Protest Group Today

There are many different protest groups in Canada. Some people have joined a protest group because of their beliefs about war.

In 1983, Canada's prime minister signed an agreement that allows the United States to test cruise missiles in Canada. Cruise missiles are war weapons. Many Canadians are against the cruise missile tests because they believe the tests may lead to war.

Thousands of people across Canada have been protesting the cruise missile tests. One protest group, called Operation Dismantle, has over 7800 members. The protesters have signed petitions and written to their elected representatives. They have spoken at meetings and joined in protest marches. They have carried signs saying, "Cruise no more, we don't want war."

Operation Dismantle does not agree with the federal government. It wants Canadians who do not want cruise missile tests to join their protests.

How Can You Let the Government Know What You Think?

"I'm sorry to announce that we may not be able to visit the local museum next month as we had planned," the teacher told the class. "The city council is thinking of closing it."

The students looked surprised—and disappointed.

"I'm sure the council doesn't want to close the museum," added the teacher. "But the city is short of funds. The council doesn't want to raise taxes this year, so it has to cut some services."

"But the museum is important to the people in this city," said Raj.

"My grandfather gave the museum his father's coal mining hat and some equipment from the city's old coal mine," said Laurel.

"It is the only place that displays our community's heritage," the teacher agreed.

"It would be terrible if the museum closed," said Andre. "We should tell city council that we want it kept open."

The students agreed. They began to talk about what they might do to let council know how they felt. The teacher wrote all of their ideas on the board:

— speak at a city council meeting
— meet with the mayor
— march in front of city hall with signs
— ask people in the community to sign a petition
— write a letter asking council to cut another service instead of the museum

The class discussed each of the ideas. Finally they decided to choose one student in the class to speak at a city council meeting. All the students would help prepare the speech. As many students as possible would attend the meeting.

- How would you let your local government know what you thought?

This student is speaking on behalf of other students at a city council meeting. Why is it important for a group to have a spokesperson?

CHAPTER CHECKUP

Recalling the Main Ideas

Imagine that you have a friend who has recently moved to Canada. You want to help your friend understand how the government provides services for Canadians. You might explain some of the following things. Fill in the words that are missing.

In Canada, local, provincial or territorial, and federal governments provide many services that you cannot easily provide yourself. People pay ____(1)____ to these governments to pay for all these services. People who earn a lot of money or own a lot of property pay ____(2)____ taxes than those who don't. Government services change as people's ____(3)____ change.

Canadians can tell governments what they need by writing to their ____(4)____. They can also communicate with governments by working together in groups, such as ____(5)____. Both the ____(6)____ and the people can gain by working together.

When citizens don't agree with the government, they can ____(7)____ the work of the government. For example, for many years, elected representatives supported a law that kept women from ____(8)____. Many people ____(9)____ that law until it was changed.

In Canada, you are more likely to receive the services you need if you communicate with the ____(10)____.

Using What You Have Learned

Imagine that the provincial government passed a law that said no animals could be kept as pets. If you wanted the government to change that law, what might you do? List at least five things.

5

How Might Government Change in the Future?

Students board an electric train for a trip to city hall. How might this transportation service be paid for?

Tuesday, May 15, 2040

"This is great," said a student boarding the monorail train with his class. "Last week we got two days off school to work in the park. Now we get this morning off."

"I think we worked harder at the park than we would have at school," said another student. "But this trip to city hall should be fun."

City hall was 20 km from the school, but the trip took only five minutes. The electric monorail train sped quietly above the buses on the road below. Then it stopped in front of a huge, see-through dome.

The students got off the train and followed their teacher through sliding doors. They stepped into the dome. Inside, it was as fresh and sunny as it was outside. The dome was a garden filled with trees, shrubs, vines and flowers.

"The people in our city love parks," explained the teacher. "If they like this indoor garden around city hall, the city may build domes over some of our parks, too. We could enjoy them in any weather."

Just then an electronic voice spoke to the class. "Welcome to city hall," it said. "We are pleased to serve you. Allow me to show you the offices at city hall."

From the doorway, the class could see all the offices at once. They were in large, see-through cubes in the middle level of the dome. There was also an office near the very top and a large hall at the bottom. A light shone on each office as the voice named it:

"Taxes and licences."

"Voters' list and council meeting information."

"Planning and permits."

"Garbage, recycling and pollution control."

"Parks, recreation and parades."

"Inspectors."

"Transportation."

The class could see many people going to and from the offices on moving ramps.

"The Public Meeting Hall is straight ahead. The office of the mayor and councillors is here," the electronic voice said. The light shone on the top cube. "Please press this button if you wish to contact the mayor or councillors."

One of the students pushed the button. The image of a secretary appeared on a screen in front of the class. When he found out who the students were, he invited them to the top cube. "The mayor is expecting you," he said.

As the class rode up the ramp, the students could see Mayor Adams waiting at the top. "I'm glad you could come," she said. "You have been a great help to your city."

The students and their teacher sat down in the office while Mayor Adams held up a framed certificate. "I am very happy to present you with this award for good citizenship," she said. "As you know, our city has created many new parks this year. It takes time and money to plant shrubs and flowers in them all. But as a class, you offered to do most of the planting in the park near your school. Now you and many others can enjoy the results. Thank you for your hard work."

As Mayor Adams shook hands with the students, she asked them what they liked to do at the park. Some played baseball there and some flew kites. Others went for picnics and fed wild birds. One small girl said she liked to walk her dog.

The mayor paused and smiled. "When I was your age, I liked to walk my dog in a park, too," she said. "I had a big old English sheepdog called Bosley. In fact, Bosley was the reason I made my first visit to a city hall. I had to buy him a dog licence—even though I was not very happy about it."

"Why not?" asked the girl.

"Oh, at that time I couldn't see the point of things like licences, laws—or even government," laughed Mayor Adams. "I'm sure I wouldn't have believed that I would be a mayor one day."

"Were the laws and government different then?" one boy asked.

"Not completely, but there have been many changes," said Mayor Adams. "For instance, when I was your age, people drove cars right downtown. Imagine all the traffic, the noise and the dirty air. Later on, many cities made laws banning cars from the downtown area. They set up clean electric transportation instead and installed moving pedestrian walkways along main streets."

Then Mayor Adams pointed through the clear wall to one of the office cubes below. "There's another change," she said. "Do you see that computer with the large screen? It's part of a program called Waste Watchers. Every day factories and businesses call city hall to list the garbage they want to dispose of. Then the computer matches them with people who can use the garbage."

"But who uses garbage?" asked one of the students.

"You'd be surprised," said the mayor. "Farmers feed pigs leftover theatre popcorn. Factories melt used plastic bags to make toys. The city finds uses for most of the garbage now. But when I was a girl, very little of that was happening. Garbage was becoming an alarming problem."

The mayor added, "Well, unless you have more questions, I had better let you get back to school."

Immediately, six more hands shot up. Mayor Adams smiled and settled down to talk some more.

Of course, this visit to city hall in 2040 is imaginary. Mayor Adams is an imaginary person, too. As you probably know, she's Catherine, from Chapter 1, about 50 years later.

Still, it is very possible that someone like Catherine—and like you—will see many changes in government 50 years from now. It's possible that a city hall will be built in a domed garden. It's possible that cities will ban cars from downtown areas and encourage people to use up most of their garbage. It's likely that government will be quite different in the future.

The next part of this chapter suggests some ways that the government *could* change. It will give you a picture of what local, provincial, territorial and federal governments might be like one day. Do you think any of these changes will really happen? Look into Canada's past for clues. Think about how the government has already changed and how it is changing now. Can you add to the list of possible changes?

Mayor Adams welcomes students to city hall. Have you ever visited a city hall?

What Might Canada Be Like in the Future?

Since 1867, Canada has changed many times. The provinces have increased in number and size. The territories have become smaller. Communities have sprung up all across the country.

Canadians have considered changes that would alter the country in other ways. Some people have thought that Canada should join the United States. Some have talked about Quebec and the western provinces leaving Canada. Others have hoped to see new provinces in the north.

Canada will likely keep changing in the future. What changes do you expect?

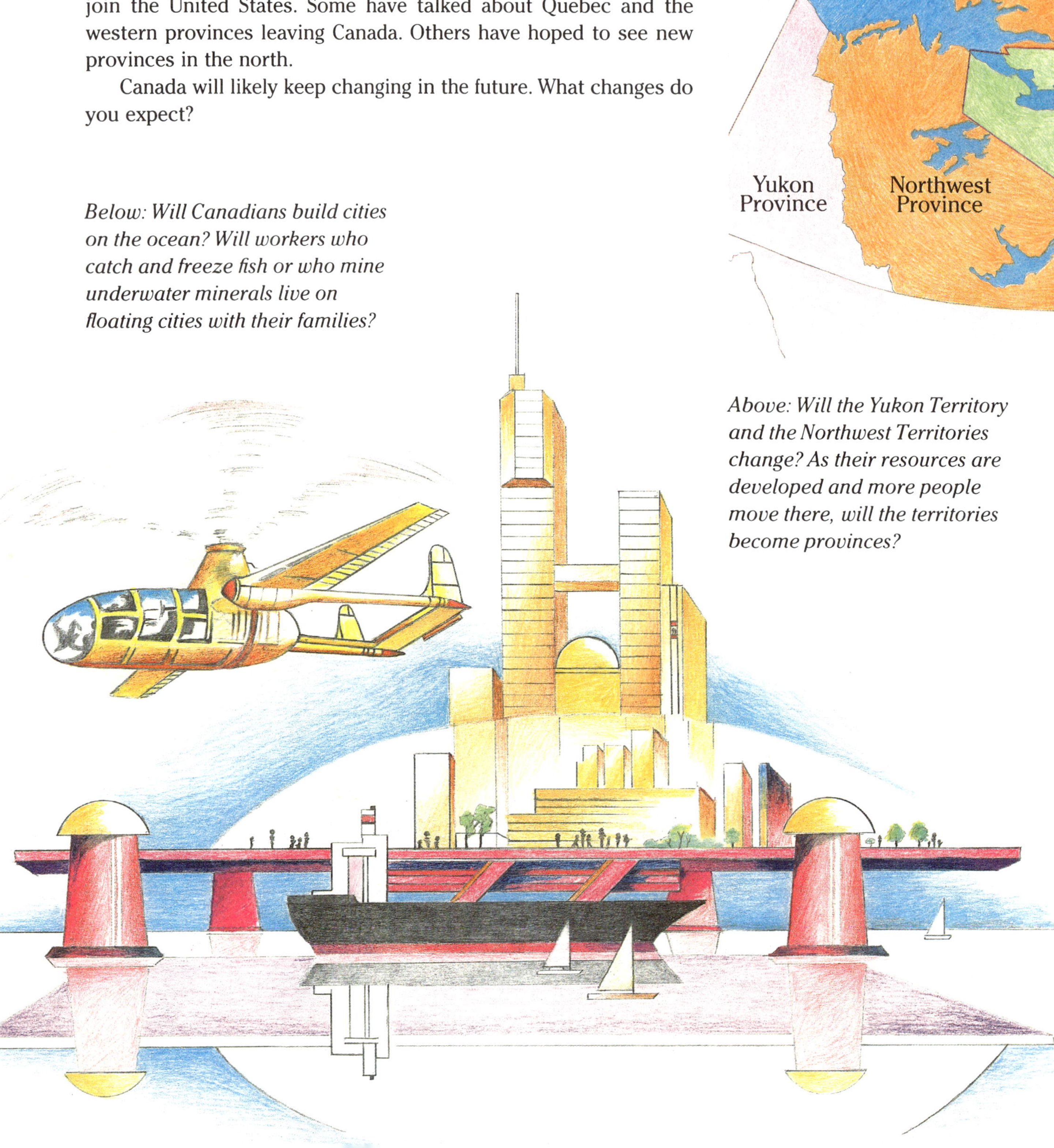

Below: Will Canadians build cities on the ocean? Will workers who catch and freeze fish or who mine underwater minerals live on floating cities with their families?

Above: Will the Yukon Territory and the Northwest Territories change? As their resources are developed and more people move there, will the territories become provinces?

Right: Will Indians have their own government for people living on Indian land? Will an Indian government be able to make laws, collect taxes and control resources like a provincial government?

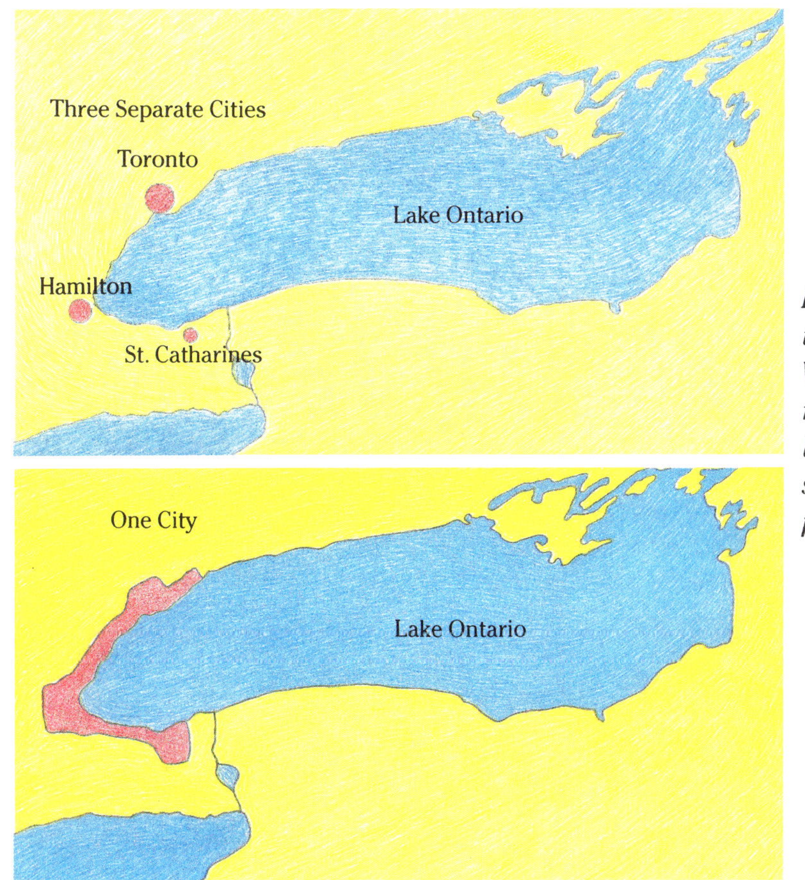

Left: Will several cities grow together and form one huge city? Will one large local government replace several smaller ones? Will large local governments take over some of the work now done by provincial governments?

How Might the Work of Elected Representatives Change in the Future?

Early colonists wanted a democratic government, so they demanded the right to elect representatives. Today Canadians still elect representatives, but there have been many changes. For example, the number of representatives has increased. Women as well as men have become elected representatives. Inventions such as radio and television allow representatives to speak to many Canadians at one time. Airplanes fly representatives between their constituencies and capital cities. What other changes might there be in the future? Can you imagine how an elected representative might work in the next century?

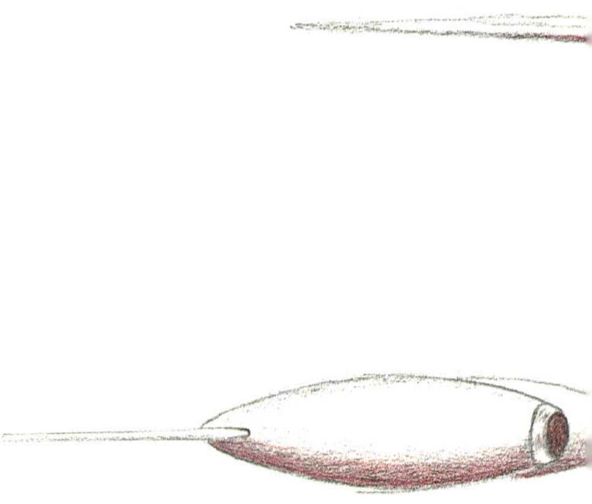

Right: Will people see more of their elected representatives? Will representatives travel on faster, cheaper superplanes to meet with their constituents more often?

Left: Will elected representatives set up computers in shopping malls or libraries so that Canadians can easily give their opinions on important bills? Will computers explain how new laws might affect Canadians?

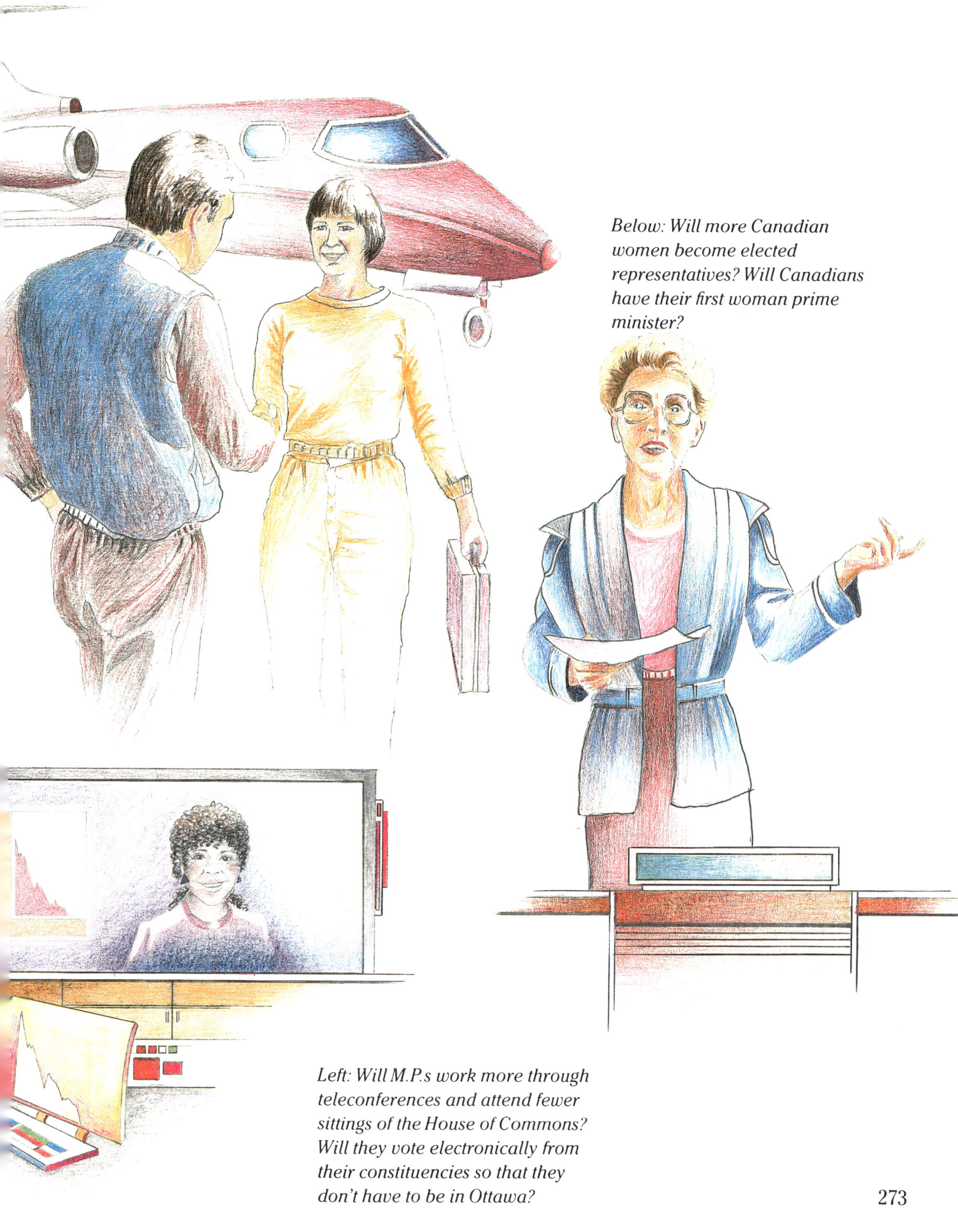

Below: Will more Canadian women become elected representatives? Will Canadians have their first woman prime minister?

Left: Will M.P.s work more through teleconferences and attend fewer sittings of the House of Commons? Will they vote electronically from their constituencies so that they don't have to be in Ottawa?

What Might Government Services of the Future Be Like?

Do you want to pay the government to inspect the safety of toy robots? Do you want the government to produce radio shows? The government can provide almost any service people want. But more services mean higher taxes.

Today the government provides many more services than it has in the past. It collects more taxes, too. What will the future be like? Will the number of government services keep growing? Will some services disappear as new services are needed? Will people work with the government to make sure they get the services they need?

Will health care cost a lot more in the future? Will people have to pay more of their own health care costs themselves?

Will the government provide more services for older people? As there will be more people over age 65 in the future, will the government provide many more recreation centres for retired people?

Above: Will the government enclose parks in domes that create summer all year round? Will people pay a fee every time they use a park?

Will letter delivery disappear? Will people hold their letters in front of a machine that can send them by satellite to home printers?

What Might the Citizen's Role Be in the Future?

If people want good government, they must be good citizens. People must always choose their representatives carefully and watch government actions closely. They must always support the actions they agree with and speak against the actions they don't.

One day computers and new inventions may make it easier for Canadians to do their part. Then people may work in different ways to have the kind of government they want.

Will protest groups use electronic petitions to gather millions of signatures? Will people who can't travel to Ottawa to protest send three-dimensional images of themselves in front of the Parliament Buildings?

Will the voting age be lowered?

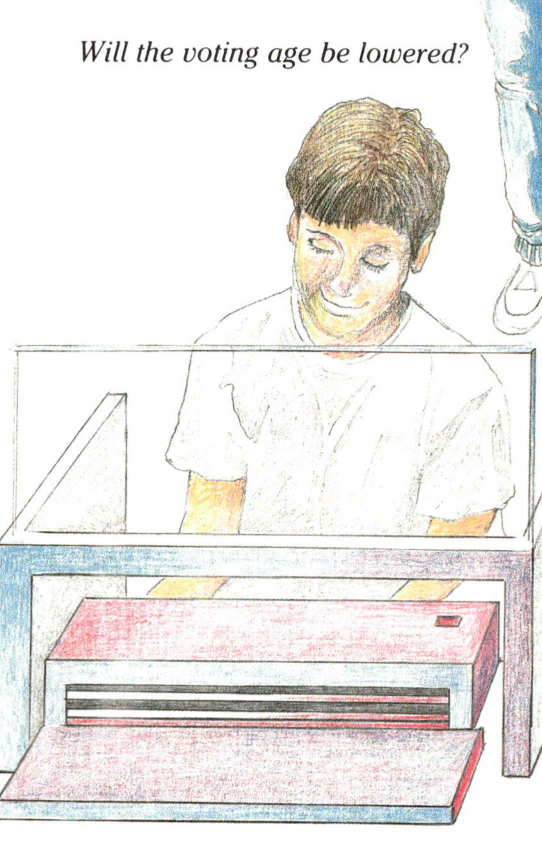

Will citizens be required to serve on committees to work with the government? Could a computer select your name to serve on a committee to help your local government?
Will people be able to vote on electronic screens in their homes? Will computers make it easier for sick and elderly people to vote?

Looking to Your Future

The future we have been discussing in this chapter is yours. It will likely be very exciting. One day you may be living in a new community in a new province of Canada. You may have a computer-run home full of things that haven't been invented yet. You may even be taking regular flights to the moon.

The government of the future is yours, too. It will likely be quite different from today's government. It will likely change as people's lives change. Whatever the government of the future is like, it will be what *you* help to make it.

Like Catherine, you will grow up to shape your government. Even if you do not become a mayor as she did, you will become a voter. You will also be free to join protest groups or committees that advise the government. You will have a say in what your local, provincial or territorial, and federal governments do.

The government of the future, like the government of today, will have its roots in the past. But it will grow and change as you become part of government in Canada.

These students are discussing an issue that affects people in Canada and other countries. How might such a discussion help students become part of government in the future?

UNIT CHECKUP

Learning from the Past

Council member Jean Talon visits a French-Canadian house in the 1600s.

This picture shows a sitting of the House of Commons in the 1980s.

Members of the Political Equality League in Manitoba pose beside a petition demanding the vote for women.

A woman votes in an election in the 1980s.

Here are some pictures of Canadians today and in the past. As each pair of pictures illustrates, Canadians have more say in their government today than they had in the past. In one or two sentences, describe the changes illustrated in each pair of pictures. Write two sentences to explain why it is important for Canadians to have a say in their government.

Looking to the Future

This is a picture of an intersection in a city today. The picture shows several government services. In the future, some of these services may change.

1. List at least four government services shown in the picture.
2. Choose one of these services and write a paragraph about what the service might be like 50 years from now.

Getting Involved

Suppose that very few citizens are turning out to vote at local government elections. What could you do to encourage more people to vote?

Summing Up

Pretend that you are at an international children's camp. The campers are learning about each other's countries and kinds of government. From what you have learned in this unit, what five things would you tell campers from other countries about government in Canada?

MIKADO
10% Discount
BITTER MELON
苦瓜
紹菜
SIU CHOY
49¢
毛瓜
BoK Choy
白菜
芋仔
CANADIAN
SPARTAN
APPLES
B.C.
CANADIAN
RED
DELICIOUS
APPLES

UNIT IV

Exploring Immigration

1

Who Are Immigrants?

Immigrants learn new skills. Do you enjoy learning a new game?

Simon's New Part

"Wait up, Simon," yelled Karen. She ran across the school playground towards her brother. "I heard that your teacher chose you to be in a play. Do you have a good part?"

"It's okay," said Simon. "But the play is just about being a new kid in Canada—an **immigrant**. It's about moving here. It doesn't sound very interesting."

"It could be interesting," said Karen. Simon could tell she was trying hard to think how.

"Being a new kid could be exciting—even scary," she said. "Suppose you are a new kid on some really strange planet where there are strange people doing strange things."

"There's no strange planet in this play," said Simon. "This new kid—that's the part I have to play—just moves here. So what's the big deal? I did that in real life when we moved to Ontario from Manitoba."

"That's not being an immigrant," laughed Karen. "Immigrants come from other countries, not just from other provinces."

"That doesn't make any difference," said Simon. "Remember when Aunt Peg came from Scotland? She spent almost a year over here, but she didn't find it so strange."

"But she wasn't an immigrant either. Aunt Peg was just visiting and doing some business here. Immigrants come to Canada to *live*. They have to get new jobs and go to new schools. They have to make new friends. Some have to learn a new language," said Karen.

She started back across the playground. "I'm going over to Amy's now. Good luck with your play."

- Have you ever tried to talk to someone who couldn't speak your language? What did you do?

Soojin's Story

Simon reached the sidewalk and headed for the store across the street from the school. He often had to stop there, so he knew the people who owned the store. He didn't know the adults very well. They didn't speak much English. But he knew their daughter, Soojin. She was in Karen's class, two years ahead of him. She helped her parents in their store after school.

"Hi, Simon," said Soojin as soon as he swung open the door.

Soojin's father glanced up from the box he was unpacking. He smiled at Simon.

"Hi. I'm just getting some bread today," said Simon. He picked up a loaf from the shelf.

"I'll ring it up for you," said Soojin, moving to the cash register. "How's it going?"

Soojin works in her family's store. How might working in the store help Soojin learn about Canada?

Soojin couldn't speak a lot of English, but Simon had no trouble understanding her. "Well—oh, okay, I guess," he said, thinking of the play again.

Simon liked the way Soojin could ring up the groceries and make change so quickly. "Thanks for the bread," said Simon, picking up his bag. Soojin's father smiled at him again. Simon felt awkward. He would have spoken to Soojin's father if he could. But it was hard trying to talk to people who know very little English.

As Soojin's father went to the back of the store, Simon said suddenly, "Soojin, are you and your dad immigrants?"

Soojin smiled. "Yes. Our whole family moved to Canada almost a year ago," she said. "My parents, my brother and I came here from South Korea."

"Did you work in a store like this before you came to Canada?" asked Simon.

"Oh no, we didn't have a store in South Korea. We worked on a farm. But the soil was very poor. Our crops were poor, too. There was not always enough to eat."

Simon could tell that Soojin felt sad just remembering the farm. "Did you know anyone here when you came?" he asked.

"Just my uncle," said Soojin.

"Did you have to find a new home and new friends and all that?" asked Simon, thinking of what Karen had been saying.

"Sure."

"Was it hard?"

Sponsoring Relatives as Immigrants

Canadians sometimes help relatives in other countries move to Canada to live. They help by becoming **sponsors**. Sponsors agree to look after their immigrant relatives and give them a place to stay in Canada. Sponsors must agree to support their relatives for up to 10 years if necessary. However, most of these relatives get jobs and do not need help from their Canadian sponsors for very long.

"It was hard for a while," said Soojin, running her fingers along the keys of the cash register. "It got easier after I learned some English."

"Didn't you know how to speak English before you came?" asked Simon, quite surprised.

"Just a bit, but I learned quickly once we got here. My brother and I learned in school. My parents are still learning, but they have to work, too. It is harder for them to find time to learn English."

"But if nobody in your family spoke English when you came, how did you find your way around? How did you buy things or talk to people?" Simon asked.

"My uncle helped us a lot," said Soojin. "We stayed with him and then he helped us find a house. The people in the Korean-Canadian Association helped, too. They are people who once lived in Korea—or their parents did. They told us about some of the Canadian ways of doing things. Sometimes they **translated** English into Korean for us, too."

Soojin stared down at the counter. "Still, it was hard. And lonely, too. If you can't talk to people, you can't make friends."

Just then a man came to the cash register with a basket of groceries. Soojin turned to help him, and Simon left.

"See you, Soojin," he said as he went out the door.

- How do groups like the Korean-Canadian Association help immigrants? How could other Canadians help new immigrants?

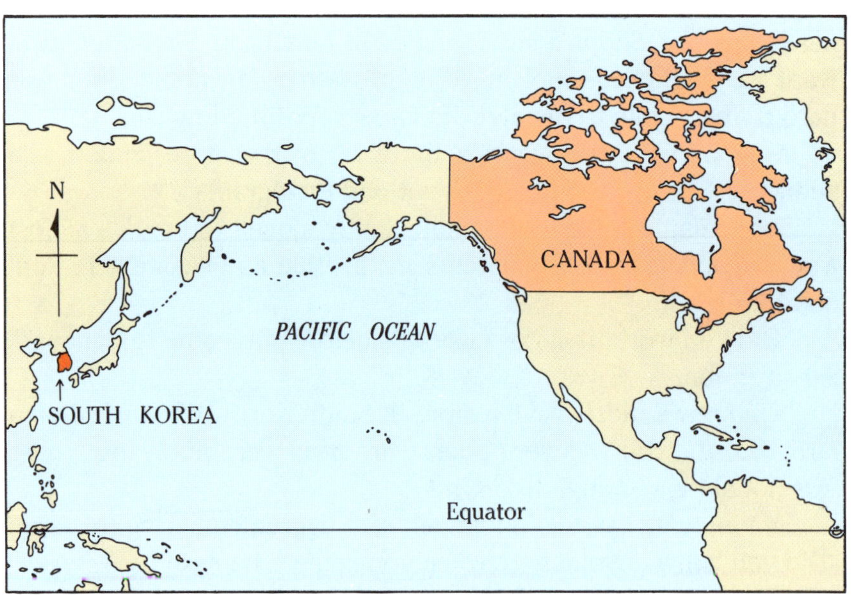

Soojin and her family have come to Canada from South Korea. What body of water did they cross to reach here?

Simon, the New Canadian Kid

The next day at school, Simon's teacher passed out copies of the play they were going to do in class. It was called *New Canadian Kid,* and it was written by a Canadian named Dennis Foon.

Simon immediately flipped it open and looked at some of the pictures. He saw a picture of the character—the immigrant—he was to play. Simon couldn't tell what country he was supposed to come from.

"Where am I coming from?" Simon asked the teacher. "It doesn't even say what country I'm from."

The teacher explained that Mr. Foon wanted his play to show the audience what it's like to be a new Canadian—from any country. So the "new Canadian kid" comes from a place called "Homeland," which could be anywhere.

"When people first come to Canada, they feel very strange," said the teacher. "They have moved to a new country. They must learn to use different kinds of money and go to different kinds of schools. Often immigrants must learn a new language."

The teacher continued. "Immigrants also find many ways of doing things that are different from their **customs** at home. Our food may be very different from theirs. The way we dress and the way we behave may be different. Even the games we play and the kinds of jokes we enjoy may seem very unusual to a newcomer."

"This play doesn't make any sense," said Simon's friend Len. He had been looking at his copy while the teacher was talking. "I'm supposed to be the Canadian boy in the play, but he doesn't talk English or French. He says, *'Eh-Mencha, ein brochney conk-you-bay-tor.'* What's that supposed to mean?"

The teacher laughed. "Hold on. Remember, I said that Mr. Foon wants the audience to understand what it really feels like to be a new immigrant. So the audience will only understand the immigrants. Everybody else in the play speaks a language of nonsense words. People in the audience won't understand it, so they will feel just as lost and confused as the immigrants do."

"Do you mean that I won't even know what's going on?" asked Simon. "When I'm the new Canadian kid, won't I be able to understand what anybody says to me?"

New Canadian immigrants learn about the bus system from their sponsors. What other public services might immigrants need to learn about?

The Language of Immigrants

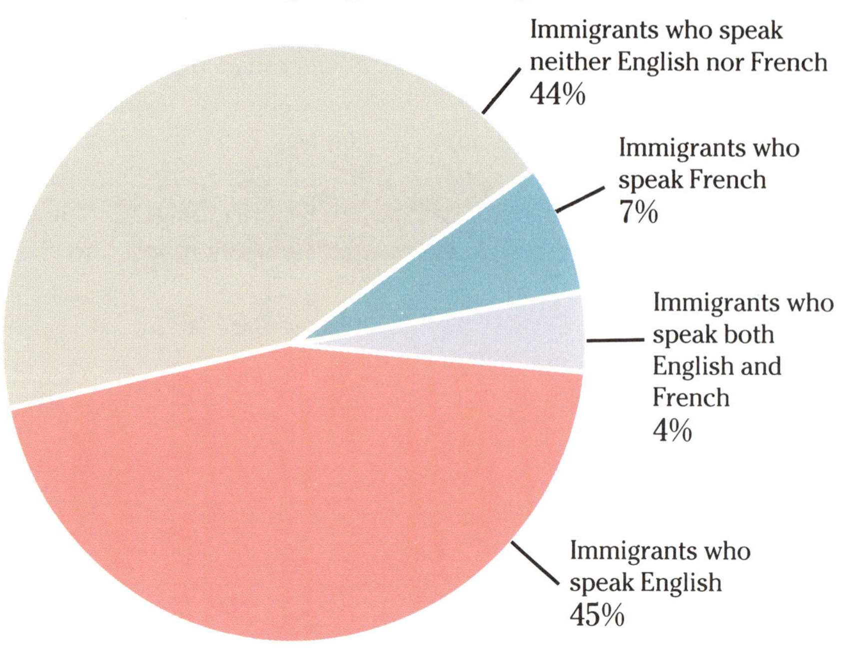

This chart shows what percentage of immigrants speak Canada's two official languages when they arrive here. Which language is spoken by the largest number of immigrants?

"Don't worry, Simon. You'll have the play script to follow," said the teacher. "But you can imagine how you would feel if this were really happening to you—as it does to many new immigrants. Almost half of the new immigrants who come to Canada cannot speak English or French when they arrive."

Over the next few weeks, the class read the play and began rehearsing. Just a few students were acting, but others were busy directing the play and making scenery. Everyone was involved. The students planned to invite their families to see the play at the end of the month.

While rehearsing the play, Simon's class was learning a little about how it feels to be a new immigrant in Canada. When the others in the play were talking, Simon didn't understand the language. So he found it difficult to talk to the other students. As the "new Canadian kid," Simon felt left out.

In the play, one of the Canadians became Simon's friend. She tried to talk to him and teach him games. Another Canadian, played by Len, was really mean. He laughed at Simon and called him names.

While acting the part of an immigrant, Simon was embarrassed many times. In the play he did not know Canada's national anthem, so he was the only one who did not stand up for it. He had never played baseball in "Homeland," so when he was handed a baseball mitt, he tried hitting the ball with it.

- Why does the "new Canadian kid" feel embarrassed in the play? What else might embarrass a new immigrant in Canada?

Len's Story

Rehearsals were going well. Then, one lunch hour, Len sat down beside Simon and began to talk really fast. Simon knew Len always talked fast when he was upset.

"I don't want to be the Canadian boy in this dumb play," he said, as he yanked his lunch out of a brown paper bag. "I don't like saying the things I have to say. I don't like doing the things I have to do."

"It's only a play, Len," said Simon, biting into his peanut-butter-pickle-and-radish sandwich. "We know you're not really mean. Anyway, I've got the awful part—not you. I'm the one getting picked on."

"But I really was picked on. And not just in a play—for real," said Len, looking away.

"What do you mean?"

"Five years ago, my family moved here from Trinidad. I was a new immigrant. And do you know what? Even though I could speak English, it really was a lot like this play. Not many kids would play with me. Sometimes they called me names—really mean names. Sometimes they made fun of me—of my hair, of what I ate."

Simon listens as Len tells him what it is like to be a new immigrant in Canada. What might Len be saying?

Len stopped for a moment. Simon didn't say anything. He didn't know what to say.

"I don't ever want to act like that. Not even in a play," said Len.

"Why did the other kids act like that? Why did they make fun of you?" asked Simon, taking another bite of his sandwich.

"I guess just because I was different. I don't know," said Len. "By the way, what is that sandwich you're eating?"

"It's just peanut-butter-pickle-and-radish. Do you want a bite?" asked Simon.

"No, but do you know what? If you were an immigrant, someone would make fun of you for eating it."

Simon stopped in the middle of a bite. Then he looked at Len and they both grinned.

After school, Len stayed to ask the teacher if he could drop out of the play. Simon waited outside for Len.

"Aren't you coming home now?" asked Simon's sister, Karen, when she saw him standing by the front door.

"I'm waiting for Len. He's talking to the teacher about the play."

"How's it going? Do you like it any better now?" Karen asked.

Simon smiled. "Do you remember saying that it might be exciting and scary to be an immigrant on a new planet? I think this planet is scary enough."

Karen gave him a puzzled look and then walked off with her friends.

In a few minutes, Len appeared.

"In or out?" asked Simon.

"Oh, I'm still in, I guess," said Len with a shrug. "The teacher said she understands how I feel. But she said plays like this can help people to understand immigrants better and to treat them better."

A Trinidadian youth stands on the bow of a sailboat. Suppose he decides to move to Canada. What things in Canada might he find familiar?

As the boys started to walk off together, Simon asked, "Were you sorry you moved here, Len? When people were being mean to you, did you want to go back to Trinidad?"

"Oh sure, I used to think about going back home. I really missed my friends and my cousins and grandparents. I missed some of the places we used to go and the special holidays we had. But coming to Canada was really exciting," said Len. "There are lots of things here that we didn't have in Trinidad. There are lots of nice people, too."

Len continued, "My parents like their jobs here. They manage a big hotel and they give courses in managing hotels. They've had experience running busy hotels in Trinidad. Lots of tourists go there."

Simon walked along, thinking. "So when immigrants move to Canada from other countries, we learn things from all over the world."

- Pretend that you are writing a report on Len's life in Trinidad. What questions would you ask Len?

Immigrants from Trinidad celebrate their way of life at a carnival in Toronto. How might events like this benefit all Canadians?

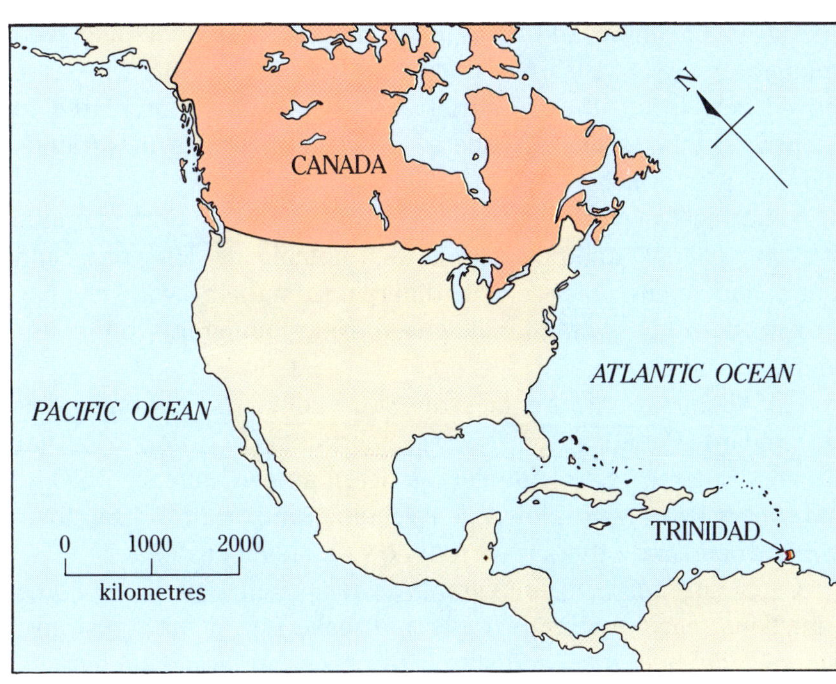

Simon's friend Len comes from Trinidad. Approximately how many kilometres did Len's family travel from Trinidad to Ontario?

Farmers work on the land in Korea. If these people decided to immigrate to Canada, what skills might they bring?

The Play

The following Thursday was the day of the play. All the students in Simon's class had invited their families to see *New Canadian Kid.* The audience was surprised when the Canadians in the play spoke in nonsense words. Everyone could see how confusing it is to be an immigrant who does not know what people are saying.

Most of the people in the audience frowned when Simon was teased and called names just because he was new to Canada. They smiled when one of the Canadians enjoyed tasting the food from Simon's homeland. The audience was also happy when Simon learned how to talk to his new Canadian friends and how to play baseball with them.

Karen walked home beside Simon after the play. "Being an immigrant sure means making lots of changes," she said. "I guess it would be exciting to move to a new country, but it would be difficult, too."

Simon was quiet for a minute. He thought about Len and Soojin and the things they had told him about coming to Canada. He thought about the play and how it had felt to play the part of an immigrant. "It's hard to imagine it, Karen," he said slowly. "It's really hard for us to imagine what it's like."

- Is the play a good way for Canadians to understand how new immigrants feel? Why or why not?

New Immigrants in Canada

The story of Simon and his friends helped you understand who immigrants are. You learned that immigrants are people who have moved here from other countries. After they have **immigrated** to Canada, they begin new lives here—finding new homes, new friends and new jobs or schools.

Learning to live in Canada can be hard for new immigrants. They miss people and places from their homelands. They often find that Canadian customs are quite different from their own. They may also need to learn another language. New immigrants often feel confused and lonely.

Not all immigrants are the same. Some come from countries that are similar to Canada in many ways. Others come from countries that are very different. Some immigrants learn a new language quickly, and others learn more slowly. Some immigrants want to keep their own **culture**, and others want to follow Canadian customs.

Canadians react to immigrants in many different ways. Some Canadians tease new immigrants and make fun of their customs. Others try to help them adjust to their new home. Some immigrants

have relatives in Canada to help them. Immigrants may also get help from Canadians who once lived in their homeland.

As you read on, you will learn more about **immigration** to Canada. You will learn about some of the immigrants who came here in the past. You will find out what it is like to be a new immigrant in Canada today. You will read about some of the **contributions** that immigrants have made to Canada. You will even look ahead 50 years and try to imagine what immigration might be like then.

Immigrants often feel lonely when they first arrive in Canada. How might you help an immigrant feel welcome?

Who Are Canadians?

The Inuit and the Indians were the first people to come to Canada. They lived here thousands of years before this country was even called Canada. Sometimes the **native people** are called the first immigrants. But the Inuit and the Indians do not think of themselves as immigrants. They are the original Canadians.

All other Canadians are immigrants or the **descendants** of immigrants. If you are the descendant of an immigrant, that means that someone in your family, like a parent or a grandparent or a great-grandparent, was an immigrant.

What is special about Canadians is that they have so many different backgrounds. Canadians are made up of more than 80 different **ethnic** groups—groups that have their own customs or history or language. Here are a few examples of ethnic groups in Canada: British, Chinese, French, Germans, Hungarians, Inuit, Jamaicans, Nigerians and Swedes.

British immigrants or their descendants make up the largest ethnic group in Canada. Still, the number of British Canadians is less than the number of non-British Canadians. No single ethnic group in Canada is larger than all the other groups put together.

*Canada is a **multi-cultural** country. It is made up of many different cultures.*

CHAPTER CHECKUP

Recalling the Main Ideas

Imagine that Simon is telling his sister Karen what he has learned about immigrants. Listed below are the beginnings of Simon's sentences.

1. Immigrants to Canada are people who ____.
2. Nearly half of Canada's new immigrants ____.
3. When they came to Canada, Soojin and her family ____.
4. When Len's parents came to Canada as new immigrants, they ____.
5. Immigrants help Canadians ____.

From the following list, choose a group of words that best completes each sentence. You may want to choose more than one group of words to finish some sentences.

- **a.** had jobs that were like their homeland jobs.
- **b.** learn things from all over the world.
- **c.** were helped by the Korean-Canadian Association.
- **d.** cannot speak English or French when they come.
- **e.** were helped by an uncle.
- **f.** spoke English.
- **g.** have moved to Canada to live.

Using What You Have Learned

Think of someone you know who has been a new immigrant to Canada. Perhaps you are a new immigrant yourself. Write down at least three things a new immigrant might enjoy about coming to Canada. Write down at least three things that a new immigrant might find difficult.

2

What Immigrants Have Come to Canada?

For thousands of years native people have lived in Canada. Today there are other ethnic groups, too, because immigrants from many different countries have made Canada their home. The first immigrants came nearly 400 years ago. The native people helped these first **settlers** by showing them new foods to grow and the best ways to travel in the new land.

In this chapter, you will read some stories about immigrants who came to Canada at different times. Although the immigrants in the stories are not actual people, the events are true. The stories will help you understand why immigrants came to Canada and what challenges they faced. These stories only tell about some of the ethnic groups. Immigrants have come to Canada from many other countries and at other times, too.

- What do you think would be the most exciting thing about immigrating to a new country? What would be the most difficult?

As you read this chapter, try to put yourself in the place of the immigrants. Try to imagine what it would have been like to immigrate to Canada when they did. That was what Simon did when he was the "new Canadian kid" in the class play. Imagining what it would have been like helped Simon understand his immigrant friends. It will help you understand Canada's immigrants, too. It might also help you understand your own family history.

Members of a pipe band talk together at a Scottish games day. Can you think of a custom that might have been brought to Canada by Scottish immigrants?

Immigrants have come to Canada from most countries in the world. Can you find the country or countries that your family came from?

Legend

1. BELIZE
2. HONDURAS
3. EL SALVADOR
4. NICARAGUA
5. JAMAICA
6. HAITI
7. PUERTO RICO
8. SURINAM
9. FRENCH GUIANA
10. PARAGUAY
11. URUGUAY
12. DENMARK
13. NETHERLANDS
14. BELGIUM
15. WEST GERMANY
16. EAST GERMANY
17. POLAND
18. CZECHOSLOVAKIA
19. AUSTRIA
20. SWITZERLAND
21. HUNGARY
22. ROMANIA
23. YUGOSLAVIA
24. ITALY
25. ALBANIA
26. BULGARIA
27. GREECE
28. TUNISIA
29. GAMBIA
30. GUINEA-BISSAU
31. GUINEA
32. SIERRA LEONE
33. LIBERIA
34. IVORY COAST
35. BURKINA FASO
36. GHANA
37. TOGO
38. BENIN
39. EQUATORIAL GUINEA
40. CAMEROON
41. CENTRAL AFRICAN REPUBLIC
42. CONGO
43. LESOTHO
44. SWAZILAND
45. BOTSWANA
46. ZIMBABWE
47. ZAMBIA
48. MOZAMBIQUE
49. MALAWI
50. BURUNDI
51. RWANDA
52. UGANDA
53. KENYA
54. SOMALIA
55. DJIBOUTI
56. YEMEN
57. PEOPLE'S DEMOCRATIC REPUBLIC OF YEMEN
58. OMAN
59. UNITED ARAB EMIRATES
60. QATAR
61. KUWAIT
62. JORDON
63. ISRAEL
64. CYPRUS
65. LEBANON
66. SYRIA
67. NEPAL
68. BHUTAN
69. BANGLADESH
70. LAOS
71. THAILAND
72. KAMPUCHEA
73. BRUNEI
74. HONG KONG
75. NORTH KOREA
76. SOUTH KOREA

ARCTIC OCEAN
UNION OF SOVIET SOCIALIST REPUBLICS
ENLAND
Arctic Circle
ICELAND
NORWAY
SWEDEN
FINLAND
UNITED KINGDOM
IRELAND
FRANCE
PORTUGAL
SPAIN
MOROCCO
ALGERIA
LIBYA
EGYPT
TURKEY
IRAQ
IRAN
AFGHANISTAN
PAKISTAN
INDIA
CHINA
MONGOLIA
JAPAN
TAIWAN
BURMA
VIETNAM
PHILIPPINES
MALAYSIA
SRI LANKA
SAUDI ARABIA
MALI
NIGER
CHAD
SUDAN
NIGERIA
ETHIOPIA
GABON
ZAIRE
TANZANIA
ANGOLA
SOUTH-WEST AFRICA (Namibia)
SOUTH AFRICA
MADAGASCAR
Equator
INDIAN OCEAN
INDONESIA
PAPUA NEW GUINEA
SOLOMON ISLANDS
FIJI
VANUATU
AUSTRALIA
NEW ZEALAND
N
W
E
S
Prime Meridian
Antarctic Circle
ANTARCTICA

This French girl has just arrived at Quebec in 1670. What difficulties might she face in this new land?

The French

The year is 1670. A 15-year-old girl is just about to step off a ship at Quebec. She feels lonely and frightened. Not so long ago, she left her family and home in a small village in France. Now she is on the other side of the Atlantic Ocean, where she knows no one.

Her priest encouraged her to come. He said France wanted people to ***settle*** *the French* ***colony****. The colony especially needed young girls to move there. Many French soldiers in the colony wanted to start farming, get married and have children.*

The priest signed a certificate to say that the young girl was healthy, strong and well behaved. He was sure she would be able to work hard and survive the freezing winters along the St. Lawrence River. But as the young girl looks out from the ship, she is not sure he was right.

The people in the colony will not think the girl is too young to become a bride. Many girls here marry before they turn 16. If they do, the king of France gives them a gift. If they don't, their fathers must pay a fine. The king encourages young girls to marry because he wants the colony to grow. He wants the ***colonists*** *to raise lots of food and make products for trade with France.*

In less than two weeks, the young girl will marry a soldier she barely knows. Then the king will give her a bull, a cow, a dog, a sow, two chickens, two barrels of salt meat and some money. But she wonders if she will ever be happy in this strange new land.

- If you were settling into a new country, what gifts would you find useful? Why?

The king of France ruled the French colony in Canada between 1663 and 1760. During that time, about 10 000 immigrants came from France. Most of them settled along the St. Lawrence River. Some went to New Brunswick and Nova Scotia, where the earliest French settlements had been.

The Loyalists

A shopkeeper is watching the cheering crowd in New York. The people are blowing bugles and tossing their hats high into the air. It is 1783, and the American colonists have just won a war with Britain. Now they are free from British laws.

The American shopkeeper watching the crowd is unhappy. He wants to continue living under British rule. Many people, even some of his friends, are angry because he did not support their fight against Britain. One day, someone throws a rock through the window of his house. Some children beat up his son. Many of his former customers refuse to come to his store.

The first Loyalists arrive in New Brunswick from the American colonies in 1783. Why might it be difficult for them to leave their homes?

Soon he and his wife decide to move away. They want to move to a colony that is still British. Packing up as many belongings as possible, the family takes a ship heading north to New Brunswick. On board, there are many other families who are moving to the British colony for the same reason. These immigrants are called ***Loyalists*** *because they have stayed loyal to the British king.*

When the shopkeeper arrives near the St. John River in New Brunswick, he does not find a city with many streets and gardens like the one he just left. He finds an empty wilderness instead. At night he doesn't go to sleep in a warm, comfortable house. He sleeps with his family in a drafty tent, with the wind and rain lashing at the canvas.

Britain rewards the shopkeeper for his loyalty. He is given some lumber, food and clothing. He also gets some free land to live on. But what land! It is shallow and rocky—very difficult to farm, especially for a shopkeeper who has never farmed before.

At the end of a day's work, he leans heavily on his shovel, his hands bleeding and blistered. As he lifts his head and looks across the empty field, he hopes the future will be better. One day he would like to have his own shop again.

- Name at least three things that might have made the family feel unhappy in their new home.

The Loyalists were English-speaking settlers in the United States who were loyal to Britain. When the United States gained **independence** from Britain in 1783, many Loyalists moved north. They wanted to live in one of the British colonies in Canada. Almost 40 000 Loyalists came. Most of them settled in Nova Scotia, New Brunswick and Ontario. A few moved to Prince Edward Island, Newfoundland and Quebec.

The Irish

The farm woman buries her head in her hands and sobs. Ugly black slime oozes from the potatoes she has dropped. "What can we do?" she asks. "What can we do?"

In 1847, Ireland is more overcrowded than any other country in Europe. Most of the Irish are very poor, and potatoes are almost the only food they have left. After 13 years of bad crops, there is a terrible crop failure. The potatoes have a disease called blight. There is nothing left to eat.

The farm woman and her husband and seven children join crowds of people at the seaports. They manage to get on a large timber ship headed for Canada.

On board there are too many passengers. Most of them stay down in the hold, where the crew will store timber on the ship's return voyage. There is no fresh air and very little food or drinking water.

During the voyage, several of the passengers complain of fever and headache. More and more of them grow sick with a dreaded disease called typhus. The woman and her husband look after their sick children, but before the ship reaches Canada, the two youngest children are dead. Many people have died during the six-week voyage.

In Quebec, inspectors check all the passengers for disease. Then many of the Irish immigrants travel up the St. Lawrence River and across Lake Ontario to a small town. There they receive a few clothes and some food from the church.

For the farm woman and her family, this is just the beginning of another journey. They will travel on foot into the forest to find land to farm. There they will struggle to build a new home and a new life.

Irish immigrants prepare to board sailing ships for North America in 1851. What might it have been like to live on board ship for six weeks?

The Loyalists and then the Irish greatly increased the English-speaking **population** of Canada. In 1847, almost 90 000 people came from Ireland to escape starvation. Like the family in this story, many Irish immigrants travelled to York, now the city of Toronto, and then moved on to clear farmland in Ontario.

During the 1840s and 1850s, many immigrants from Ireland and Britain came to Canada. They were leaving hardship in their homelands and looking for a better way of life.

The Black Americans

It is nighttime. The man runs out of the trees, down the bank and up the dry creek bed. The next night, he runs again. Sometimes he cuts through swamps and sometimes over rocky areas. He runs because his freedom depends on it.

It is 1850, and the United States has just passed a new law, the Fugitive Slave Act. *It says that everybody must help to capture runaway* ***slaves****. Under the law, a judge who decides that a black person is a runaway slave is paid twice as much money as a judge who decides that a black person is* ***free****.*

The man is furious about this unfair law. Like many black people, he feels he can no longer live safely in the United States. He heads north to the British colonies.

After weeks of running in fear, the man reaches Ontario. He is desperate for food and a place to stay. Charities are able to help only a few of the new immigrants. The man finds a job as a road builder. He works at least as hard as he did as a slave, and many people treat him badly. Some even think that black people cannot be trusted.

When slavery ends in the United States in 1865, many of the black Americans in Canada go back. But by that time, the man has saved enough money to buy a small farm. He decides to stay.

Between 1850 and 1860, about 43 000 American blacks came to Canada. Most of them had been slaves in the United States. They were in great danger as they tried to escape. Most of the blacks went to communities in Ontario, but 600 to 800 of them moved to British Columbia.

- Both the black American and the Loyalist ran away from the United States. Why did each leave?

This picture shows members of the Pioneer Rifle Corps in Victoria, British Columbia, around 1860. These men were black immigrants from the United States. How might the corps have contributed to life in early Victoria?

The Chinese

The young Chinese man has heard about Canada. In China it is known as **gum san**, *the land of the golden mountain. The young man decides to go there. He hates to leave China, his parents, his brothers and sisters and his friends. But in* gum san *there is work. He will be able to send money home to his family.*

The voyage by ship is long and difficult. Yet when the young man arrives in Victoria, British Columbia, he continues to travel. He takes a sternwheeler up the Fraser River to the great, looming mountains. There he finds the rough campsite he will call home.

It is 1882, and Canada has encouraged thousands of Chinese men to help build the Canadian Pacific Railway through the mountains of British Columbia. Like most of the men in his work gang, the young man does not understand English. Each gang has a Chinese ***interpreter*** *who speaks Chinese and English and explains the work.*

And what difficult, dangerous work it is. The men blast through solid rock along very steep slopes. Then they shovel the path clear before laying the track. Sometimes the blasts cause slides that can kill or injure the workers. The young man works 10 to 12 hours a day for less than a dollar. What's even worse, he is paid less than non-Chinese railway workers are paid.

In the fall of 1885, the railway is finished and the men are out of work. Some of the Chinese railway workers head to the prairies or to eastern Canada, but most stay in British Columbia. The young man decides to go to Vancouver with three of his friends from the work gang. They hope to start a small laundry or a grocery store. They plan to work hard so that they can continue to send money back to their families in China.

Chinese workers arrive in Canada around 1900. How do you think they felt when they first stepped off the ship?

- How might the Chinese men have felt about Canada before they came? How might they have felt about Canada after they came?

The Canadian Pacific Railway could not have been built without the help of immigrants. Many workers were needed. Between 1882 and 1885, over 15 000 Chinese men came to British Columbia to work on the railway. Most of them worked in order to send money back to their families in China.

These Chinese workers helped build the Canadian Pacific Railway in the 1880s. What kinds of problems do you think the workers faced?

Today Chinese celebrations are an important part of Canada's culture. Have you ever attended a Chinese New Year's Day Parade?

Ho Inn
Ho Inn

Unfair Treatment of Asians

Thousands of Chinese men came to Canada in the 1880s to help build the Canadian Pacific Railway. They were hard workers. But many Canadians did not like the Chinese, because they were different. When the railway was finished, many Canadians wanted to prevent other Chinese workers from coming to Canada. So the government passed a law saying that every Chinese immigrant had to pay a **tax** of $50 to enter Canada. Later the tax, called a "head tax," was raised to $500. Since most Chinese people could not afford to pay the tax, few Chinese immigrants came to Canada.

Canada also tried to keep out immigrants from other parts of Asia. For example, in 1914 a ship carrying nearly 400 immigrants from India arrived in Vancouver. The ship waited in the harbour for many weeks. Finally the government sent back the ship and its passengers.

In the 1940s, Canada was helping to fight a war against Japan. During this war, the Canadian government made Japanese Canadians move away from the west coast. The government was afraid that Japanese Canadians would help Japan win the war. They had to give up their houses, land, fishing boats and personal belongings. Many had to live in special camps, separated from their families. They were not free to come and go as they wanted. Some were forced to work on roads and farms. Yet, of the 21 000 people involved, 13 000 had been born in Canada and another 3000 had become Canadians. Most of the others had lived in Canada for 25 to 40 years.

These are examples of **discrimination** against people from Asia. Asians were discriminated against because of their **race**. Discrimination against people because of their race is called **racism**. Today people who want to immigrate to Canada cannot be prevented from doing so because of their race, colour, **religion** or country of origin. Nor can people in Canada be discriminated against. The Charter of Rights and Freedoms protects them.

These Japanese Canadians are being sent to the interior of British Columbia.

NOTICE TO ALL JAPANESE PERSONS

AND PERSONS OF JAPANESE RACIAL ORIGIN

TAKE NOTICE that under Orders Nos. 21, 22, 23 and 24 of the British Columbia Security Commission, the following areas were made prohibited areas to all persons of the Japanese race:—

LULU ISLAND (including Steveston)	SAPPERTON
SEA ISLAND	BURQUITLAM
EBURNE	PORT MOODY
MARPOLE	IOCO
DISTRICT OF QUEENSBOROUGH	PORT COQUITLAM
CITY OF NEW WESTMINSTER	MAILLARDVILLE
	FRASER MILLS

AND FURTHER TAKE NOTICE that any person of the Japanese race found within any of the said prohibited areas without a written permit from the British Columbia Security Commission or the Royal Canadian Mounted Police shall be liable to the penalties provided under Order in Council P.C. 1665.

AUSTIN C. TAYLOR,
Chairman,
British Columbia Security Commission

Above: This notice was posted by the British Columbia government during the 1940s.

Canada's Multi-cultural Policy

Canada is a multi-cultural country. For hundreds of years immigrants have brought their own cultures or ways of life to Canada. People from many different cultures now live here. All of these ethnic groups are equally important, and they all contribute to Canadian culture.

The federal government supports **multi-culturalism**. This means that the government encourages ethnic groups to keep their culture. For example, the federal government provides money to volunteer ethnic groups to help them share their culture with other Canadians.

The Ukrainians

Bump. Jiggle, jiggle. Bump. Jiggle, jiggle. The little girl sits in the back of the swaying ox cart and holds her baby brother tightly. If she weren't so tired, she'd be very excited. After a long train trip from the Ukraine, a voyage across the Atlantic Ocean to Quebec and a second train ride to Alberta, she has almost reached her new home. It is 1913.

The girl's parents are good farmers and hard workers, but land in the Ukraine was scarce and expensive. Here they can have 64 ha (hectares) of free land. The Canadian government is anxious to settle the prairies.

The Ukrainians reach their farmland in the spring. The little girl and her family start working right away to make a simple home. They lay strips of sod like bricks on top of one another. Both the roof and the walls of the house are made of sod. That's where they must live while they build their log house.

In early summer, they plow the hard prairie soil. Thick clouds of mosquitoes attack their faces, necks and hands. While her father steers the steel plow, the little girl walks ahead, waving mosquitoes away from the poor horse.

The worst thing about being in Canada is the loneliness. The nearest neighbours live at least a kilometre away. And they do not seem very friendly. But the little girl and her parents cannot speak English, so they can't talk with their neighbours anyway.

One day the neighbours need help building their house. The little girl and her parents help them make plaster out of clay, water and grass. They help the neighbours fill the holes between the logs in the walls of the house.

The two families still can't talk much to each other, but they shake hands and smile. The little girl hopes her family has made some friends in this new, lonely land.

- How would you describe the people in this Ukrainian family? Would you like to have them as your neighbours?

Between 1897 and 1914, almost 3 million immigrants moved to Canada. The greatest number of immigrants ever to come to Canada in one year was 400 000. That was in 1913.

The immigrants came to work in mines, lumber camps and factories. They also came to farm. The railway could easily carry settlers to the prairies and carry out shipments of wheat from the new farms. The Canadian government was anxious to have farmers from Europe to settle the prairies. It offered free land to the immigrants. More than 150 000 Ukrainians moved to Canada during those years.

Left: Immigrants arrive in Quebec City from Eastern Europe around 1900. What might they have brought with them in the bundles on the station platform?

After 1914, things changed. For many years Canada did not receive many immigrants. From 1914 to 1918, Canada was helping to fight World War I in Europe. The 1930s were not a time for large numbers of immigrants, either. Many Canadians were out of work. There were few jobs for immigrants. However, Canada did accept about 11 000 Jewish immigrants from Europe in the 1930s. They were being badly treated in Europe because of their religion and ethnic origin. Then, from 1939 to 1945, Canada was helping to fight World War II in Europe. During the war Canada accepted almost no immigrants. Thousands of Jews were refused entry to Canada. Many of the Jews who could not leave Europe were killed.

This map shows the Ukraine, or the Ukrainian S.S.R. Today it is part of the Soviet Union. Find the Soviet Union on the map on pages 298 and 299. Can you find the location of the Ukraine?

Who Are Refugees?

The **United Nations** defines refugees as people who have left their homeland because of their race, religion, nationality or **political** ideas. They are afraid that they will be harmed in their homeland, and so they try to find another country to live in. Canada uses the United Nations definition when it takes in immigrants as refugees. About 6000 refugees came to Canada in 1984.

The Hungarians

There is a loud knock and a voice calls, "Hurry, please answer." Inside the house, a young woman runs to the door.

"You must leave right now," her friend tells her. "The government has found out that you write for the secret newspaper."

The young woman is shaking. Quickly she throws a few belongings into a small bag. Then she hurries down the road to say goodbye to her parents.

This is Hungary in 1956. The young woman is a university student who has been writing for a secret newspaper. The newspaper encourages Hungarians to work for a better government.

Ever since the 1940s, many Hungarian people have been unhappy with their government. They were not allowed to say or write anything against the government. They were not allowed to leave the country either.

In 1956, the Soviet Union invades Hungary to help the Hungarian government. There is a **rebellion***: some of the people are fighting against the government. Thousands of people, like the university student, must run away from Hungary. It is not safe for them to return there. They would be badly treated because of their ideas about the Hungarian government. These people are known as* ***refugees****. The Hungarian refugees crowd into nearby countries. Some of them hope they can move on to another country from there.*

Several other countries want to help the Hungarians. The Canadian government sends planes and ships to bring some of the refugees to Canada.

The university student is pleased to go to Canada. She flies to Toronto, but at the huge airport, her heart sinks. She knows no one and she can't speak a word of English.

Then suddenly a woman in the crowd rushes forward and greets her warmly. She is from the Hungarian-Canadian Society, a group of Hungarians who are already living in Canada. She will help the student find a place to live and a class that teaches English to new immigrants. She will also help the student find a university to attend.

The student is grateful to be in Canada, where she is safe, but she misses her family terribly. So much has happened that she feels almost dizzy. She thinks sadly, "Just one week ago, I was at home in Hungary, not expecting to go anywhere."

In the past, as well as today, some people have not felt safe in their own homeland. They were afraid of being badly treated because of their race, religion or ideas about government. They left their homeland and became refugees. After World War II ended in 1945, thousands of refugees came to Canada. Some of them were Hungarians. These refugees learned how hard it is to leave their homes suddenly and move to a strange country. They were a great help to the Hungarian refugees, like the university student, who came to Canada later, during the rebellion in Hungary. Canada accepted 37 000 Hungarian refugees between 1956 and 1958.

- Why did Canada accept so many Hungarian refugees during these years?

A member of the Hungarian-Canadian Society greets a refugee from Hungary. How might the society help to make the refugee feel at home in Canada?

The Fijians

The young Fijian man has finished school and is ready to look for work. He has a fine record to show: high marks in his subjects, good behaviour at school and a letter from the principal saying he is a hard worker. What more could he need?

Sadly enough, he needs much more. Somewhere, he needs to find a job that isn't already filled. It is 1969 and there are few jobs in Fiji.

Fiji is made up of a group of tiny tropical islands that are green with fields of tall sugar cane. There are few other crops and few industries. Yet there are many well-educated young people looking for jobs.

The Fijian applies to immigrate to Canada, where more workers are needed to fill the available jobs. Soon he is on his way to British Columbia, the closest province to Fiji. He will have a job in a lumber mill near Vancouver. There are many Fijians there. He will also have a chance to go to a technical school and learn more about the lumber industry.

The Fijian has heard that Vancouver is not as cold as many Canadian cities. That pleases him. His life in Fiji has not prepared him for snow and ice. He knows that many things in Canada will seem strange to him, that he will often feel confused, lost and alone. But the Fijian also knows that Canada offers him a chance to work and to develop his own life. He is ready to take that chance.

- The Fijian moved to Vancouver, where there were other immigrants from Fiji. How might these other immigrants help him? If you were moving to another country, would you want to live in a city where there are other Canadians?

After 1967, immigrants of any race, colour, religion or country were free to come to Canada if they had jobs, were going to start businesses or had someone to support them. Before that, immigrants from some countries were more likely to be accepted than others.

The Fijians are one of the smallest ethnic groups in Canada. But in Vancouver, there are more than 5000 Fijians—the largest group outside Fiji.

Each year, Fijians come to Canada from their homeland in the tropics. Why do you think most of them settle on the west coast?

Today's Immigrant

After spending 14 months in prison for disagreeing with her government, a refugee from El Salvador arrives in Canada. A couple from Sweden comes to start up a new business. A Spanish-speaking 10-year-old boy flies from Ecuador to live with his aunt and go to school here. A scientist from Nigeria comes to work in Canada.

These people are the immigrants of today. They come to Canada from all over the world. Some come to join relatives that already live here. Some, like the refugee from El Salvador, come for their own safety. (Since 1945, about 1 out of every 14 immigrants has been a refugee.) But many immigrants come because Canada offers them something they cannot get in their own countries: a job, an education or, possibly, land and a house of their own.

Two children and their grandmother look at photographs and old newspaper clippings together. How might these materials help them understand their past?

Looking Back at Canada's Immigrants

You can see that immigrants have come from many different countries. For nearly 400 years, they have been coming to Canada to live. Some have come because they wanted to find new opportunities. Others have come because they wanted to escape starvation in their homeland. Some immigrants have been refugees, who left their homeland to escape punishment for their race, religion or political ideas.

When times have been good in Canada, there have been many jobs available. Sometimes free farmland was offered to attract new settlers. Immigrants have taken advantage of these opportunities. At the same time, immigrants have helped to meet Canada's needs for more workers. They have helped create new jobs, too, by starting businesses and buying Canadian goods. However, in hard times, fewer immigrants have been allowed into Canada.

For early immigrants, coming to Canada meant long, hard journeys. When they arrived, they often settled in undeveloped parts of the country. They built communities and cleared land for farms. They faced years of hard work and loneliness.

Later, immigrants generally came to more settled parts of Canada. Their journeys were easier and their work was not as backbreaking. However, they, too, had to adjust to life in a new country.

Although immigrants have had many challenges to face, they have worked hard to build new lives in Canada. And in the process, they have also worked hard to help build Canada itself.

- Do you think it would be easier to be an immigrant today or an immigrant in the past? Why?

nigration

Below: Immigrants to Canada make their way towards their new home in 1849. What kinds of items might their wagon contain?

An immigrant couple and their six children pose beside a railway station around 1900. What problems might a family with young children face when they move to a new country?

New immigrants are welcomed to Canada by their sponsors. How do you think the two groups of people are feeling?

CHAPTER CHECKUP

Recalling the Main Ideas

In Chapter 2, you read about a number of events in the past. Here are some of those events:

1663: King of France encourages people to settle in the French colony.

1783: United States gains independence from Britain.

1847: Potato blight occurs in Ireland.

1850: *Fugitive Slave Act* is passed in the United States.

1882: Canadian Pacific Railway is being built in British Columbia.

1913: Canadian government offers free land to immigrants.

1956: Soviet Union invades Hungary.

1967: Race, colour, religion or country of origin no longer considered when selecting immigrants to come to Canada.

Each of these events brought many new immigrants to Canada. Choose at least three events. For each one write

1. the event and its date,
2. where the immigrants came from,
3. the reason the immigrants came.

Using What You Have Learned

In this chapter you read about a Ukrainian family that came to Canada in 1913 and settled on a farm. Today immigrants still come to Canada to settle on farms. Choose at least two of the following questions. Write your answer to each question in two or three sentences.

1. Was farming harder in 1913 than it is today? Why or why not?
2. The Ukrainian family received free farmland from the government. Would an immigrant receive free farmland today? Why or why not?
3. Do you think the Ukrainian family was lonelier on the farm than immigrants on a farm today? Why or why not?

3

What Is It Like to Be an Immigrant in Canada?

Every year, thousands of immigrants move to this country. Some come from places that are similar to Canada. Others come from places that are very different from Canada. Still, all immigrants face the excitement and challenge of learning to live in a new country.

In this chapter, we will look at what it is like to be an immigrant in Canada today. You will read about the members of an imaginary family who came here from India. Although they are not real people, the kind of experiences they have are common to many new immigrants.

Coming to Canada

"There go two more," called Sanjit to his sister in a language called **Punjabi**.

Mahinder glanced out the open window. Two teenagers wearing headphones were walking up the street. They were snapping their fingers to music that no one else could hear.

"They look funny," said Sanjit.

Mahinder grinned. "No one in our village in India had headphones. But we saw some when we visited New Delhi. Remember?"

"Yes, but lots of people have them here," said Sanjit. He leaned on the window sill, thinking. People in Canada had quite a different way of life from people in India. In many ways, moving here was like coming to a whole new world.

Just one month ago, Sanjit was living in a small village in India. For years, his parents had talked about moving to Canada. They wanted to join his uncle there. His uncle agreed to help them. Then Sanjit's father found a job in southern Alberta and applied to move to Canada.

Sanjit and Mahinder have recently moved to Canada from India. What might they be thinking as they watch these two Canadian teenagers?

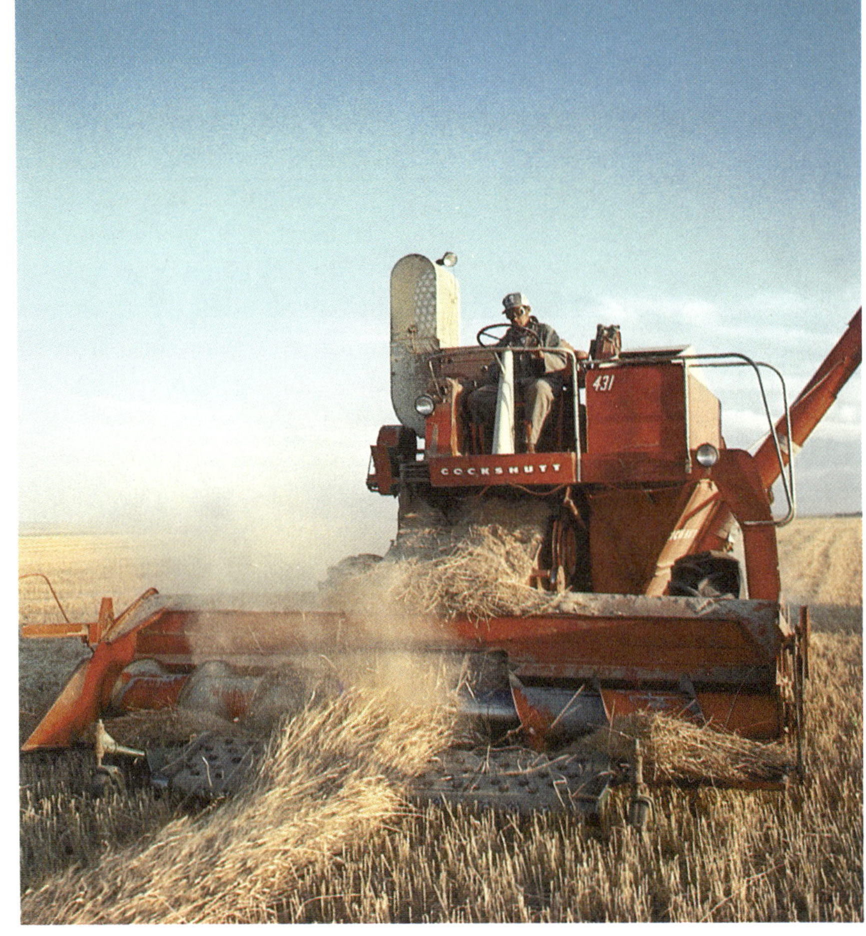

Like farmers in Punjab State, farmers in Alberta grow wheat. Here an Alberta farmer works on a combine. Why is Alberta a good place for the Samras to settle?

431
COCKSHUTT

This map shows the Samras' homeland in Punjab State and their new home in Alberta. About how many kilometres is Alberta from Punjab State?

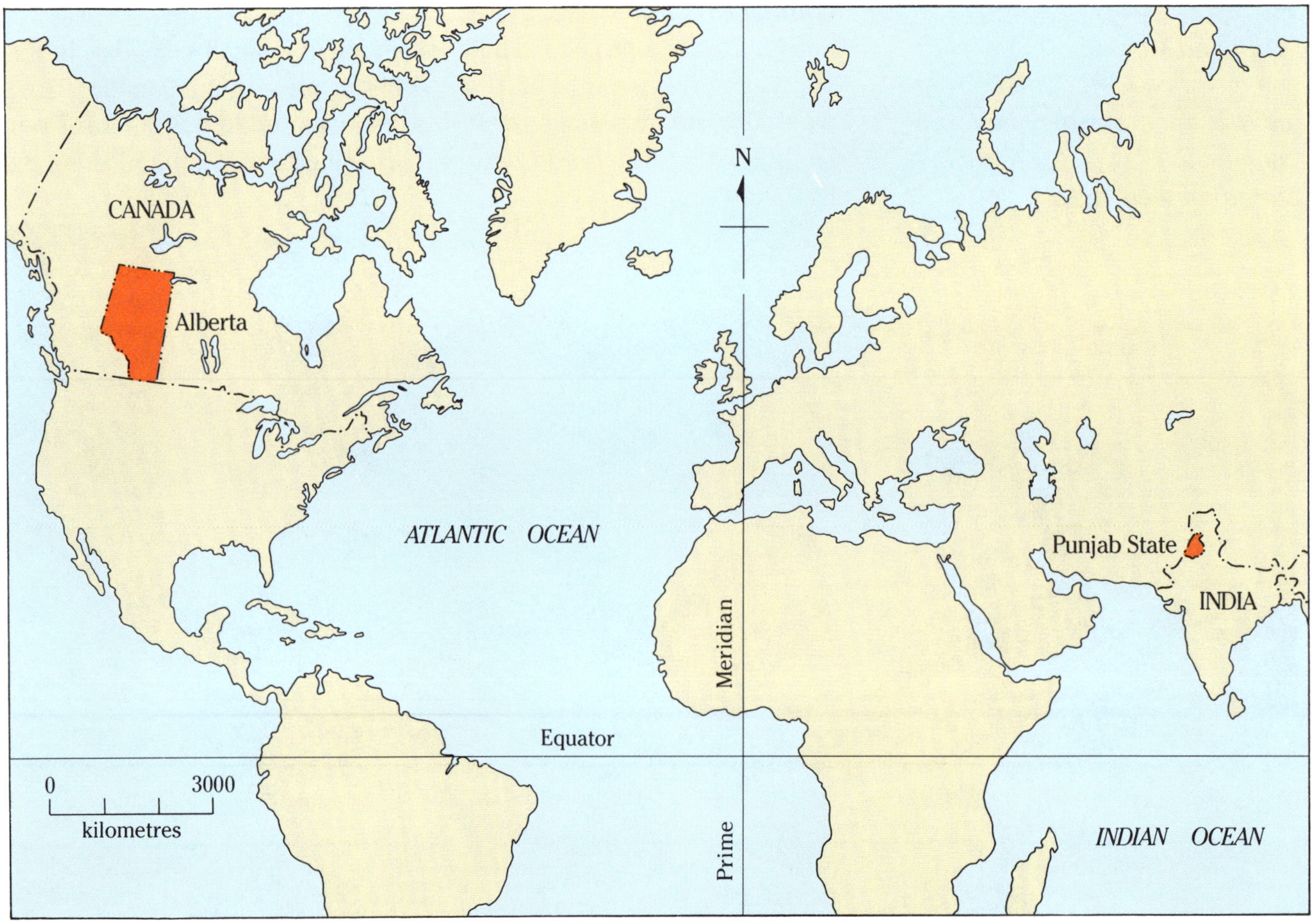

CANADA
Alberta
N
ATLANTIC OCEAN
Punjab State
INDIA
Prime Meridian
Equator
0
3000
kilometres
INDIAN OCEAN

Sanjit and Mahinder's father, Mr. Samra, is a water technician. In Punjab State in northern India, he helped to develop irrigation systems for wheat fields. Irrigation is a way of bringing water to fields to help crops grow.

Farmers in southern Alberta also use irrigation to grow crops. A research station hired Mr. Samra to work with other water technicians and engineers in Alberta. They are looking for ways to make better irrigation systems.

The Samras were pleased to come to Canada. They looked forward to the excitement of living in a new country. And they were happy to be joining Mr. Samra's brother and family. Sanjit and Mahinder's grandmother came with them to Canada, too.

- If your family moved to another country, what relatives might go with you?

Facts about India

Capital: New Delhi
Official Language: Hindi
Population: 713 million
Area: about 3 300 000 km^2 (square kilometres)
Climate: from very hot in the south to very cold in the mountains of the north
Main Crops: rice, grains, coffee, sugar, corn, spices, tea, cashews and cotton
Main Industries: textiles, steel, processed food, cement, machinery, chemicals, fertilizers, appliances and cars
Main Resources: timber, minerals and rubber

People at Varanasai, India, attend religious ceremonies at a temple on the waterfront. How is this city different from cities in Canada?

Learning about Canada

A cowboy rides a bull in a rodeo. What would it be like to see a rodeo for the first time?

Sanjit's mother called him. "Take this money," she said in the Punjabi language. "I want you to buy milk at the store."

Sanjit was glad to have something to do. School was not starting for a month and he had not made any friends yet. He walked out of the apartment, folding and unfolding the dollar bills. They still looked strange to him. In India, he had spent ***rupees*** and ***paise***. Canadian money was one of many things Sanjit had to learn about here.

At the store, Sanjit saw a woman from his apartment building. She smiled at him and asked, "Are you going to the rodeo this afternoon?"

Sanjit looked at her blankly.

"The rodeo," she repeated. "Are you going?"

Sanjit paused to think what she meant. He spoke English well, but there were some words, like "rodeo," that he didn't know. Whenever Sanjit had trouble with a word, some people thought he hadn't heard. They spoke louder, and that embarrassed Sanjit. Sometimes people assumed he was not very smart, and that hurt his feelings.

However, the woman understood. She knew that Sanjit was new to Canada. "Oh, I guess you wouldn't know about a rodeo," she said.

"No," Sanjit smiled, relieved.

"You'd like it. People ride wild horses and bulls. There are lots of races, too. It's starting today. Look, the paper tells you all about it," she said. She pointed to the front page of a newspaper.

Sanjit hurried home. His family was eager to learn about Alberta, so everyone was interested in the rodeo. Mr. Samra called his brother and suggested that they all go the next day.

The Samras were not disappointed. They found the rodeo very exciting. They cheered during the chuck wagon races and laughed at the clowns. Sanjit and Mahinder felt happy they had come to Canada. They thought there would be lots of exciting things for them to see and do.

- Pretend that you are showing Mahinder and Sanjit around your community. Where would you go? What special events or places would you want to show them?

Right: Sanjit and Mahinder do not yet have friends to walk home with from school. What are some of the reasons they have not yet made friends?

Going to School in Canada

When school started in September, Mahinder and Sanjit found that much of their excitement died down. They had to work very hard. They were excellent students, but English was not their **mother tongue**, and they could not read and write English as well as the other students could. In social studies, they knew little about Canada. Naturally, at school in India, they had studied more about that country.

Still, all the hard work was not as bad as the loneliness Sanjit and Mahinder felt. At recess, Sanjit usually couldn't find anyone to play with. The other students all knew each other, and they all knew the same games. While they played, Sanjit just watched. After school, Mahinder's classmates walked home in twos and threes. They talked and laughed together, but none of them walked with Mahinder.

Sanjit and Mahinder thought that they were left out partly because their way of life was different from most. Some students stared at Mahinder's brown skin. Some giggled and whispered about Sanjit's long hair gathered on top of his head. Once, some students laughed at the turban Mr. Samra wore when he visited the school. Sanjit and Mahinder wondered if their family would ever fit in.

One day, Mahinder had to stay after school. Sanjit waited for her on their apartment steps.

"I guess I'll have to stay in after school a lot," said Mahinder when she got home. "But I'm not going to wear shorts in the gym."

Sanjit's eyes widened. "Is that what they want you to do?"

"All the students are supposed to," said Mahinder.

"But you can't let your legs show," said Sanjit. "Didn't you tell the teacher? Won't she let you wear slacks?"

"I just told her that I wouldn't wear shorts. What's the use of explaining our way of life? Everybody thinks I'm strange enough already," she said angrily. She dashed past Sanjit up the stairs and into the building.

The following week, Mahinder continued to wear slacks in gym class even though all the other students wore shorts. Her teacher sent a note to Mrs. Samra about the gym shorts, but Mahinder didn't deliver it. She thought it might upset her mother, who was already unhappy.

Mrs. Samra and her mother-in-law were feeling very lonely. In Canada, it was hard for them to meet people. Although Mr. Samra's brother and sister-in-law lived nearby, they were at work all day. In India, Mrs. Samra and her mother-in-law had had many relatives and friends.

The Samras began to think of all they had left behind in India. They missed their friends and relatives in the village. They missed the festivals and special holidays they used to enjoy. Most of all, they missed the feeling that they belonged.

Indo-Canadians enjoy an outing to a city park. Why might they have decided to adopt North American dress?

- Do you think it is easier for children to adjust to a new country than it is for their parents or grandparents? Why or why not?

One evening, Mahinder was surprised to see the school counsellor at her door.

"Hello, Mahinder," said Mr. Nagano. "I've come to speak to your parents. They're expecting me."

Mr. Samra came to the door and greeted the counsellor. Mrs. Samra joined them in the living room. She served tea and ***samosas***—small pieces of dough filled with vegetables. Then Mr. Nagano told the Samras how hard Sanjit and Mahinder were working. He said he was very pleased that they were doing so well. Then he talked about how difficult it can be for immigrant students to make friends. "It takes time to feel at home and to get to know others," he said. "And it takes time for other students to understand that Sanjit and Mahinder came from a country with a different way of life."

"It takes time for us to adjust, too," said Mr. Samra. "I have to get used to my job here, and we would all like to meet more people. Next week my mother begins English classes."

"Good," said Mr. Nagano. "There's one more thing. Mahinder's teacher is concerned that Mahinder has refused to bring gym shorts to school. The teacher sent a note home, but she hasn't heard from you."

"I know nothing about it," said Mr. Samra. He and Mrs. Samra spoke together. Then he said, "My wife received no note."

"Mr. Samra, there are very few people from India living in southern Alberta," said Mr. Nagano. "There's a lot we don't know about your way of life. When I heard that Mahinder refused to wear shorts, I wondered if it was because of some Indian belief. The teacher has no other problem with her."

"You are right, Mr. Nagano. We believe that older girls and

Mr. and Mrs. Samra talk to Mr. Nagano, the school counsellor. Why is it a good idea for Mr. Nagano to visit the Samras?

women should always have their legs covered. But Mahinder should have told my wife about this," said Mr. Samra.

"She likely wanted to save you a problem," said Mr. Nagano. "And it may have been easier for her to refuse to wear shorts than to explain why she couldn't. She wants to feel more like other students, not less."

Mr. Nagano stood up to leave. "Don't worry. I'll explain to Mahinder's teacher. I'm sure she'll allow Mahinder to wear slacks in gym. I'm glad we had this talk," he said. The next day Mr. Nagano spoke to the teacher, and she agreed to let Mahinder wear slacks in gym.

During October, the students decorated the school for Thanksgiving. Then they hung witches and ghosts in the windows for Hallowe'en. As soon as that passed, they began to practise for the Christmas concert, which was just six weeks off. It all seemed so new and strange to Sanjit and Mahinder.

Mr. Nagano spoke to them after school one day. "I was just thinking," he said. "You've been learning so much about our way of life and what we celebrate in Canada. But we know very little about life in India. Would you like to talk to some of the classes about it?"

At first Sanjit and Mahinder refused. They felt uneasy. They didn't want to talk about all the things that made them different from the other students. But Mr. Nagano convinced them that most students would be interested to hear about Indian culture.

Telling about India

During the next week, Sanjit and Mahinder listed things to tell the students about India. Mr. Samra gathered up some pictures of India and some records. Mrs. Samra offered to cook some Indian food for the students to sample.

On the day of the talk, Mr. Nagano gathered two classes together in the gym. "Probably very few of us will ever travel to India," he said. "We are lucky that Sanjit and Mahinder have brought a bit of India here to us."

First, Sanjit and Mahinder showed photos of the village where they had lived. They also showed pictures of farms, schools and temples in India. Then they played a record of Indian music.

"We sang songs like this one at the beginning of winter," explained Sanjit. "In the middle of January, there's a special Punjabi festival called **Lourdie**. People sing, dance and eat special sweets. They feel thankful for life and for their children."

"A few months later, we **Sikhs** celebrate our new year, **Baisakhi Day**," said Mahinder. "It is the most important event of the year to Sikhs. We dress in new clothes and join in a three-day festival. People dance and swirl to drums like these." She paused so that the students could hear the drums on the record.

Then Mr. Nagano carried a big box into the gym. "You're in for a special treat," he said to the classes. "Mrs. Samra has cooked some Indian food for you to try."

Sanjit passed out Indian bread called ***chapati***. The *chapatis* were round and flat like pancakes. Mahinder passed around a big bowl of ***dhal***. It was like thick soup, made from lentils, onions and spices. Sanjit showed the students how to scoop up the *dhal* with pieces of *chapati*.

"This is a fun way to eat," said one girl, taking another scoop of *dhal*. "It tastes good, too."

"While you're eating, do you have any questions?" asked Mr. Nagano.

Several students wanted to know more about food in India. Others asked about clothing. Sanjit and Mahinder usually wore Canadian-style clothes to school, but that day they had dressed in their clothes from India.

"I once saw an Indian woman wearing a long dress. It was sort of wrapped around her. I think it's called a ***sari***," said one girl. "Don't you wear that?"

"Yes, but I also wear this ***salvar-kamiz***—a long shirt and pants. Women often wear these in Punjab State," said Mahinder, pointing to her clothes. "We also wear a long scarf called a ***dupatta***."

"Why do you wear your hair on top of your head like that?" one boy asked Sanjit.

Above: A young Indo-Canadian bride and groom pose for a picture after their wedding. How does the bride's clothing differ from the clothing worn by most Canadian brides?

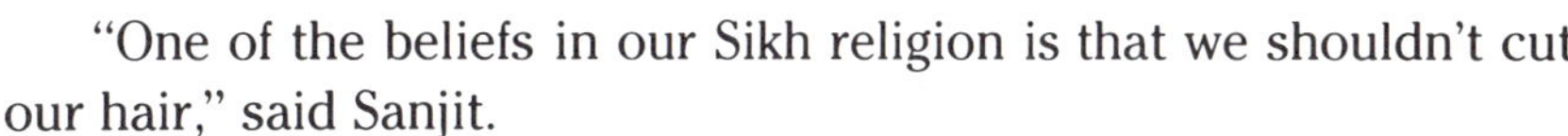

"One of the beliefs in our Sikh religion is that we shouldn't cut our hair," said Sanjit.

Mahinder explained something else about the Sikh religion, "In India, I would be called by my full name, Mahinder-Kaur Samra. Sikh girls and women use *Kaur* in their names."

Sanjit added, "And my full name is Sanjit-Singh Samra. Sikh boys and men include *Singh* in their names. The name is important in my religion. But there are many different religions and ways of life in India."

"Aren't there many different languages, too?" asked Mr. Nagano.

"Sixteen main ones," said Mahinder, "and hundreds of others."

"Wow," said one boy. "I thought it was something that Canada had two official languages. Can you speak all those languages?"

Sanjit and Mahinder laughed. "Oh, no," said Mahinder. "We just speak three: Punjabi, Hindi—which is India's national language—and English."

"You speak English very well—especially when it's your third language," said one student.

Mahinder and Sanjit smiled. They felt proud. The talk had gone better than they had hoped.

The rest of the school year went a bit better, too. Mahinder and Sanjit still had to work very hard in class, but they were beginning to catch up. They still felt left out by many students, but they were starting to make a few friends.

Mahinder's class decided to learn more about immigrants from India. Studying about immigrants helped Mahinder and her classmates feel that she belonged.

Mr. and Mrs. Samra were getting to know more people, too. They visited some of their neighbours and some of the people working with Mr. Samra. As Mahinder and Sanjit's grandmother learned more English, she felt more comfortable talking with people.

- There are different languages, religions and customs in India. What does this tell you about the culture of immigrants from India?

Young Indo-Canadians wear traditional clothing at a Canada Day celebration. At what other times might they wear these clothes?

Immigrants from India
Past to Present

Most of Canada's early immigrants from India were Sikhs from Punjab State. In 1897, some Sikh soldiers travelled through Canada. When they got home, they told other Indians about a country full of opportunities. Between 1905 and 1908, about 5000 Sikhs came, mainly to British Columbia. Most of them were men who worked in logging, mining and railway construction. Later some found jobs on dairy and fruit farms. These immigrants helped to develop Canada's natural resources.

Then the government began to limit immigration from India. For many years, very few immigrants came to Canada from India.

In 1951, the government of Canada agreed to accept 150 immigrants from India each year. Later 300 immigrants a year were accepted. In 1967, Canada stopped restricting immigrants according to country of origin. The number of Indian immigrants continued to grow. In 1974 alone, almost 15 000 came to Canada. During the 1980s, about 5000 immigrants have come from India each year.

Today's Indian immigrants have different religions and come from different Indian states. In Canada, they have settled in every province and territory. Ontario now has the largest number of Indian immigrants and their descendants.

In the early 1900s, many Indian immigrants worked in the forest industry in British Columbia.

Above: These Indians were not allowed to stay in Canada when they arrived here by ship in 1914.

Many Indian immigrants have settled in Canada in recent years.

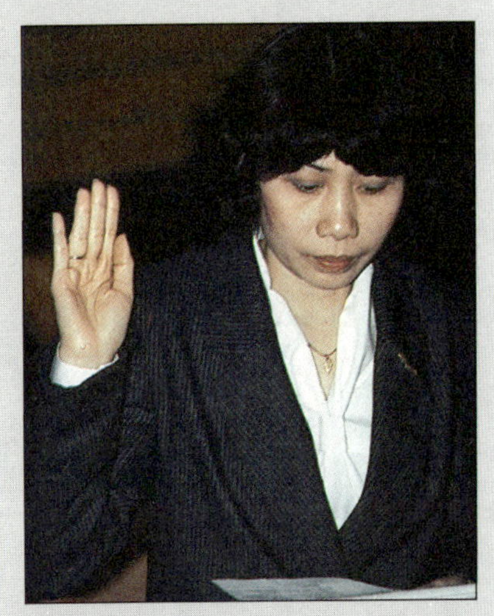

Citizenship

People born in Canada are Canadian citizens. Immigrants from other countries can also become Canadian citizens. At a citizenship ceremony they give their **allegiance** to Canada.

Canadian citizens have certain rights. For example, they have the right to vote and run for office in federal elections and some provincial elections. Only Canadian citizens may have Canadian passports. These allow people to travel to other countries and return to Canada. Certain jobs, such as being a police officer or practising law in some provinces, may be filled only by Canadian citizens.

Becoming a Canadian Citizen

Three years passed. While the Samras kept many of their Indian customs, they also began to feel more at home in Canada. Sanjit, Mahinder and their parents decided to apply for Canadian **citizenship**. Mr. Samra's mother did not want to apply.

When immigrants want to become Canadian **citizens**, adults must be interviewed by a citizenship judge. Mahinder and Sanjit decided to go to the interview, too. The Samras spent weeks getting ready for their interview. They learned something about Canada's government and history. They studied Canadian maps. They read about the rights and responsibilities of a Canadian citizen.

Sanjit and Mahinder had already learned many of these things in school. They were able to help their parents a lot. But when it was time to meet the citizenship judge, the Samras were all a bit nervous.

"Good morning," said the judge as they arrived at her office. She smiled and shook hands with each of them. Sanjit thought she looked friendlier than he had expected.

The Samras sat down while the judge glanced over some papers. "So, I see that you are all applying for citizenship," she said. "That's wonderful. Your application looks fine."

"Now, I just need to talk a bit to each of you," she continued. "As you know, new Canadian citizens must be able to speak either English or French. They must also know something about Canada."

The judge leaned back in her chair and began to chat with the Samras. She asked Mr. and Mrs. Samra how Canadians vote and how they make laws. She asked Sanjit and Mahinder to name Canada's Governor General and their city's mayor. The Samras pointed out capital cities on a map. They talked about some important dates in Canada's history, such as July 1, 1867. Then they discussed what citizenship means.

At the end of the interview, the judge sat quietly for a moment. Then she leaned forward and smiled. "I was just thinking," she said. "Many people born in Canada would not have answered those questions as well as you have."

- Why did the citizenship judge think that many Canadians could not answer the questions as well as the Samras could? Could you answer them?

The next month, the Samras attended a citizenship ceremony. They sat in court with 20 other immigrants from various countries. Friends and relatives of the immigrants sat at the back.

A citizenship judge, a court clerk and an RCMP officer stepped up on the platform. The audience stood and everyone sang "God Save the Queen."

A citizenship judge congratulates two new Canadians. How might they be feeling at this moment?

Then the judge stepped forward. "You probably made one of the biggest decisions of your lives when you decided to come to Canada," he said. "It's not easy to make a fresh start in a new country. Still, thousands of immigrants have done it. And they have become valuable citizens of Canada."

Then the judge asked the group of immigrants to stand to say the Oath of Citizenship. He invited Canadian citizens to join in, too. "It is good for all of us to repeat the oath from time to time. It helps to remind us to be good citizens," said the judge. Together, everyone said the Oath of Citizenship:

> I affirm that I will be faithful and bear true allegiance to Her Majesty Queen Elizabeth the Second, Queen of Canada, Her Heirs and Successors, according to law and that I will faithfully observe the laws of Canada and fulfil my duties as a Canadian citizen.

One by one, the new citizens walked up to the platform. They shook hands with the judge as he gave them their citizenship certificates.

When they were all seated again, the judge said, "Congratulations! Now you are citizens of Canada. Like all Canadians, you should do everything you can for your country. But don't ever lose the culture you brought from your homeland. That's a very important part of what makes this country so special."

Then everyone stood and sang "O Canada," the national anthem. Like the other new citizens, the Samras felt proud. "We'll always be Indian," whispered Sanjit to Mahinder. "But now we are Canadian, too."

Being a New Immigrant in Canada

In this chapter, you have seen a little of what it is like to be an immigrant in Canada today. Although our country offers immigrants many advantages, there's a challenge in learning to live in a new place. And it's a special challenge for immigrants from countries that are very different from Canada.

When immigrants come to Canada, they leave friends and relatives behind. They have to learn about many new things, such as Canadian school systems, government, money and customs. If immigrants have to learn a new language, too, they face an especially difficult challenge.

For many immigrants, settling in Canada is a lonely experience. It often takes a lot of time to make friends. Some Canadians are not willing to accept people from another ethnic group. Sometimes Canadians expect new immigrants to do things they wouldn't be allowed to do in their homelands.

In spite of the challenges, most immigrants adjust well and contribute much to Canadian life. They bring special skills and training to Canada. They enrich our lives with customs and ideas from their homelands. And because they have to earn their citizenship, they often value it even more than people who are born here.

- Are you a Canadian citizen? What does being a citizen mean to you?

Below: A tour boat takes sightseers around Toronto's waterfront. What might a new immigrant learn from a tour like this?

Friends share a snack after playing baseball together. What do you think they might learn from playing with each other?

Far left: Mahinder and Sanjit play soccer. How has their life changed since they first arrived in Canada?

MAKING A DECISION

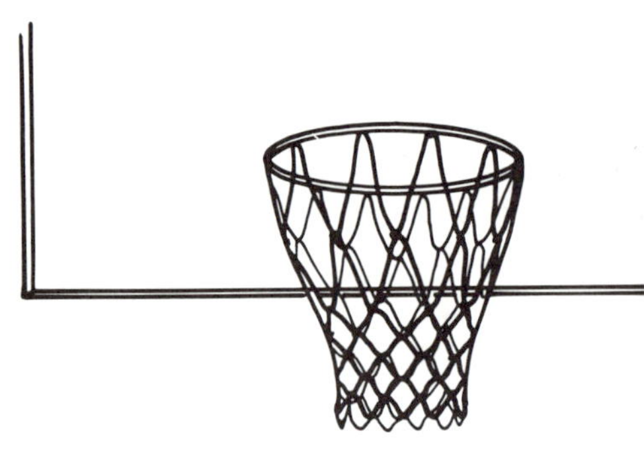

How Can We Make Immigrants Feel Welcome?

"Immigrants move to Canada every year," the teacher was saying. "But I'm sure it's not an easy thing to do."

"It would be really hard," said Alex. "My grandfather moved to Canada after the war and he told me that he felt very lonely. It took him a long time to make friends."

"When my neighbours first came to Canada," said John, "people made fun of them just because they were different. No one could understand their ways."

"I came to Canada four years ago," said Donja. "I remember feeling really confused. School seemed so different here. Many of the games and sports were new to me, too."

"Canadians should try to help new immigrants feel welcome," the teacher said. "We all benefit when they come to Canada. We should try to make Canada the kind of country newcomers want to move to. Do you think there is anything our class could do to help make immigrants feel more welcome?"

The students decided there were things they could do at school to help newcomers to Canada. The class decided to form a committee to meet new students and introduce them around the school. The committee would explain how the school worked. It would help immigrant students learn any games or sports that were new to them.

The committee might also appoint a "buddy" for each immigrant who might need help with English or French. The "buddy" might also learn to speak a few words in the immigrant student's language.

The class also planned to set up a display of books and pictures about other cultures. The students decided that immigrants would feel more welcome if they were asked to tell other students about their homeland. This would help the whole class learn about other countries and cultures.

- How could you help an immigrant student feel welcome at your school?

Students play basketball together. How might learning to play this game make a new immigrant feel more welcome in Canada?

CHAPTER CHECKUP

Recalling the Main Ideas

Imagine that Sanjit writes the following letter to his friend in India. Fill in the words that are missing.

Dear Surinder,

Yesterday I became a Canadian citizen. At a special ceremony, Mahinder, my parents and I said the ____(1)____. To become a Canadian citizen, you must be able to speak ____(2)____ or ____(3)____ and know some facts about ____(4)____.

I feel quite at home in Canada now. But when we first moved here, many things seemed strange. I had to learn to spend Canadian dollars instead of Indian ____(5)____ and ____(6)____. In our first year here, we learned about the days Canadians celebrate, like ____(7)____ and ____(8)____. Then we told some of the students about special days we celebrated in ____(9)____ State in India. We told them about ____(10)____, when people feel thankful for life and for their children. Mother cooked some ____(11)____ and ____(12)____ for the students to try.

Helping students understand our Indian ____(13)____ seemed to help them understand us. Anyway, we feel more comfortable in Canada now.

I hope you will write soon.

Your friend,
Sanjit

Using What You Have Learned

In the letter to his friend, Sanjit mentioned some of the challenges he and his family faced as new immigrants. There were many more. Choose four of the challenges Sanjit and Mahinder faced. For each,

1. write down the challenge,
2. write a sentence or two about what you might have done if you had been there to help Sanjit and Mahinder.

4

How Have Immigrants Contributed to Canada?

Immigrants from around the world have contributed to Canada in many ways. In this chapter, we will look at some of the contributions they have made. First you will read about the ways immigrants have helped Canada, past and present. Then you will read about a few individual immigrants and their personal contributions to Canada.

Along with Australia and the United States, Canada receives more immigrants than any other country. Even so, Canada doesn't receive all the people who would like to immigrate here. The federal government decides how many immigrants may come each year. It looks for people who can make a contribution to Canada. Let's look at some of the contributions immigrants have made over the years.

Ukrainian settlers stand in front of their home in northern Alberta around 1900. What materials have they used to build their house?

Immigrants Help Settle Canada

Try to imagine what Canada was like when only the native people lived here. Most lived in small villages. Some native people farmed, and others fished or hunted. Then, almost 400 years ago, people from Europe came here. Since then, millions of immigrants have settled in Canada. They have built cities and factories, railways and highways.

The first immigrants were French colonists. French settlers started farms and built towns along the St. Lawrence River. Some people settled in parts of Atlantic Canada. But Canada is a huge country, and the French settlements were just a small part of it.

Gradually, immigrants from Europe and the United States cleared farmland and built villages. Some immigrants, particularly the Chinese, helped to build the railway joining the country from coast to coast. The railway opened up new areas for settlement on the prairies. Immigrants started farms, ranches and small communities there.

As Canada developed, it needed thousands of workers to build roads, canals, harbours and dams. Immigrants from many countries helped. They also continued to help develop new settlements. Since the late 1940s, for example, many immigrants from Portugal have moved to new towns built near natural resources, such as the mining towns of Thompson, Manitoba, and Kitimat, British Columbia. Immigrants have settled in every province and territory of Canada.

There are many areas of wilderness in Canada today. Immigrants will probably help to settle new parts of Canada in the future, just as they have in the past.

Immigrants Help Populate Canada

People in Canada do not have enough children to replace the number of Canadians who die or leave the country. In order for the population to increase, many more births are needed or people from other countries must immigrate to Canada.

Why does Canada need more people? The country needs many people to buy its products. Also, the population is getting older. More and more Canadians are retiring every year. There are fewer working people to support older Canadians. Canada needs younger, working people to share the costs of services such as fire protection, hospitals and schools.

- How can Canada's population grow? Name two ways.

Left: French colonists greet each other in front of a fort around 1640. What might they be saying to each other?

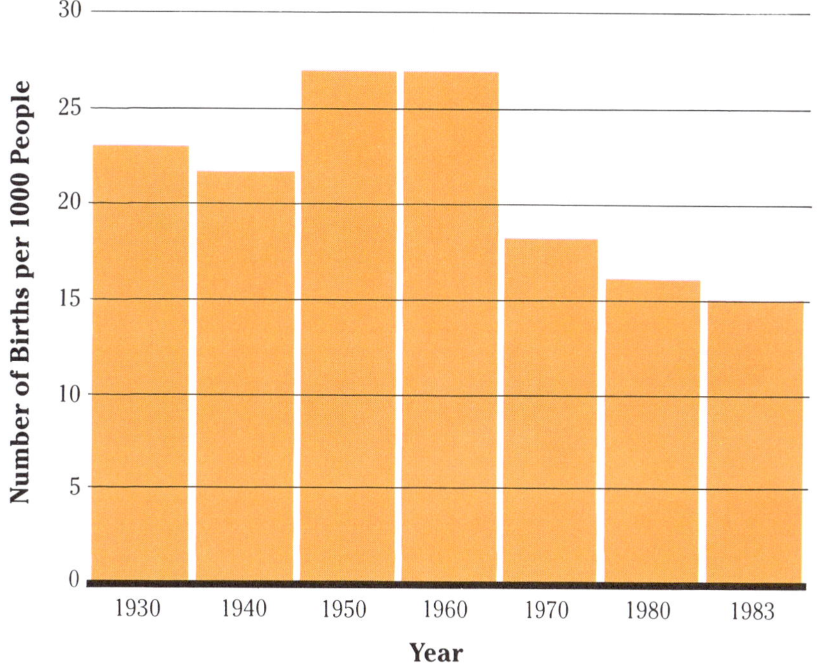

Above: This graph shows the birth rate in Canada from 1930 to 1983. What has been happening to the birth rate since 1960?

Left: Many immigrants have settled in new towns near natural resources. This is the mining town of Tumbler Ridge in British Columbia. How might an immigrant contribute to this new community?

Immigrants Bring Their Customs to Canada

Have you ever played soccer? Have you ever hung lights on a tree at Christmas? If so, you've enjoyed doing something that immigrants have contributed to Canada. The British introduced soccer, and the Italians, Poles and Ukrainians helped to make it a popular game here. The Germans started the tradition of putting lights on Christmas trees.

All year round, we enjoy contributions made by immigrants. They have come from over 200 countries, bringing their customs, games and foods with them.

Besides soccer, immigrants have encouraged several other sports in Canada. Scottish immigrants introduced golf and curling. American immigrants helped develop baseball and football. Austrian and Hungarian immigrants created an interest in fencing. Japanese immigrants introduced judo and karate.

Immigrants have even affected what Canadians eat. Today you probably enjoy Chinese egg rolls, Italian spaghetti and Mexican tacos. Different ethnic foods are so common and so popular that they have become part of the culture of many Canadians.

Immigrant groups often hold festivals and celebrations with dancing, singing and craft displays. You don't have to belong to an ethnic group to enjoy its celebrations. Some celebrations are so popular that Canadians outside the ethnic group take part. For example, many non-Chinese Canadians celebrate Chinese New Year in February, and many non-German Canadians join in the fun of Oktoberfest, a German fall festival.

- Think of some celebrations in Canada that originally came from other countries. Which ones do you enjoy?

Each year many Canadians celebrate Oktoberfest, a German fall festival. Can you think of other German customs or foods that Canadians enjoy?

Right: Scottish immigrants introduced curling to Canada. How do you think the game got its name?

Far right: Soccer was introduced to Canada by British immigrants. Can you name another ethnic group that has helped to make it popular?

This woman is making shoes at the Bata shoe factory in Batawa, Ontario. The Bata Shoe Company was started by an immigrant to Canada. How might this company help Canada?

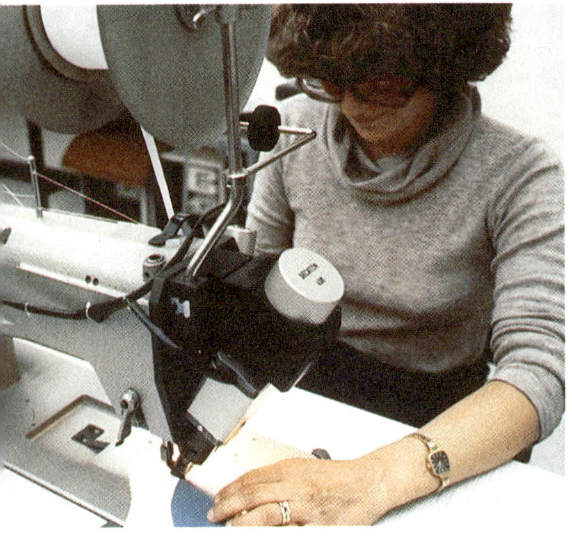

Immigrants Bring Their Skills to Canada

Through immigration, Canada has gained skilled people in every field of work. Many immigrants have years of training and work experience when they arrive. They help other Canadians by introducing new skills and creating new jobs.

- Think of some of the immigrants you know. Name some of the skills they have brought to Canada.

Immigrants in Business

French and British immigrants started businesses here as early as the 1600s. They built many trading posts. Both native Indians and new immigrants from Europe worked in the fur trade. Scottish immigrants opened Canada's first bank, the Bank of Montreal, in 1817. Over the years, thousands of immigrants started businesses like the ones they had run in their homelands—stores, restaurants and construction companies.

The new businesses often created jobs for other Canadians. Between 1950 and 1964, for example, 14 000 immigrants started small businesses in Canada. Other immigrants opened huge companies, such as Bata Shoe Company and Bick's of Canada, a company that makes pickles. Companies started by immigrants have hired thousands of Canadians. From 1980 to 1983, immigrants invested over two billion dollars in businesses that created over 14 000 jobs for Canadians.

Right: The grey building on the right in this picture is Canada's first bank, the Bank of Montreal. It was opened by Scottish immigrants in 1817. What skills are needed in the banking business?

Left: In the early 1900s, prairie farmers took their grain to the wheat market by wagon. What first attracted immigrants to the prairies?

Immigrants in Farming

Immigrants from many different countries cleared land and developed farms all across Canada. The promise of free farmland on the prairies attracted many immigrants in the early 1900s. Some religious refugees, such as the Russian Doukhobors and the Hutterites and Mennonites from Europe, established grain farms on the prairies.

Some immigrants made special contributions that improved farming for other Canadians. In the early 1900s, immigrants from the United States showed farmers how to irrigate Canada's dry prairie lands. Dutch immigrants built greenhouses in order to grow vegetables and flowers indoors. They also drained marshland in Ontario and British Columbia, creating thousands of hectares of rich farmland.

Immigrants in Fishing, Forestry and Mining

Large numbers of immigrants have helped develop Canada's resources. They brought skills in fishing, logging and mining from their homelands. In the 1870s, for example, Japanese immigrants introduced new fishing methods to the west coast. They started the herring fishing industry there. Hungarian immigrants worked with other Canadian foresters to improve the way forests are logged. American immigrants brought their knowledge of oil drilling to develop Canada's oilfields.

An oil rig is drilling for oil off the coast of Newfoundland. How do new resources help Canada?

Immigrants in Trades

Canada has always needed people trained in the **trades**. Early British immigrants brought their shipbuilding skills to Canada and helped create an important industry. During building booms, many of Canada's carpenters came from Europe. Italian immigrants did most of the mosaic work on buildings. Since the 1970s, Canada has gained tradespeople, such as goldsmiths from Ecuador, who have very specialized skills.

Immigrant journalists and commentators like this popular television host have brought their interests and opinions to Canada. How might other Canadians benefit from hearing the views of immigrants?

Immigrants in Professions

Professionals, such as teachers, doctors and lawyers, have settled in Canada since the 1600s. Since the 1940s, many more professionals have come. A large number of them have been refugees. They have contributed their skills to Canada's universities, research centres, hospitals, industries and government. During the 1960s, when Canadian universities were growing quickly, Canada needed more teachers and researchers. Immigrants from many countries responded.

Canada has also gained professional artists from around the world. Musicians, conductors, composers, opera singers, dancers, actors, painters, sculptors and architects have brought their special talents to Canada.

- How does Canada benefit by receiving immigrants who have been educated and trained in other countries?

Musicians from other countries bring their musical skills to Canada when they settle here. How might you benefit from their skills?

How Canada Chooses Immigrants

Anyone from any country may apply to immigrate to Canada. The Canadian government decides how many immigrants may come each year. It tries to choose immigrants who will settle successfully in Canada. There are three groups of immigrants who come to Canada: the family class, refugees and a group called "independent and other immigrants."

Immigrants in the family class must be sponsored by a close relative in Canada. They must also be of good health and character.

Some refugees are sponsored by groups of five or more Canadian residents. The government helps refugees without sponsors to settle in Canada.

The group of independent and other immigrants includes retired people, self-employed workers and people who come to start businesses. This group also includes those who have relatives (but not sponsors) in Canada to help them. Except for retired people, immigrants in this class are chosen according to a point system. The more points they receive, the better chance they have of coming to Canada.

Points are given for things such as education, job training, experience, age and ability to adjust to Canadian life. People also receive points if they have a job to come to or if they can work in areas where Canada needs people. Points are also given for knowing French or English and for having relatives in Canada who are willing to help a new immigrant.

This chart shows the three groups of immigrants who come to Canada today. Which group is the largest?

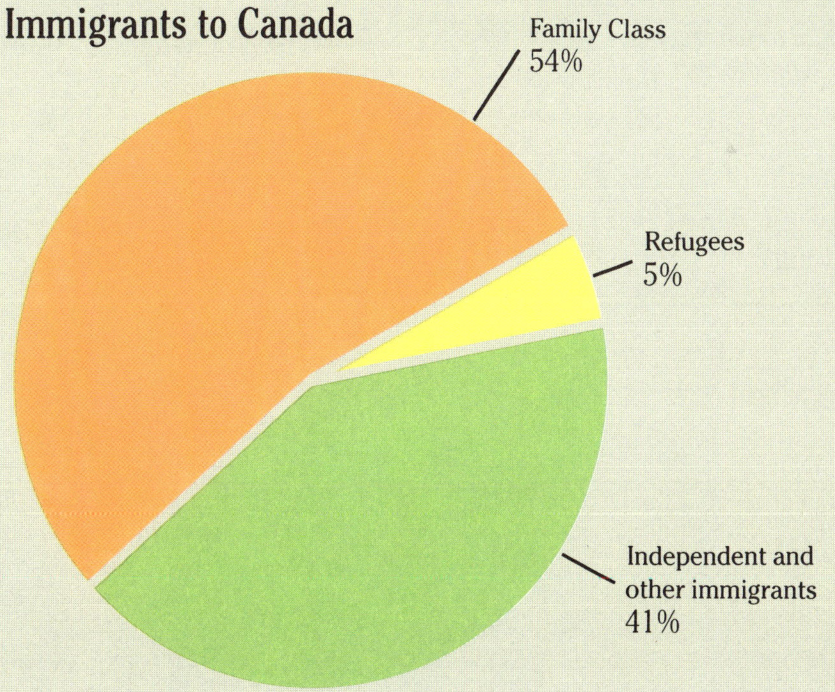

Contributions of Individual Immigrants

You have read about some of the many ways immigrants have contributed to Canada. Now let's look briefly at seven individual immigrants who settled in Canada at different times. Each of them came from a different country. Each of them made a different kind of contribution to Canada.

Jeanne Mance, Nurse

Jeanne Mance was a nurse who came to a French colony in Canada in 1641 to establish a hospital for the colonists. She lived and worked in a small settlement that later became the city of Montreal. What kind of person do you think she was?

Jeanne Mance was born in France in 1606. She became a dedicated, hard-working nurse. When she heard that a French colony in Canada needed a hospital, Mance decided to go.

In 1641, Mance set out for the colony with a small group of soldiers, labourers and nurses. They came to a small settlement that grew to become the city of Montreal. To Mance, the settlement seemed almost lost in the wilderness.

Right away, she organized the building of a small, temporary hospital. After three years, she moved her patients to the new hospital, called Hôtel-Dieu, in Montreal.

Although it was hard to run a hospital in the wilderness, Mance was determined to continue. Sometimes there were battles and her life was in danger. Sometimes she was short of staff and money to run the hospital. She had to make several trips back to France for more nurses and money.

Until her death, Jeanne Mance was devoted to helping the people in Canada. In her honour, a statue stands in front of the Montreal hospital she founded.

John Ware, Rancher and Settler

In 1845, John Ware was born a slave in the southern United States. When slavery ended 20 years later, he became a cowboy. He learned to ride horses and rope cattle.

In 1882, Ware was hired to drive some cattle to Canada. He crossed the border into the Canadian prairies and never went back to the United States. Although there were few black people in that area, he decided to make Canada his home.

Sometimes people treated Ware very badly. Just because he was black, they insulted him on the streets. Sometimes hotel keepers refused him a room. When he took jobs at ranches, he often had to work harder and longer than the cowboys who were not black.

- Why did John Ware have to work harder and longer than cowboys who were not black? Do you think that could happen today?

By 1890, life in Canada had grown easier for Ware. He had saved enough money to buy his own ranch near Calgary. He had married and started a family. The settlers began to respect him. They knew he was good with horses and often asked for his help breaking in wild horses.

John Ware became one of the best-known successful ranchers in the area. Today a hill, a creek, a museum and a Calgary school are all named after him.

John Ware and his family stand in front of their home near Calgary. Ware was born in the United States and worked there as a cowboy. What skills did he bring to Canada?

This is a picture of Margret Benedictson and her family. Benedictson was born in Iceland and left her homeland in 1886. She later became a suffragette in Canada. How has her work as a suffragette helped you today?

Margret Benedictson, Suffragette

Margret Benedictson was born in Iceland in 1866. When she was 20, she left Iceland for North America. In 1889, she settled in an Icelandic community in Manitoba.

Benedictson had grown up in a country where both men and women had the right to vote. She was shocked to find that women in Canada did not have that right. She became a suffragette.

In 1898, Benedictson began publishing a monthly newspaper in the Icelandic language. It was the first paper in Canada that encouraged people to work for women's rights. Then, in 1908, she founded an organization of suffragettes in Winnipeg. The group tried to convince the Manitoba government to give women the vote.

As the suffragette movement grew, other women's rights groups joined Benedictson and the Icelandic women. In Unit III you read about Nellie McClung, who led these groups in their struggle to get the vote. In 1916, the women of Manitoba became the first in Canada to get the right to vote in their province. Margret Benedictson had worked many years for this victory.

- Suppose you moved to a country where women couldn't vote. Would you try to change that law? Why or why not?

Celia Franca, Dancer and Director

Celia Franca was born in England in 1921. As a girl, she begged her parents to give her dancing lessons. After years and years of hard work, she became a leading ballerina.

In 1951, Franca was invited to Toronto to form a ballet company for Canada. She went to work immediately, travelling right across the country to find excellent dancers. That same year, she founded the National Ballet of Canada with only 29 performers.

Franca worked hard to make the ballet company a success. She was the company's artistic director and a leading dancer. She helped to start the National Ballet School so that the ballet company would have a supply of well-trained dancers. Under her leadership, the National Ballet grew larger and more popular. It became one of the finest companies in the world.

Celia Franca has won many awards, including the Order of Canada, for her contributions to ballet in Canada.

Order of Canada

The Order of Canada was created in 1967 to honour Canadian citizens for outstanding achievement or service to their country. Every year the Governor General presents Order of Canada medals to many deserving Canadians. They become members of the Order of Canada for their contributions in recreation, literature, music, art, science, medicine and many other areas of life.

Celia Franca has appeared as the lead dancer in many ballets. She also established the National Ballet of Canada. How has Franca's work made a difference in the lives of Canadians?

Edith Andody, Forester

Edith Andody was born in Hungary in 1932. She wanted to become a forester and began studying at Hungary's Sopron School of Forestry. Then, in 1956, the Soviet Union invaded Hungary. Many Hungarians fled the country. Two hundred students and 29 professors from the Sopron School fled, too. Andody went with the group to nearby Austria.

The students and professors came to Canada in January 1957. The refugees spent several months studying English and learning about Canadian forests. In the fall, the Sopron School became a special part of the University of British Columbia. The professors continued to teach forestry, in Hungarian, until all their students graduated.

Andody was part of the first graduating class. But she couldn't find a job as a professional forester. At that time, many people felt that the work and the forest camps were too rough for women. No women had been hired as professional foresters in British Columbia.

Andody took a low-paying job as an office assistant with the British Columbia Forest Service. Nine years passed before the government gave her a position as a professional forester. Today she is still working as a forester for the British Columbia government.

Canada gained the skills and knowledge of many Hungarian foresters like Edith Andody. One president of the University of British Columbia said that the coming of the Sopron School was "one of the greatest immigrant dividends this country has ever had."

- Pretend you are a new immigrant in Canada. How would you feel if you couldn't get the job you were trained to do?

In 1957 Edith Andody came to Canada as a Hungarian refugee. Today she is a professional forester with the British Columbia government. What challenges do you think she faced when she arrived here?

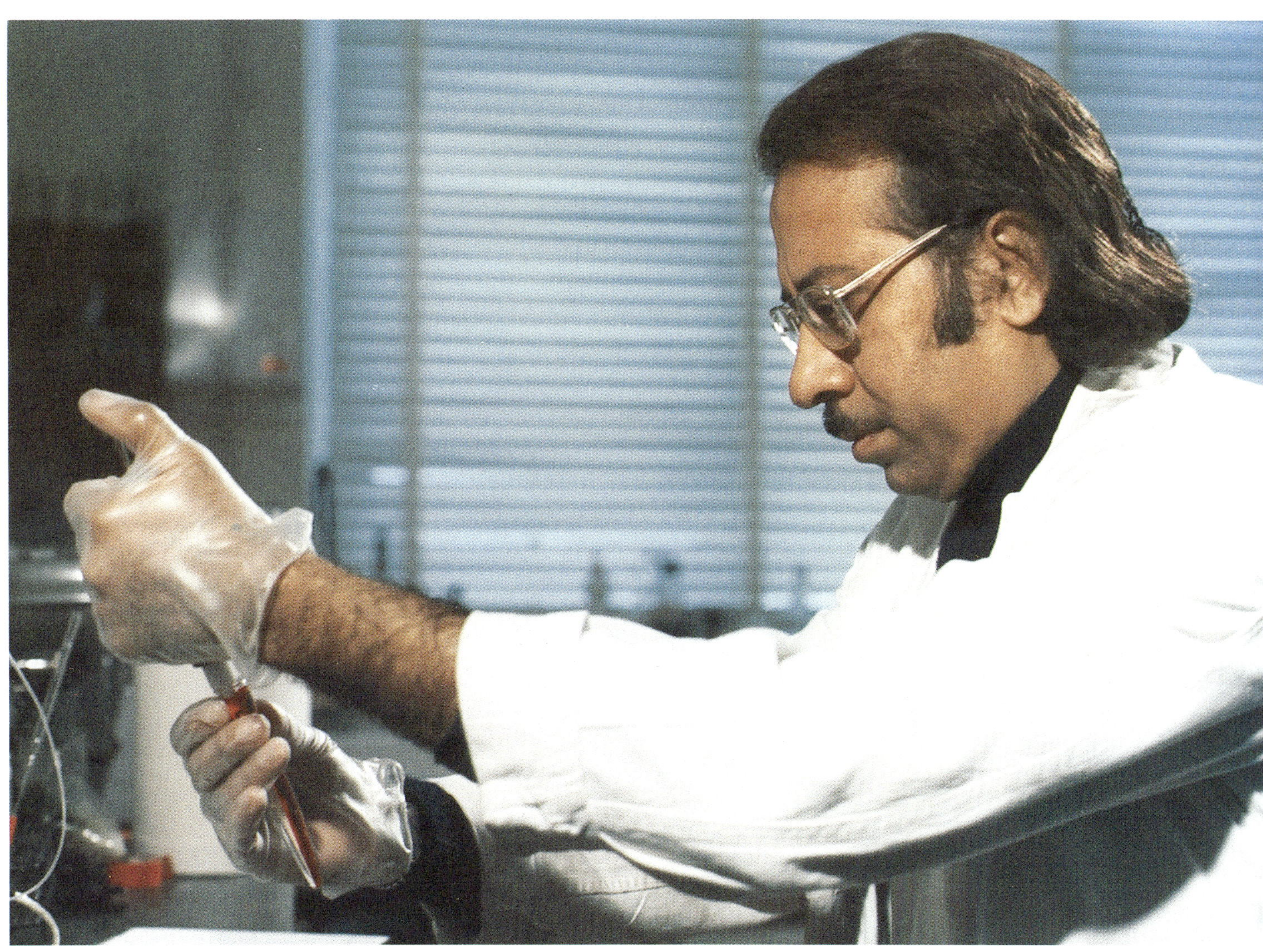

Saran Narang was born in India. Today he works for the National Research Council in Ottawa. His research has helped to develop life-saving drugs and some vaccines. How might Saran Narang's work help you and your friends?

Saran Narang, Scientist

Saran Narang was born in India in 1930. He studied science at university there and graduated with three degrees. When he was 32, he moved to the United States to do scientific research.

In 1966, Narang came to Canada. He thought that the Canadian government's National Research Council in Ottawa offered him a better opportunity to do the type of research he wanted to do.

Narang's research is very important because it helped to develop methods to make drugs, like insulin, and some kinds of vaccines. His work may also help scientists learn more about cancer.

Today Saran Narang is a Principal Research Officer at the National Research Council. He has won many awards, including the Order of Canada, for his scientific research.

- How will people in other countries, as well as Canadians, benefit from Saran Narang's research?

David Chuenyan Lai is a professor at the University of Victoria. For several years he helped to redevelop Victoria's Chinatown. How do you think it feels to be awarded a medal?

David Chuenyan Lai, Professor

David Chuenyan Lai was born in China in 1937, but he grew up in Hong Kong. He went to the University of Hong Kong, where he specialized in geography. Later he won a scholarship to finish his university education in England.

Lai taught at the University of Hong Kong. He enjoyed his work there, but he was attracted by the opportunities to do research in Canadian universities. In 1968, he joined the Geography Department of the University of Victoria in British Columbia.

As Lai settled into Victoria, he became interested in the city's history. He worked with several committees to help preserve historical buildings and papers. During Lai's research into the history of Victoria's Chinatown, he studied some 100-year-old Chinese paintings that had been stored in an attic. For many years, he worked to redevelop Canada's oldest Chinatown.

Since 1980, David Chuenyan Lai has won many awards for his work. He was made an Honorary Citizen of the City of Victoria. In 1983, Canada's Governor General made him a member of the Order of Canada.

How Immigrants Help Canada

In this chapter, you have read about some of the contributions immigrants made to Canada. You saw that they helped to populate and settle the country. They helped to build cities, farms, highways and railways. They introduced many new customs. They brought to Canada a wide range of skills and experience in business, resource industries, trades and professions.

Some immigrants have won awards or have become famous for their contributions to Canada. Still, most immigrants, like most other Canadians, are ordinary people. They have contributed to Canada by settling here, working hard and introducing their own particular skills and ideas. They have become part of the millions of people that keep this country running. You probably know some of them in your own neighbourhood.

Thousands of immigrants came to Canada because they found greater acceptance and opportunity here than in many other countries. All Canadians benefited. In the future, Canada will need the help of many more immigrants. Canadians must try to keep Canada the kind of country newcomers want to make their home.

- What do you think is the most important contribution immigrants have made to Canada?

Two immigrants play with their child in a city park. How might they contribute to Canadian culture?

MAKING A DECISION

How Can We Learn More about the Contributions Immigrants Make?

The class had just watched a film about immigrants. Some of the students were surprised at how much immigrants had contributed to Canada.

"I didn't know that immigrants started hockey here," said David.

"They introduced many of the sports we play, and many of our customs," said the teacher.

"If immigrants hadn't come, we wouldn't have many people in Canada," said Teresa.

"No," the teacher agreed. "Millions of immigrants helped Canada grow. And they contributed their labour and skills, too. They have worked at everything from logging our forests to teaching in our universities."

"The film showed that thousands of Chinese immigrants helped to build the railway," said Paul. "I've seen pictures of the last spike being hammered into the railway. But there were no Chinese people in them."

"You're right," said the teacher. "Many immigrants weren't given credit for the contributions they made to Canada. That's one reason many Canadians, like you, don't know how much immigrants have done for this country—or how much they are doing today."

The class decided that was unfair. The students thought it was important for Canadians to know about the contributions of immigrants to Canada. They decided to help students in their school to become more aware of these

These students are showing their teacher the script of a filmstrip they have produced. If you were preparing a filmstrip about the contributions immigrants make to Canada, what pictures would you want to include?

contributions. The students talked about how they could do this. They decided to show films—like the one they had seen—in the lunch room at noon hour. They planned to set up a bulletin-board display of contributions immigrants have made to Canada.

One student offered to ask the art teacher for help making posters on the contributions of immigrants. Another student suggested that the school could run an essay contest on "What Immigrants Have Done for Canada."

- How might you help others learn more about the contributions of immigrants to Canada?

CHAPTER CHECKUP

Recalling the Main Ideas

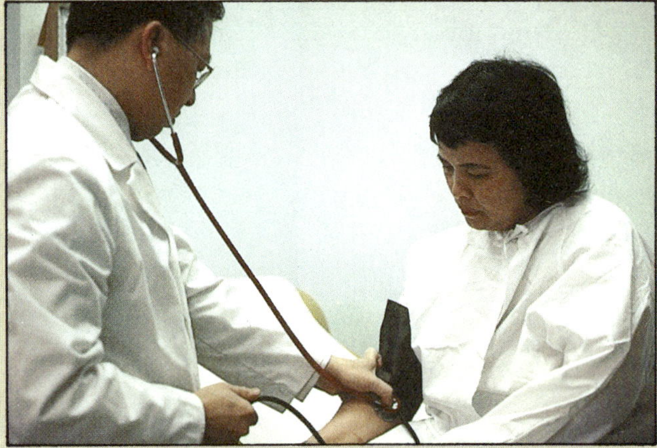

Each of these pictures shows immigrants making a contribution to Canada. For each picture,

1. name the contribution,
2. write why the contribution is important to Canada.

Using What You Have Learned

Immigrants have made many other contributions to Canada. Think of contributions, both past and present, that immigrants have made to your community. Name at least three contributions. Write them down and explain how each contribution is important to you.

5

How Might Immigration Change in the Future?

Friday, January 28, 2039

Irene Spoulos pulled a portable TV from her pocket and turned on the news channel. "Look at these shots of the island," she called to the man across the room. "It's a disaster. That volcano really blew."

Simon Mills joined her. He looked over Irene's shoulder and shook his head sadly.

"A volcano erupted, completely destroying this tiny island," the TV announcer was saying. "It is one of 13 000 Indonesian islands in the Pacific Ocean. Farms, homes and entire communities were destroyed. However, injuries were few. Airships from Canada, Australia, India and China helped with the evacuation. They flew everyone to Indonesia's capital, Jakarta. For about 200 000 islanders, there's no going back. Scientists say it will be at least 10 years before anyone can live on the island again."

"I wonder if many of those people will stay in other parts of Indonesia," said Simon.

"Some will, but Indonesia is very crowded," said Irene. "Some people may go to nearby countries like Malaysia or Thailand. Many people, like the ones coming here to Canada, will go to the countries that helped evacuate them."

"One of our airships will arrive here late this evening," said Simon, glancing at his watch. "The airship is slow, but it was ideal for this rescue. There was no place to land a jet on that island."

"Well, we'd better get to work," said Irene. "There's a lot to do before the airship gets here."

Simon and Irene are volunteers at one of the Canadian Centres for New Immigrants in 2039. The centres offer many services to help immigrants adjust to Canada. In emergencies, they also provide a place to stay until immigrants have their own homes.

Simon, Irene and the staff at the centre were loading memory capsules into electronic language translators. They could use the translators to talk with the new immigrants. When the Indonesians spoke their language into the translator, English would come out. When the centre workers spoke English into the translator, the language of the Indonesians would come out.

It was late in the evening when Simon heard the airship hovering above the centre. Men, women and children entered the roof

Irene Spoulos and Simon Mills look at a portable TV. What are some advantages of a small TV?

lobby. They looked tired, worried and confused. Children were clinging to their parents. Babies were crying. The staff and volunteers worked quickly to find places for everyone to spend the night.

Later, as Simon pulled on his coat to leave, Irene said, "I'm coming back in the morning. How about you?"

"Sure," said Simon, "I'll be in."

"You spend a lot of time here, Simon," said Irene. "Were you a new immigrant once—like I was when I came from Greece?"

"No, but I was a 'new Canadian kid,'" said Simon, grinning.

"What do you mean?"

"It's a long story," said Simon. "I'll tell you sometime when we're not so tired. But I understand a little bit about how hard it is to move to Canada."

When Simon returned to the centre the next day, lots of things were happening. Several members of the Canadian-Indonesian Society had arrived. They were talking with the new immigrants, trying to reassure them.

The workers in one of the offices were helping some immigrants reach relatives in Canada. Volunteers in the home-finders office were searching computer listings to find houses or apartments for those who needed them. In another office, the staff was arranging emergency funds for immigrants who had arrived with little money.

Simon knew that after the Indonesians had settled in, the centre would help them find jobs. If necessary, it would help retrain them. It would run language classes so that they could all learn French and English. Immigrants could also use the computer to look up information about Canada in their own language.

But Simon knew that computers and classes are not enough. New immigrants, like anyone else, need friends to make them feel at home. Simon had come back to the centre to get to know some of the Indonesians.

We have been imagining an event in the future, in the year 2039. We made up a volcano that erupted and islanders who came to Canada. And, of course, we made up Simon Mills. He's the same Simon you read about in Chapter 1, about 50 years older.

We can easily imagine that immigrants, like these Indonesians, will be coming to Canada in the future. This country has been receiving immigrants for hundreds of years. Some of them really did leave their homelands during a **crisis**. When they came, many were helped by the government, ethnic groups and volunteers.

But will the future change immigration in other ways? Will the government build many "Centres for New Immigrants"? Will inventions like electronic translators help with language problems? The rest of this chapter raises questions for you to think about. No one knows what changes will take place, but you can try to imagine what future immigration to Canada will be like.

An erupting volcano glows in the background as airships take people away from their island home to safety. These people know that they may never be able to return home again. How might they be feeling?

How Might the Number of Immigrants Change?

Can you picture a world that is always peaceful? Can you imagine people who have all the food, homes, skills, services and opportunities that they want? In a world like that, there would be few immigrants. Few people would want to leave their homelands. And there would be few countries needing immigrants.

The number of immigrants changes as the needs of people and countries change. When Canada wanted people to settle the prairies, thousands of immigrants came to farm. During the rebellion in Hungary, many refugees fled to Canada. Just as it has in the past, the number of immigrants will likely rise and fall with changes in Canada and other parts of the world.

Right: Will there be fewer jobs in Canada for immigrants to come to? Will the work of computers and robots eliminate many jobs for both Canadians and immigrants?

Will there be new communities in Canada for immigrants to come to? As we find ways to develop the north, will immigrants help settle more of Canada?

Above: Will fewer people need to immigrate to Canada? Will scientists find more ways to grow food in deserts? Will countries be able to grow enough vegetables and fruit in factories?

Birth Rate in Canada
1990–2040

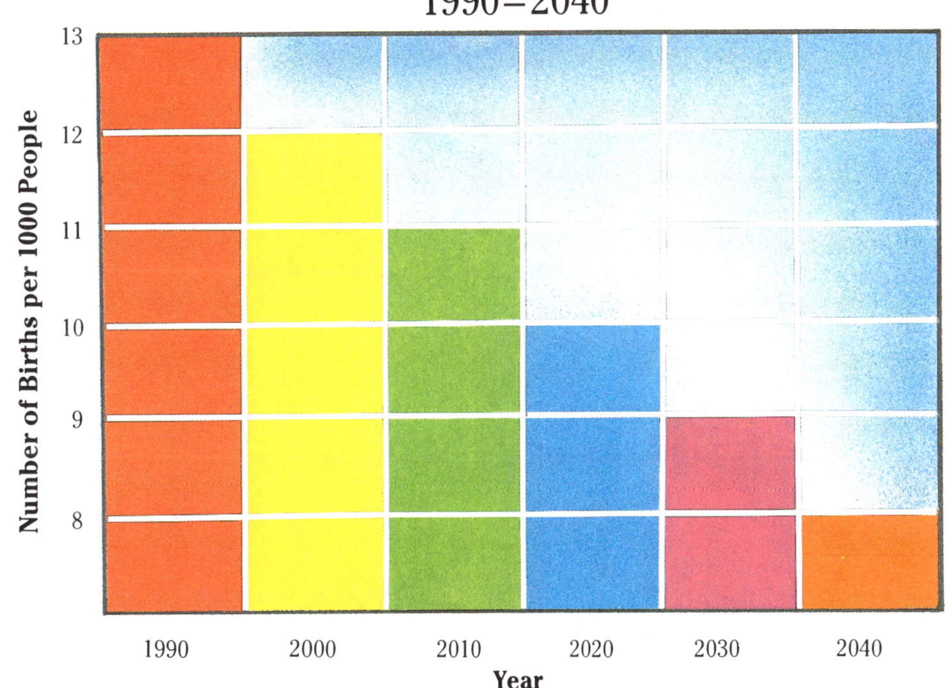

Will the number of Canadians being born affect future immigration? Will the birth rate rise, creating a bigger population for Canada without any immigration? Or will the birth rate drop, as shown in this graph? If so, will this drop create a greater need for immigrants?

Where Might Immigrants Come from in the Future?

Who will have the skills and ideas that Canada needs? Who will need or want what Canada has to offer? If you could answer those questions, you would know where Canada's future immigrants will come from.

Immigrants, both in the past and the present, have come from overcrowded countries and countries at war. They have also come from rich countries and peaceful countries. Early immigrants came mainly from France, Britain, the United States and Ireland. Today Canada receives immigrants from countries all around the world.

Will more immigrants come from countries where the land is overcrowded and the people cannot grow enough food? Will Canadians share more of their land and resources with people who have very little?

Will more immigrants come from French-speaking countries? Will Quebec encourage more French immigrants?

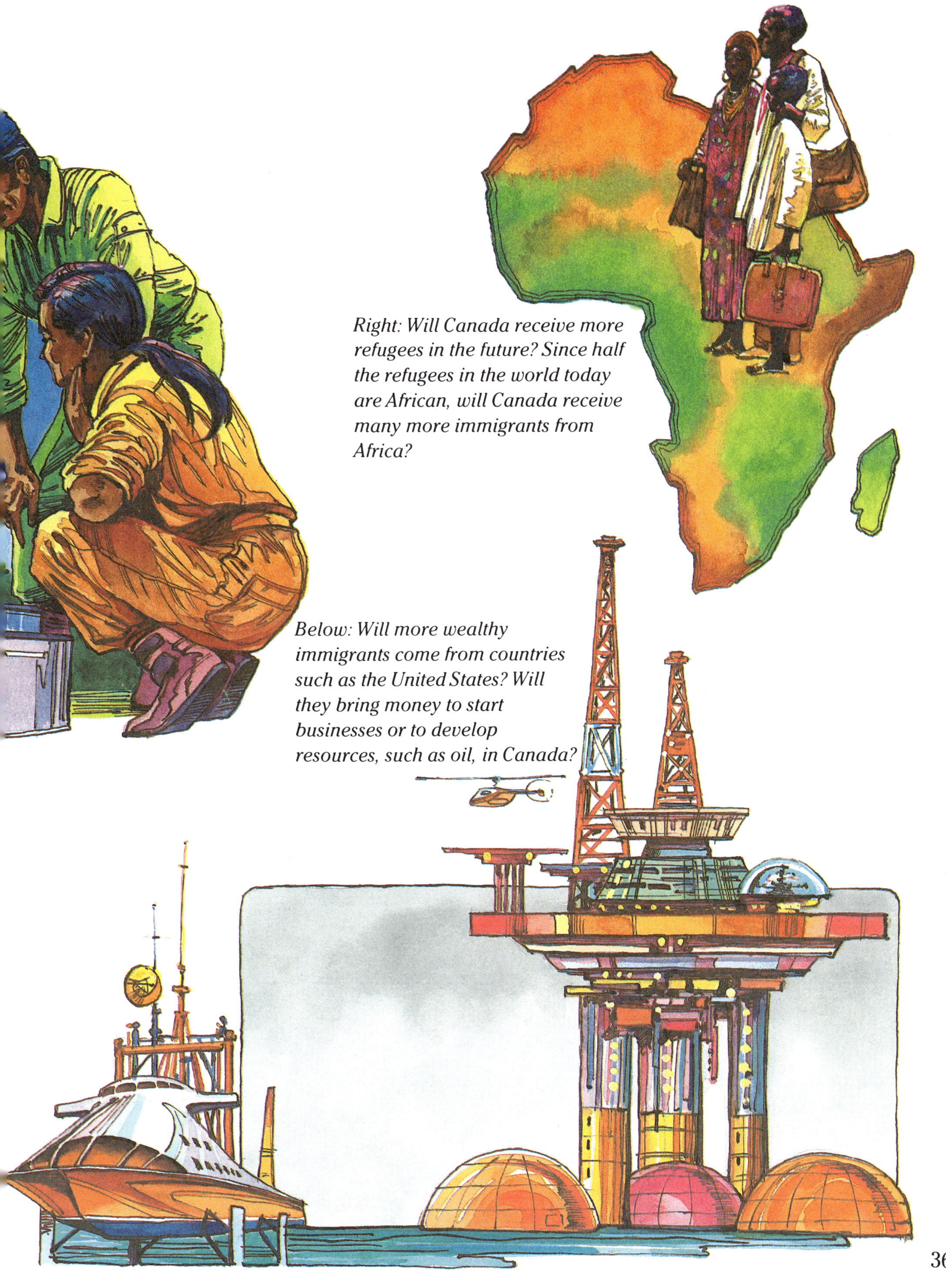

Right: Will Canada receive more refugees in the future? Since half the refugees in the world today are African, will Canada receive many more immigrants from Africa?

Below: Will more wealthy immigrants come from countries such as the United States? Will they bring money to start businesses or to develop resources, such as oil, in Canada?

What Might Contributions from Immigrants Be Like in the Future?

For almost 400 years, immigrants have contributed important skills and ideas to Canada. They have built hospitals, opened businesses, improved farming and taught school. They have worked with other Canadians in almost every field. In the future, immigrants will also make important contributions to Canada. But the kinds of contributions will depend on Canada's needs and the needs of other countries.

Just as these needs have changed in the past, they will likely change in the future. Can you imagine what some of those needs will be? Can you imagine how the contributions made by immigrants in the future might be different from those made today?

Will Canada want more immigrants with the money to start new businesses and create new jobs?

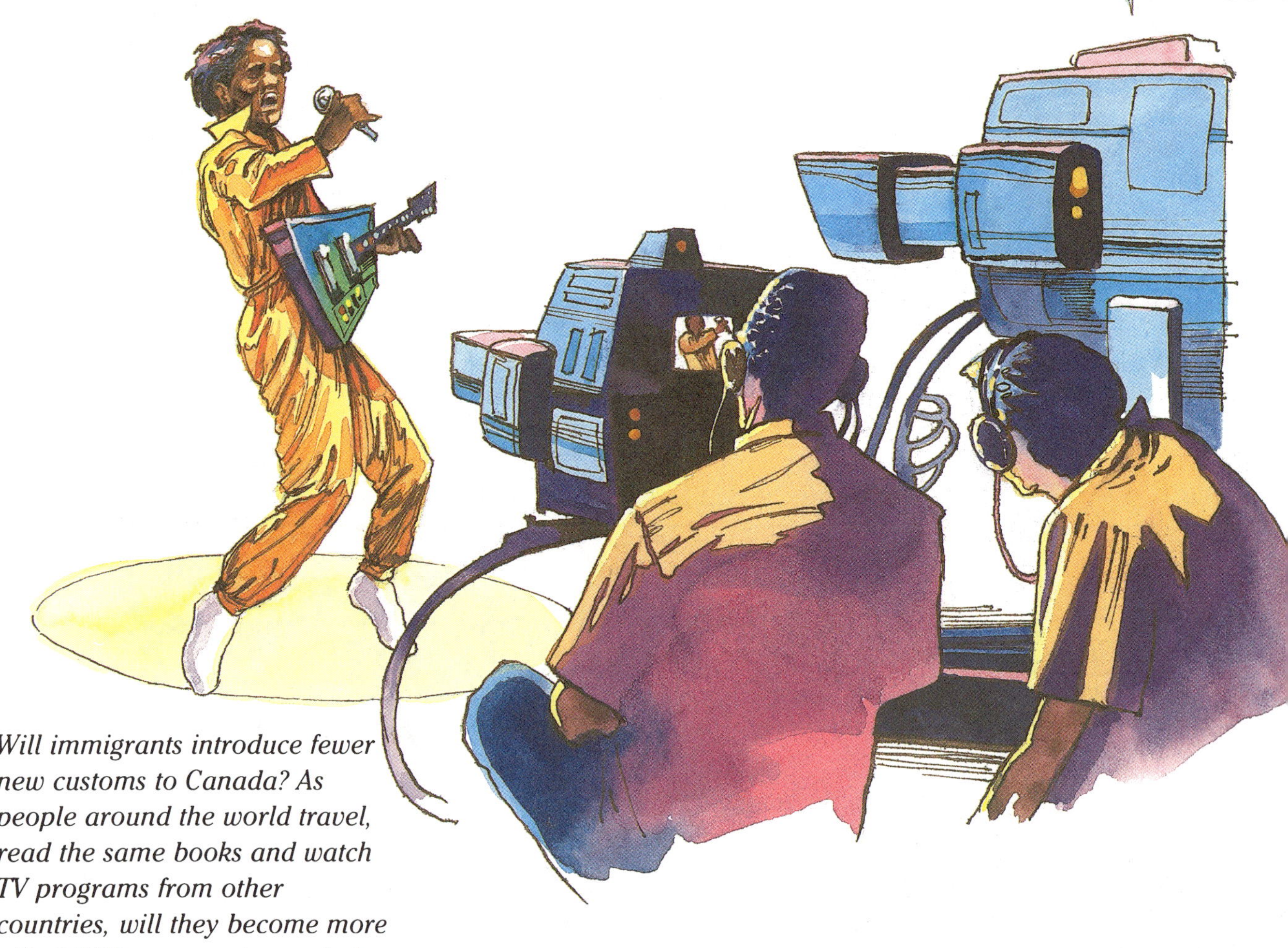

Will immigrants introduce fewer new customs to Canada? As people around the world travel, read the same books and watch TV programs from other countries, will they become more alike? Will many customs, clothes and foods be the same throughout the world?

Right: Will immigrants contribute special new skills? Will Canada encourage scientists from around the world to help develop Canadian travel in space? Will immigrants help Canadians develop farming in the far north?

Will students learn more about different countries and ethnic groups from each other? Will schools hold monthly "Ethnic Days" when new immigrants explain life in their homelands?

How Might Canadians Help the Immigrants of the Future?

For many years, immigrants have been coming to Canada. Sometimes they have been given jobs or farmland. Volunteers and ethnic groups have often helped them settle in. Still, most immigrants have been lonely when they first moved here. Immigrants need more than a job and a place of their own to feel at home. Individual Canadians, like you and your family, can welcome new immigrants to the community.

When future immigrants come to live in Canada, they may receive a lot of government aid. They may be able to get information from computers and help from machines such as electronic language translators. In the future, immigrants will still need your help and understanding. Individual Canadians can help immigrants to feel at home.

Above: Will people who meet new immigrants in their work receive training to help them understand different ethnic groups? Will people like teachers, doctors and store managers be more aware of the challenges immigrants face?

Will Canadians have more free time to help people in their community? Will most Canadians do volunteer work at a Centre for New Immigrants?

Will Canadian citizens feel more responsible to help new immigrants? Will communities pair a Canadian with each new immigrant to help the newcomer adjust to Canada?

Will computers help new immigrants understand their communities? Will libraries have computers that can answer questions on laws, taxes and community services in any language?

Looking to Your Future

In this chapter, we have been discussing the future. The year 2039 sounds very far away, but it is part of your future. By that time you will likely be living in a very different world. You might have a full-time job but work only 20 hours a week. You might spend some of your free time repairing a robot that cleans your home.

Your future in Canada will be shared with many other Canadians. Some of them will have always lived here. Others will be new immigrants to Canada. Working together, you will shape the multicultural country you share.

Because immigrants are newcomers, they need special support and understanding from other Canadians. You may never work at a Centre for New Immigrants as Simon did. But you will have many chances to help newcomers in your neighbourhood or at work.

The immigrants of the future, like the immigrants of the past, will benefit all Canadians. It is your responsibility to help them make Canada their home.

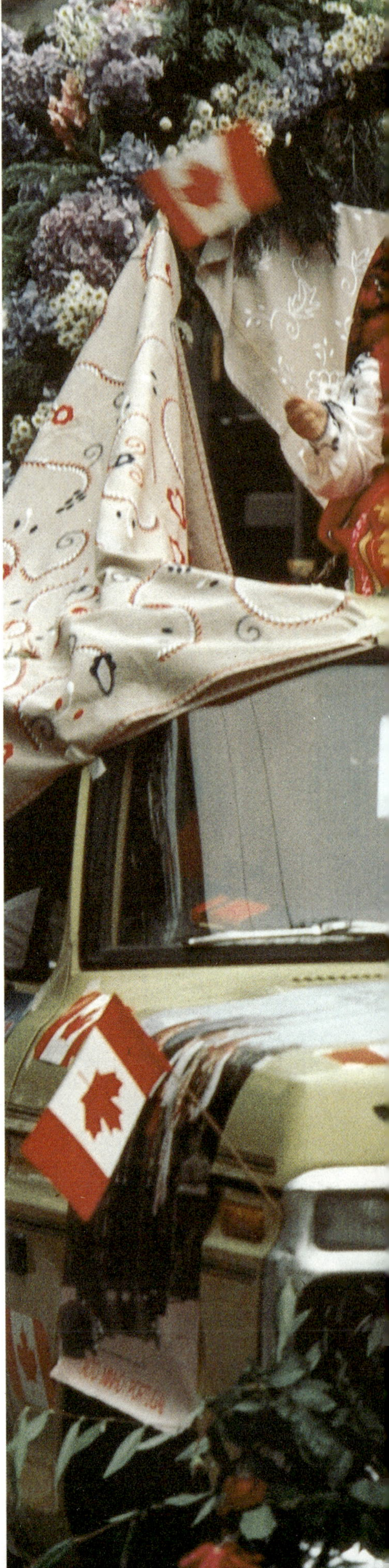

Many new Canadians celebrate their cultural heritage on Canada Day. How do you celebrate Canada Day?

Above: Friends from different cultures play together. Do you think friendship will be important to you in the future?

UNIT CHECKUP

Learning from the Past

Chinese immigrants look for work on the prairies in the late 1800s.

Chinese immigrants are welcomed at the airport by a Canadian volunteer.

Irish immigrants prepare to leave Ireland for the long sea voyage to Canada.

Today Irish immigrants travel to Canada in a matter of hours, often by plane.

Each pair of pictures shows immigrants to Canada in the past and in the present. For each pair of pictures,

1. describe how immigration would have been harder in the past than it is today,
2. name one way that immigration would have been easier in the past than it is today.

Looking to the Future

As Canada develops more resources in the north, it will likely develop new towns and cities. Canada will need the help of many people to settle new areas. How might immigrants help Canada develop its land in the north? Name at least two ways. How might it be harder to immigrate to a newly settled part of Canada? How might it be easier? Name at least two ways.

Getting Involved

Imagine that some refugees have arrived in your community. They need food, clothing and a place to stay. They need help learning English and understanding Canada. They need friends. What could you and your family do to help?

Summing Up

Imagine that you are training volunteers to work at a Canadian centre for new immigrants. From what you have learned in this unit, what five things would you tell the volunteers about immigrants that would help them in their work?

Conclusion

How old will you be in the year 2039? Can you imagine what you might be doing then? One way to imagine the future is to look at your past experiences. Of course when you grow up, you will have many new experiences. But the things you do as a child can affect what you do in the future.

For example, think about the children who started and ended the units of this book. You probably were not surprised that Michelle in Unit I had a forestry job when she grew up. Her visit to Vancouver Island introduced her to the importance and excitement of the forest resource. David, the boy who sent his message of friendship around the world, later worked for a communications company. Catherine's concern about government influenced her decision to become a mayor. And Simon's understanding and appreciation of immigrants led him to help out at a Canadian centre for new immigrants.

Like people, countries develop from past experiences. Some surprising events and new discoveries will likely change Canada in ways no one can predict. Events and people of the past and present affect the kind of country you will live in when you grow up.

In this book, you learned about Canada by exploring its forests, its communications, its government and its immigrant people. They all have played an important role in developing Canada. You read about people and events in the past and saw how things have changed. You took a close-up look at examples of what is happening in the present. Then you tried to look ahead to see what might happen in the future.

In Unit I you saw how valuable forests are to Canada. For years, the forest industry has used wood to make lumber, pulp and paper and other products. The forest industry has provided jobs to some

A faller walks along a tree he has just cut down. How might this person have learned to be a faller?

The Anik C-1 *satellite, at the top of the picture, is placed in orbit from the space shuttle* Discovery. *How has Canada contributed to new developments in communications and space travel?*

Canadians and benefits to all of us. Forests are also important for fish and wildlife, for clean water and for activities such as hiking and camping. If Canadians make sure new trees grow up to replace the ones that are cut, forests will be just as valuable to people in the future.

In Unit II, you learned how important communication is to people spread out across a country as large as Canada. Communications networks help people send messages, receive information and keep in touch with others. Through the years, Canada has used better and better communications equipment, such as telegraphs, telephones and satellites. New inventions will help Canadians in the future, too.

In Unit III, you read about how the colonies united under one central government to form a single country. Our country has federal, provincial or territorial, and local governments that provide many services for all Canadians. Citizens can affect the work of these governments through their elected representatives, public committees and protest groups. In the future, Canadians will probably continue to meet their needs by working together through government.

In Unit IV, you learned about immigration. Despite the challenges of moving to a new country, many immigrants have come to Canada from all around the world. They helped to populate and settle this country. They contributed their customs, ideas, skills and hard work to Canada. All Canadians benefit from the contributions made by immigrants. Immigrants will continue to play an important role in Canada's future.

A young black Canadian attends a public event in Toronto. How might immigrants from other cultures contribute to Canada?

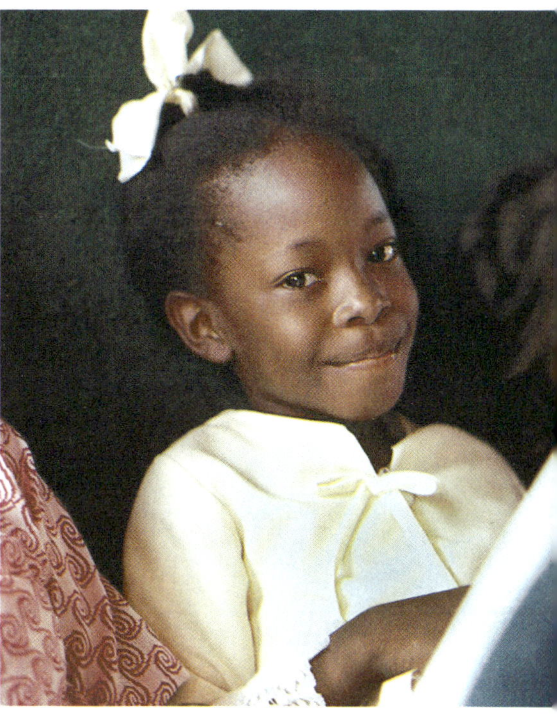

A protest group marches for peace. How might this action help change government decisions?

Your future is linked to the future of Canada. Your understanding of Canada's past and present can help to prepare you for your future. For instance, you now know that the wise use of the forest resource benefits you and every other Canadian. So you can try to make sure Canada does not run out of trees. You might do things such as recycling your newspapers or asking your government to support tree-planting programs.

You have seen that a system of communications links Canadians in different parts of the country. So you might want to make sure that communications networks are used well. For example, you might want to campaign to limit the number of advertisements on television.

You have seen that good citizenship is important to good government. Like Canadians today and in the past, you will be able to work for good government by voting for your representatives. You might also want to improve the work of government by joining a planning committee or a protest group.

You understand how important immigrants are to Canada. So you might help to make Canada a country that more immigrants will choose. You might help immigrants adjust at work or make them feel at home in your neighbourhood.

Your future life in Canada will be an exciting exploration of its own. Not long from now, you will enter a new century filled with new ideas, new inventions and new challenges. You will find that the people and experiences of the past can help prepare you for the future.

Right: Three students use computers in school. What schoolwork might they be doing?

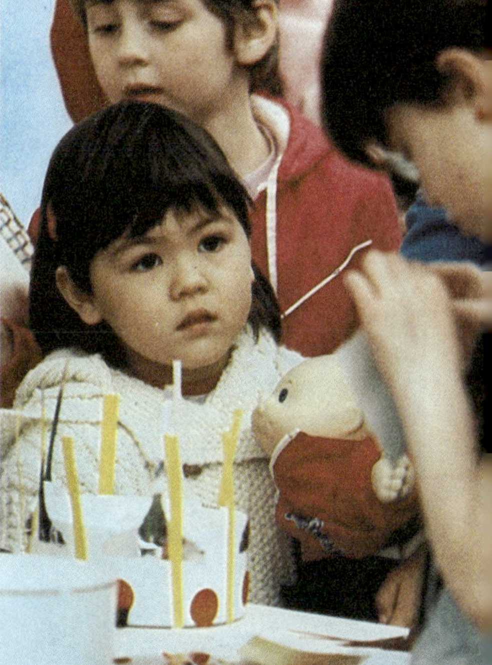

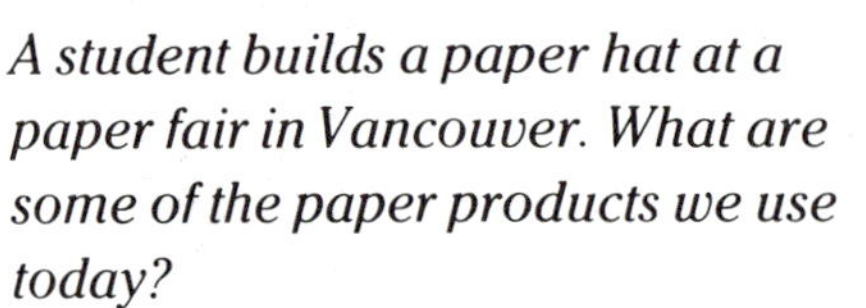

A student builds a paper hat at a paper fair in Vancouver. What are some of the paper products we use today?

Below: *Immigrants are an important part of Canada's population. How might you make a new immigrant feel more at home in Canada?*

Two people picnic on a sunny day in a park. How do parks make life more enjoyable for Canadians?

GLOSSARY

This glossary tells you the meaning of some new words used in this book. Some of these words have other meanings, too. You will need a dictionary to find the other meanings.

If a word is important to understanding the ideas in a unit, it is included in the glossary. The number listed after each meaning tells you the page in that unit where the word is first used. The word is in heavy print on that page. Sometimes a glossary word is in heavy print in more than one unit. Then a page number for each unit is shown.

Some of the new words are hard to say. The marks below will help you to pronounce the words:

a = cat	i = it	u = up
ā = say	ī = ride	u̇ = look
ah = father	o = dog	ü = school
e = red	ō = go	ə = pocket
ē = he		

′ is an accent mark. It points to the part of the word that you say most strongly.

jump′ ing   good bye′

allegiance (a lē′ jəns): the loyalty owed by citizens to their government. (p. 328)

antenna: a piece of equipment for sending or receiving radio and television signals. Metal rods, wires, microwave dishes and microwave horns are different kinds of antennas. (p. 128)

Baisakhi Day (ba su′ kē): New Year's Day celebrated by the Sikhs of India. (p. 324)

band: a group of native Indians who live and work together. (p. 227)

bill: a suggestion for a new law put forward in Parliament. (p. 235)

boom town: a new town that grows quickly. (p. 22)

braille (brāl): a system of writing for the blind in which raised dots indicate letters and numbers. Braille is named after its inventor, Louis Braille. (p. 178)

broadcast: to share information with the public by radio or television. (p. 128)

Cabinet: a group of people in the Government party in the House of Commons who decide on programs for departments of the federal government. Sometimes a senator is also part of the Cabinet. (p. 239)

cabinet minister: a person appointed by the prime minister to head a government department; a member of the cabinet. (p. 239)

cable: a wire rope. In communications, cables contain wires or fibres for sending messages. (p. 130)

cambium (kam′ bē um): a soft layer of a tree just under the bark that grows into new wood. (p. 32)

campaign (kam pān′): to try to convince people to vote for a candidate or to accept an idea or proposal. (p. 237)

candidate: a person trying to win an election as a representative in government. (p. 236)

capital: the city where elected representatives meet. (p. 218)

caucus (ko′ kus): the elected members within a political party who decide on a plan of action for the party. (p. 235)

cellulose fibre (sel′ ü lōs fī bər): thread-like material in wood used to make paper. (p. 78)

chamber: the hall in the House of Commons where M.P.s meet. Senators meet in the Senate Chamber. (p. 239)

chapati (chu pa′ tē): in India, a flat bread made from flour, water and salt. (p. 324)

chemical (kem′ i kəl): a substance that causes a change in another substance. (p. 38)

citizen: a member of a nation, by birth or by choice. A citizen has both rights and responsibilities. (p. 228, p. 328)

citizenship: the state of being a citizen. (p. 328)

city hall: the building where the business of local government is carried out. (p. 198)

clearcut: an area of the forest where all the trees have been cut down. (p. 25)

colonist (kol′ ən ist): a person who started or lives in a colony. (p. 211, p. 300)

colony (kol′ ən ē): a group of people who live in a settlement far from their homeland but are still governed by the homeland. (p. 211, p. 300)

committee: a group of people formed to study a problem or to do a job. (p. 60)

communicate (ko myün′ i kāt): to share information, thoughts and feelings with others. (p. 8, p. 109)

communication (ko myün i kā′ shən): sharing information, thoughts and feelings by speaking, writing or using signals. (p. 109)

communications (ko myün i kā′ shənz): the sending and receiving of messages, using equipment such as telephones and radios. (p. 118)

computer (kom pyü′ tər): a machine that does calculations, solves problems, and stores and retrieves information very quickly. (p. 42, p. 109)

Confederation (kon fed′ ər ā shən): the joining together, in 1867, of the Province of Canada (now Ontario and Quebec), Nova Scotia and New Brunswick to form Canada. Six other provinces have joined Confederation since then. (p. 217)

constituency (kon sti′ tyü en sē): a voting area from which one or more government representatives are elected. In the federal government, each constituency elects one representative. In some provincial governments, some constituencies elect more than one representative. (p. 233)

constituent (kon sti′ tyü ent): a resident in a constituency, represented in the government by the elected member or members for that area. (p. 233)

constitution (kon′ sti tyü shən): the basic laws by which a country is governed. (p. 218)

contribution (kon tri byü′ shən): the giving of help, skills or money. (p. 293)

control room: a room from which a television director controls production of a TV show. (p. 116)

council (kown′ səl): a group of people who govern by making decisions or by giving advice. (p. 212)

councillor (kown′ sil ər): a member of a council. (p. 226)

crisis (krī′ sis): a time of danger or great anxiety. (p. 356)

cross-section: a cut across something that shows the inside parts. (p. 33)

crude oil: a thick, dark liquid found underground, also called petroleum. (p. 20)

culture (kul′ chər): the way of living that a group of people has developed. Beliefs, language, art, food and dress are all part of a group's culture. (p. 292)

custom: a long-established tradition or habit. (p. 287)

cutting plan: a plan explaining how a logging company will cut the trees in an area of the forest. (p. 50)

democracy (dem o′ kra sē): a form of government in which the people elect representatives. (p. 212)

descendant (dē sen′ dənt): a person born into a certain family or group. (p. 294)

dhal (dol): in India, a soup or stew made by cooking dried beans or lentils with spices and vegetables. (p. 324)

director: the person in charge of the music, words and actions in a radio or television show. (p. 111)

discrimination (dis krim′ in ā shən): the treating of people differently because of their race, colour, religion or country of birth. (p. 306)

dupatta (du pa′ tə): in India, a long scarf, often with a fringe, worn by girls and women. (p. 324)

earth station: a place on earth equipped to send signals to satellites in space and to receive signals from them. (p. 134)

editor: a person who selects and prepares material for broadcast, publication or performance. (p. 144)

elect: to choose by voting. (p. 212)

election (ē lek′ shən): the process of choosing by vote. (p. 228)

electricity (el ek tri′ si tē): a form of energy carried through wires. Electricity is used to run machines and to produce light and heat. (p. 124)

electronic (el ek tron′ ik): having to do with electrons, which are tiny particles that travel through wires and produce electricity. (p. 124)

employ: to hire someone to do a job. (p. 67)

ethnic: having to do with people who are grouped by their common culture, language and history. (p. 294)

export: to sell things to another country. (p. 81)

faller: a forest worker who cuts down, or falls, trees. (p. 14)

federal: having to do with the government of a whole country, not a province or a city alone. (p. 205)

fertilize (fer′ tə līz): to make land capable of producing crops, by adding substances that enrich the soil. (p. 62)

foreign (fōr′ ən): having to do with another country. (p. 81, p. 114)

forester: a forest worker who plans the harvesting and renewing of the forest. (p. 25)

forest inventory (in′ vən tōr ē): a list of everything, including trees, streams, wildlife and soil types, found in an area of the forest. (p. 72)

forestry (fōr′ es trē): the science of planting and taking care of forests. (p. 28)

free: not owned or controlled by others. (p. 303)

generation (jen′ ər ā shən): people born in the same 25-to-30-year period. A generation goes from the time parents are born to the time their children are born. (p. 43)

ghost town: a town where no one lives any more. (p. 22)

gold rush: a rapid, sometimes frantic movement of people to where gold has been found. (p. 22)

goods: things that can be bought or sold. (p. 81)

govern (guv′ ərn): to rule or control. (p. 211)

government (guv′ ərn mənt): the people who rule, or govern, a country, province, territory, city or other community. (p. 200)

Government party: the political party that has the most elected representatives. (p. 235)

governor (guv′ ər nər): a person who governs or rules. (p. 212)

Governor General: the representative of the Queen in Canada, appointed for five years. (p. 242)

growth ring: the layer of wood produced by a tree in one year. (p. 31)

gum san (gum sahn): a Chinese phrase meaning "land of the golden mountain." Some Chinese called Canada *gum san.* (p. 304)

habitat (ha′ bi tat): the place where a plant or an animal naturally lives or is most likely to be found. (p. 54)

harvest: to gather a crop when it is ready to be used or sold. (p. 25)

hauling (hol′ ing): pulling or moving. In forestry, moving logs from the forest. (p. 36)

heritage (hār′ i tij): something passed down from people who lived earlier. (p. 7, p. 208)

House of Commons: in Canada, the group of elected representatives that meets in Ottawa. (p. 233)

hydro-electric power: electric power produced from falling water. (p. 16)

immigrant (im′ i grənt): a person who moves into another country to settle and make a home. (p. 284)

immigrate: to move into another country to live. (p. 292)

immigration (im i grā′ shən): the act of moving into another country to live. (p. 293)

import: to buy things from another country. (p. 81)

income tax: money that working people give from their earnings to the government to help pay for services. (p. 200)

independence (in dē pen′ dəns): freedom from the rule or control of others. (p. 301)

industry (in′ dus trē): all the businesses or manufacturers that make or sell similar goods. Logging companies, pulp and paper mills and lumber traders are all part of the forest industry. (p. 28)

information bank: all the facts stored in a computer. (p. 136)

interpreter (in tər′ pre tər): a person who changes the words of one language into another language so that people who speak different languages can communicate. (p. 304)

knot (not): a hard, round spot on a tree marking where a branch grew out of the trunk. (p. 36)

land claim: a demand for land as one's own or as one's right, especially by a native group. (p. 227)

law: a rule made by the government that must be obeyed. (p. 198)

licence (lī′ səns): a paper, card, plate or tag that gives official permission to do something or to own something. (p. 198)

log drive: moving logs from the forest by floating them down rivers. (p. 36)

logging: the cutting down of trees and removing them from the forest. (p. 36)

Lourdie (lōr dē): in India, a festival in which people celebrate life and the birth of children. (p. 324)

Loyalist: a settler in the United States who moved to Canada after 1783, when the United States became independent from Great Britain. (p. 301)

lumber: boards and planks cut from logs. (p. 26)

manage (man′ əj): to take care of and control something. (p. 40)

media (mēd′ ē ə): ways of communicating, including newspapers, magazines, radio and television. (p. 112)

Member of Parliament (par′ le mənt): a person elected to the federal government; a member of the House of Commons. (p. 233)

microwave: a short radio wave that can carry radio, television and telephone signals. (p. 130)

mineral: a valuable natural substance found in the ground. Coal, silver and oil are minerals. (p. 18)

monitor: a machine that receives television pictures and shows them on a screen. (p. 91, p. 116)

mother tongue: the first language a person learns to speak. The mother tongue of most Canadians is English or French. (p. 321)

M.P.: *See* Member of Parliament.

multi-cultural (mul′ tē kul′ chər əl): of many cultures. (p. 295)

multi-culturalism (mul′ tē kul′ chər əl izm): in Canada, a government policy to encourage ethnic groups to keep their culture and share it with other Canadians. (p. 308)

national (na′ shən əl): belonging to a country or nation. (p. 205)

native people: the first people to live in Canada. The Inuit and Indians are the native people. (p. 294)

natural resource (na′ chər əl rē′ sōrs): a thing occurring in nature that people can use, such as water, trees and minerals. (p. 8, p. 15)

network: a way of connecting parts of a system. A communications network is a system of wires, satellites and microwave stations. (p. 118)

newscast: a news show that is broadcast on television or radio. (p. 108)

newsletter: a printed report containing news of interest to a particular group of people. (p. 111)

newsprint (nyüz′ print): the type of paper used in newspapers. (p. 38)

nominate (nom′ in āt): to name someone as a candidate for an election. (p. 236)

nomination (nom in ā′ shən): the naming of someone as a candidate for election. (p. 236)

non-renewable (non rē nyü′ ə bl): unable to grow again or to be replaced after being used. (p. 18)

old growth: trees in a forest that has never been cut down. (p. 92)

Opposition: in the Canadian House of Commons, the political party or parties with fewer M.P.s than the Government party. (p. 235)

optical fibre (op′ ti kəl fī′ bər): a thread of glass along which light beams move. (p. 136)

paise (pī sā′): coins used in India. Each *paisa* is worth less than one cent Canadian. (p. 320)

Parliament (par′ lə mənt) **Buildings:** the buildings in Ottawa where M.P.s and senators meet and work. (p. 233)

party: *See* political party.

passport: a paper or book that states a person's identity and citizenship. It is used to help a person enter other countries. (p. 234)

petition (pə ti′ shən): a request to the government for some privilege, right or benefit. A petition is often signed by many people. (p. 258)

plywood (plī′ wu̇d): a strong board made by gluing together many thin sheets of wood. (p. 69)

political (pōli′ ti kəl): having to do with politics or government. (p. 310)

political party: a group of people who have the same ideas about what the government should do. A political party tries to influence government decisions. (p. 235)

politician (pol ə ti′ shən): a person who works in government or for a political party. (p. 63 or p. 130)

population (pop ü lā′ shən): the total number of people living in a place. (p. 303)

premier (prē′ mē yer): in Canada, the leader of the Government party of a province. (p. 130, p. 216)

prime minister: in Canada, the leader of the Government party in the House of Commons; the head of the Cabinet. (p. 216)

producer (prō dyü′ ser): the person in charge of the money, equipment and other needs of a radio or television show. (p. 111)

product (prod′ ukt): something people have made. Lumber is a forest product. (p. 16)

property tax: money that people who own land, or property, give to the government to help pay for services. (p. 207)

protest (prō′ test) **group:** a group of people formed to speak out against some decision or action. (p. 247)

province (pro′ vins): one of 10 areas of Canada that have their own elected government. (p. 204)

public: belonging to all the people. (p. 40)

public committee: a group of people who help and advise the government. (p. 254)

public meeting: a meeting that everyone may attend. (p. 49)

pulp: a soft, wet substance formed from wood. Pulp is used to make paper. (p. 38)

Punjabi (pun ju′ bē): the language spoken in Punjab State, India. (p. 317)

Queen of Canada: Canada's official head of state. Queen Elizabeth II has been Queen since 1952. (p. 242)

race: one of several broad groups of people with common physical characteristics. (p. 306)

racism (rās′ iz əm): the belief that another race is not as good as one's own. (p. 306)

rebellion (rē bel′ yən): a disagreement between citizens and the government or people in power. (p. 310)

recommendation: advice or suggestion. (p. 152)

refugee (ref′ yü jē): a person who is in danger in his or her homeland because of race, religion, nationality or political ideas and who flees to another country for safety. (p. 310)

religion (rē li′ jən): the belief in a God or gods and in a particular system of faith and worship. (p. 306)

renewable (rē nyü′ ə bl): able to grow again or to be replaced. (p. 16)

represent: to speak or act for another person or group of people. (p. 228)

representative (rep rē zen′ tə tiv): a person who speaks or acts for another person or group of people. (p. 212)

research: careful study to learn as much as possible about a subject. (p. 39)

reseed (rē sēd′): to seed an area where the plants have been removed. In forestry, trees can reseed a logged area. (p. 25)

reserve: land set aside for a certain use or for certain people. (p. 226)

right: a privilege given to a person by the law. (p. 212)

rupee (rü′ pē): in India, a unit of money worth about three cents Canadian. (p. 320)

sales tax: money charged on items when they are sold. Sales tax is given to the government to help pay for services. (p. 208)

salvar-kamiz (sil′ var kə mēz′): a suit, including a long shirt and pants, worn by girls and women in Punjab State. (p. 324)

samosa (su mō′ su): a small pastry, shaped like a triangle, filled with vegetables, meat or sweets. (p. 322)

sari (sa rē): in India, a dress made by wrapping a length of cloth around the body. (p. 324)

satellite: a manufactured object that orbits the earth. (p. 72, p. 111)

sawyer (so′ yər): a person who operates a saw in a sawmill. (p. 42)

second growth: a second forest, growing where the original trees have been logged or burned. (p. 92)

seedling: a very young tree. (p. 62)

self-government: government of a group by its own members. (p. 227)

Senate (sen′ ət): in Canada, a group of appointed people, from all the provinces, who help make laws. The Senate may include up to 104 members. (p. 242)

senator (sen′ ə tər): a member of the Senate. (p. 242)

service (sər′ vis): the supplying of help that is necessary and useful. (p. 9, p. 80, p. 202)

session (se′ shən): a set of meetings, or sittings, of the House of Commons. A session lasts for several months. (p. 242)

settle: to establish a permanent home in a new country; to set up a community. (p. 300)

settler: a person who moves into a new area to live and work. (p. 21, p. 297)

share: a part of something. Many people buy shares of land or of a company. (p. 256)

shareholder: a person who buys shares. (p. 256)

Sikh (sēk): a member of a religious community founded around 1500 in Punjab State, India. (p. 324)

silviculture (sil′ ve kul chər): the planting of and caring for a forest. (p. 39)

sitting: a meeting of the House of Commons. A sitting lasts one day. (p. 239)

slave: a person owned and controlled by another person. (p. 303)

Speaker: in Canada, the Member of Parliament who acts as chairperson at sittings of the House of Commons. (p. 239)

sponsor (spon′ sər): a Canadian, usually a close relative, who supports an immigrant. (p. 286)

suffragette (suf rə jet′): a woman who tried to get the right to vote for all women. (p. 258)

tax: money paid by people to the government for public services such as education, crime protection and medical care. (p. 54, p. 200, p. 306)

technology (tek no′ lo jē): the tools, equipment and methods used to do a job. (p. 42, p. 122)

telegraph (tel′ ə graf): a system that sends signals electrically along wires. (p. 124)

telephone exchange: a building where many telephone wires meet and can be connected to each other. (p. 127)

teletypewriter (tel′ ə tīp rī tər): a typewriter that prints out messages it receives electrically along wires. (p. 125)

terminal (tər′ min əl): a small machine connected to a computer in order to send and receive messages. (p. 91)

territory: one of two regions of Canada governed by a representative of the federal government. A territory also has a territorial government and representatives in the House of Commons. (p. 205)

timber: wood used for building or making things. (p. 36)

time zone: a region where the time is the same in all places. There are 24 time zones on earth; Canada has 6. (p. 154)

trade: the buying and selling or exchanging of goods. (p. 241)

trades: types of work that require skill with one's hands; crafts. (p. 342)

translate: to change words from one language into another. (p. 286)

translation (tranz lā′ shən): changing of one language into another. (p. 182)

transmitter: a machine that sends or broadcasts signals. (p. 164)

transportation: ways of getting people and things from one place to another. (p. 122)

treaty: in Canada, an agreement between the federal government and an Indian tribe. Usually the tribe gives up rights to land in return for a payment of money and a land reserve. (p. 226)

tribe: a group of people with the same ancestors, language and culture. (p. 226)

union (yün′ yun): workers who join together to improve their working conditions. (p. 75)
unite (yü nīt′): to join. (p. 214)
United Nations (yü nīt′ əd nā′ shəns): an international organization formed in 1945 to promote world peace. (p. 310)

video: television. (p. 112, p. 144)
videophone: a machine like a telephone that can also send and receive video pictures. (p. 91, p. 184)
videotape: a tape used to record video pictures and sound for television. (p. 100, p. 144)
videotex: information from a computer shown on a television screen. (p. 136)
vote: to choose in a formal way some person or some action. (p. 228)

wage: money received for work. (p. 79)

INDEX

This index will help you to find information in this book. Topics are listed in alphabetical order. Some of the topics are then divided into subtopics.

Page numbers are listed after the topic or subtopic. If you turn to the pages listed after a certain topic, you will find information about it.

Some page numbers are in heavy print. This means there is a map on that page that relates to the topic.

I

J

K

L

M

N

O

P

Q

R

S

T

U

V

W

Y

Acknowledgements

Authors

Vivien Bowers: Introduction, Unit I, Unit II

Diane Swanson: Unit III, Unit IV, Conclusion

Editors

Anne Norman, Kathy Butts, Nancy Flight

Art Director

Ken Seabrook

Word Processing

Camille Cloutier

Glossary

Madeline O'Keefe

Photographic Research

Alex Roe

Commissioned Illustrations

Kenneth Robert Campbell: Unit II.
Soren Henrich: pp. 46-47; p. 172; p. 246; p. 281, pp. 332-333.
Deryk Houston: Unit III.
Ron Lightburn: Chapter 3 of Unit I.
Brent Lynch: Chapters 1, 2, 4 and 5 of Unit I; Unit IV.

Commissioned Photographs

Jürgen Vogt/Photo/Graphics: p. 9, bottom right; p. 30, top left; p. 77, bottom; p. 78, bottom; pp. 86-87; pp. 88-89; p. 111; p. 112, all photographs; p. 114; p. 116; p. 117; pp. 132-133, bottom; p. 142, top right, bottom left and bottom middle; p. 152, middle and bottom; p. 153, all photographs; pp. 168-169, bottom; pp. 192-193; p. 198; p. 203, bottom; p. 207; p. 208; p. 210, right; p. 247; p. 249, bottom right; p. 250, bottom; p. 251, bottom; p. 263, left; pp. 278-279; p. 284.
Kate Williams: front cover, unit openings, p. 348 and pp. 372-373, top.

Maps

Karen Ewing
Amely Jurgenliemk
Rosemary Hadley

Other Photographs and Illustrations

Carolyn Angus/Photo/Graphics: p. 201; p. 319, both photographs.
Craig Aurness/Image Finders: p. 294, bottom right; p. 297.
Bata Limited: p. 340, left.
The B.C. Canada Day Committee, Department of the Secretary of State: p. 211 — *The Canadians* by Dorothy Oxborough.
Bell Canada: p. 126 — photograph courtesy Library of Congress, Washington, D.C.; p. 127, both photographs courtesy the Bell Canada Telephone Historical Collection.
Elliott Bernshaw/Image Finders: p. 294, right middle.
Gravel Boorg/Photo/Graphics: p. 318.
British Columbia Forest Products Limited: p. 27, both photographs; p. 38; p. 41; p. 52, top; p. 53, top; p. 57, left and right; p. 58, left; pp. 58-59, top; p. 68, both photographs; p. 69, left; p. 71, top; p. 73, bottom; p. 74, top; p. 75; p. 76, both photographs; p. 78, top; p. 90, left; p. 104, top right and middle right; p. 370, left.
British Columbia Television: p. 342, top.
Petra Bruckbauer/Image Finders: pp. 294-295, upper middle.
Canadian Aviation Safety Board: pp. 164-165, top.
Canadian Broadcasting Corporation: p. 143 and p. 151 — both photographs by Fred Phipps; p. 157.
Canadian Forestry Association: p. 40; p. 64.
Canadian National Institute for the Blind: p. 179 — photograph from the *Sarnia Observer*.
Canadian National: p. 129, top.
Canadian Red Cross Society: p. 310.
Canapress Photo Service: p. 146, left; p. 227, right; p. 233; pp. 240-241; p. 243, both photographs; p. 280, top right.
Edgar J. Cheatham/ The Image Bank Canada: p. 371, right.
Chemainus Festival of Murals: pp. 84-85 — all photographs by Karl Schutz.

Confederation Life Collection: p. 122 — *Canada's First Printing Press* by Rex Woods; p. 212, bottom — *Founding of Halifax* by J. D. Kelly; p. 213 — *Canada's First Shipyard* by Rex Woods; p. 216, left — *Prelude to Confederation* by Rex Woods; pp. 216-217 — *Fathers of Confederation* by Rex Woods; p. 301 — *United Empire Loyalists* by J. D. Kelly.
Council of Forest Industries of B.C.: p. 39; p. 72.
Crown Forest Industries Limited: p. 42, both photographs; p. 70; p. 73, top; p. 77, top; p. 104, bottom right.
Department of Communications: p. 119; p. 136; p. 137; p. 142, bottom right; p. 165, photograph and illustration; p. 166, both photographs; p. 174; p. 175, right; pp. 176-77.
Department of the Secretary of State: p. 328; p. 329.
Joe Devenney/The Image Bank Canada: p. 294, upper left.
Mel DiGiacomo/The Image Bank Canada: pp. 294-295, bottom; p. 295, top.
Dome Petroleum Limited: p. 145, middle left; p. 147, left.
Koos Dykstra/Image Finders: p. 294, top right.
E. B. Eddy Archives: p. 45, top.
R. A. Farquhar/Image Finders: p. 312.
Celia Franca: p. 347, left.
Tony Frontino/Image Finders: p. 148, left.
Edward M. Gifford/Photo/Graphics: p. 4, left; p. 21; p. 30, bottom right; p. 49; p. 90, middle; p. 142, top left; p. 145, left; pp. 236-237, all photographs; p. 251, top; p. 262; p. 280, bottom right; p. 325, bottom; p. 373, bottom; p. 368, bottom right.
Gary Gladstone/The Image Bank Canada: p. 331, right.
Arne Glassborg: p. 146, right.
Glenbow Museum: p. 224, left (NA-1320-5) and right (NA-3682-1); pp. 226-227 — *Treaty No. 7* by A. B. Stapleton; p. 250, lower middle (NA-2003-44); p. 345 (NA-263-1); p. 368, top left (NA-2798-6).
Government of British Columbia: p. 17, bottom; p. 19, right; p. 37, right; p. 56, bottom; pp. 58-59, bottom; p. 71, bottom; p. 87; p. 104, top left; p. 105; pp. 248-249, top; p. 249, top right.
Ralph Greenhill/Miller Services: p. 5, top; p. 218.
R. Hamagouchi/Image Finders: p. 258.
George Hausman/The Image Bank Canada: pp. 330-331.
Bob Herger/Photo/Graphics: pp. 8-9, bottom; p. 30, top right; p. 43; p. 63; p. 65; pp. 102-103; p. 109; p. 147, right; p. 210, left; p. 339.
Fred Herzog/Image Finders: p. 290; p. 322; p. 327, bottom.
Hydro-Québec: p. 17, top.
Imagination Market Association: p. 372, bottom left — photograph by Gary Fiegehen.
Immigrant Services Society of British Columbia: p. 286; p. 287; pp. 314-315, bottom; p. 354, bottom left; p. 368, top right.
Inco Limited: pp. 18-19; p. 30, bottom middle.
Jericho Hill School for the Deaf: p. 171 and p. 173, right — photographs by Marianne Gilbert; p. 173, left.
Ted Kawalerski/The Image Bank Canada: p. 313.
Knowledge Network: p. 170, top.
J. A. Kraulis/Photo/Graphics: p. 16; p. 145, middle right and right; p. 291.
David Chuenyan Lai: pp. 256-257; p. 257, right; p. 350.
Elyse Lewin/The Image Bank Canada: pp. 230-231.
Tom McCarthy/ The Image Bank Canada: p. 367, right.
McCord Museum, McGill University, Montreal: p. 104, left middle — photograph courtesy Notman Photographic Archives; p. 340, right — *The Gibb House, Montreal 1819* by J. Milbourne.
MacMillan Bloedel Place: p. 8, left — photograph by Edward M. Gifford.
George McNutt: p. 160.
Rick Marotz/Photo/Graphics: pp. 366-367.
Gunter Marx/Photo/Graphics: p. 9, top; p. 53, bottom; p. 54, top; p. 294, bottom left; pp. 304-305; p. 320.
Greg Maurer/Photo/Graphics: p. 69, right; p. 81.
Toby Molennar/The Image Bank Canada: p. 294, middle left.
Pat Morrow/First Light: p. 144, left; p. 148, right.
Saran Narang: p. 349.
National Aeronautics and Space Administration: pp. 138-139; p. 175, left; p. 370, right.
National Museums of Canada, National Museum of Man: p. 34, bottom (72-180064).
NFB Photothèque: p. 23, bottom — photograph by Crombie McNeill; p. 45, bottom — photograph by Alex Onoszko; p. 56, top — photograph by Geoffrey Silver; p. 90, right — photograph by T. Waterfield; p. 129, bottom — photograph by P. St. Jacques; p. 159 — photograph by K. H. Raach; p. 228 — photograph by Dave Burcsick; p. 250, upper middle — photograph by T. Waterfield; p. 252 — photograph by K. H. Raach; p. 341, bottom — photograph by Murray Creed; p. 373, right — photograph by Gera Dillon.
Parks Canada: p. 25 — photograph by John Woods; p. 52, bottom — photograph by P. St. Jacques; p. 103; p. 205 — photograph by W. Lynch.
Marin Petkov/Photo/Graphics: p. 5, bottom; p. 115; p. 263, right; p. 371, left.
Beatrice Pinsley/The Image Bank Canada: pp. 294-295, lower middle.
Provincial Archives of Alberta: p. 259 (B-1138); p. 335 (A-1614).
Provincial Archives of British Columbia: p. 37, left (34515); p. 48 (62425); pp. 124-125 (92406); p. 125, right (92383); p. 142, middle top (3289); pp. 254-255 (54020); p. 255, right (31069); p. 303, right (19617); p. 304, bottom (72553); p. 327, top (75600).
Public Archives Canada: p. 4, bottom (C-27791); p. 35 (C-2401) — *First Settlement* by W. H. Bartlett; p. 104, bottom left (C-44633); p. 128 (C-5940); pp. 132-133, top (PA-111390); p. 133, right (C-64048); p. 167 (C-29471); pp. 168-169, top (B-25658); p. 212, top (C-16952); pp. 214-215 (PA-127287); p. 215 (C-21497); p. 222 (C-24522); p. 223, left (PA-122796); p. 225, left (PA-110813) and right (PA-11199); p. 235 (C-21557); p. 250, top (C-52362); pp. 260-261 (PA-5544); p. 280, top left — *Intendant Talon Visiting Settlers* by L. R. Batchelor (C-11925); p. 302 (C-3904); p. 309 (C-5611); p. 314 (C-4986); pp. 314-315, top (C-4745); pp. 336-337, top (C-73429) — *Meeting of Françoise Marie Jacquelin and Charles de la Tour* by C. W. Jefferys; p. 338, right (PA-8498); p. 344 (C-7038); p. 347, right — National Medal Collection; p. 368, bottom left (C-18682) — *Emigrants leaving home in the west of Ireland* by Clarence O'Dowd.
Public Archives of Manitoba: p. 219, bottom.
Public Archives, Prince Edward Island: p. 221, left (2301) and right (2755).
Saskatchewan Archives Board: p. 341, left (R-B-2969).
Saskatchewan Government Photograph: p. 204.
Ken Seabrook: p. 295, bottom and top right.
Shaughnessy Hospital: p. 80.
Carol Simowitz/The Image Bank Canada: p. 295, top middle; p. 351.
Tom Sloan/Photo/Graphics: pp. 134-135; p. 152, top; p. 354, top left.
Bonnie Spence/Photo/Graphics: p. 7.
John Lewis Stage/The Image Bank Canada: pp. 294-295, top.
Ken Straiton/Image Finders: p. 295, middle; p. 308; p. 354, right.
V. Stroheim/Image Finders: pp. 324-325.
Graeme Stuart/Photo/Graphics: p. 130; p. 155; p. 175, middle; p. 177, right.
Harold Sund/The Image Bank Canada: p. 293.
Lloyd Sutton/Photo/Graphics: p. 118.
Vancouver City Archives: cover; p. 31; p. 34, top; p. 36.
Vancouver Public Library: pp. 6-7 (7681); p. 23, top (8637); p. 123 (7647); p. 194, left — *Prairie Schooners* by John Innes (22900); p. 219, top (12825); p. 220, left (8634) and right (698); p. 223, right (9416); pp. 248-249, bottom (10440); p. 304, top (22859); pp. 306-307 (1380); p. 307, right (12851); p. 326 (7641).
Vancouver Symphony Society: p. 342.
Jürgen Vogt/Photo/Graphics: p. 158; p. 170, bottom; p. 194, right; pp. 202-203, both photographs; p. 210, middle; pp. 336-337, bottom.
Westcoast Productions Ltd.: p. 338, left.
Western Canada Pictorial Index, University of Winnipeg, Manitoba: p. 261, right; p. 280, bottom left; p. 346.
Weyerhaeuser Canada Ltd.: p. 33; p. 55; p. 74, bottom.
Eric Wheater/The Image Bank Canada: p. 292.
J. Williamson/First Light: pp. 144-145.
Richard Wright/Photo/Graphics: p. 30, bottom left; p. 54, bottom.